Dedication...

I dedicate this book to Debbie, James, Jon, Jason, my Mom and Dad, Dellis, Lois, Art Lewis Kimball, Mark and Carole, Glen and Debbie Webster, Scott, Bob, Bob, Kathy, Kevin, Aaron, Aaron Christopher, Aaron Hurley, Aaron James, Aaron Matthew, Aaron Michael, Aaron Ray, Ab, Abbey Nichole, Abby Elaine, Harry and Virginia, Abigail, Abijah, Abraham, Abraham Christopher, Marilyn S. and Leona, Ada, Ada Larena, Ada S., Adah Isabella, Adam, Adam Charles, Adam Lee, Gene and Nancy, Addah May, Addaline, Addie, Addie Pearl, Addison Dewey, Addison Monroe, Addison Shane, Adelaide, Adell, Adler J., Brian, Agnes, Agnes Marie, Alan, Albert, Albert (III), Albert Adolf, Albert Allen, Albert Clyde, Albert Franklin, Albert G., Albert James, Albert L., Albert N., Albert S., Alberta, Alberto Elias, Albina Myrtle, Aleon, Aleta Kristine, Aletha, Alexander, Alexandra Suzanne, Alfonso, Alford Herman, Alfred, Alfred Franklin, Alfred Porter, Alhe Cleo, Alice, Alice Avaria, Alice Dell, Alice Edwina, Alice Faye, Alice Jean, Alice Viola, Alicia LeAnn, Alisa May, Allan, Jennie and Francis, Allansyn, Bub and Carol, Carolyn, Norma, Uncle Pete, Janet and Tom D., Allen Carter, Allen Earl, Allen F., Peg and Oz, Allen Terill, Aunt LaVerne and Uncle Jim., Uncle Gaylord, Aunt Goldie, Linda and Walt, Allie, Allie Mae, Paul and Heather Benson, Alma, Cousin Babs, Alma Mae, Alma Marie, Alma Wilhelmina, and hundreds more, Bucky Ward, Almond H., Alois Bernard (Al), Alonzo, Alonzo (Lon) Claude, Alta Frances, Alta May Keller, Alton, Alton Eugene, Alva, Alva Clinton, Alvin, Alvin Jackson, Alvin Wallace, Alvis Hardy (Allen), Alvis L., Alyson, Amadora Leigh, Amalia Sophia, Cynthia and Jean Myers, Jean Landers, Shirley Billings, The Dunhams, Rob Yoder, Wayne and Gayle Thomas, Amanda, Amanda Belle, Amanda Elizabeth (Mandy), Amanda Ethel, Amanda Faye, Amanda Joyce, Amanda L. (Maud), Amanda Lorene, CUCUG members, Starship BBS, Amanda Minerva, Amanda Mitchelle, Amanda Nicole, Amanda Rae, Amanda Rochelle, Amber Dawn, Amber Irene, Amber Leigh, Ambert Lee, Ambia Kathryn, Amelia, America M., Dawn, Mike, Steven and Kelsey, Amy, Amy Bea, Amy Beth, Amy Eileen, Amy Gail, Amy Kathryn, Amy Louise, Amy Lucille, Amy Margaret, Amy Marie, Amy Ruth, Amy Sue, Amy Susanne, Ancil, Andrea Susan, Andres Alberto, The Lord, Andrew, Andrew, Andrew, Andrew, Andrew, Andrew (Andy) Keith, Andrew Brent, Andrew David, Andrew David, Andrew Duncan, Andrew Floyd, Andrew Graham, Andrew Griffith, Andrew Hilas, Andrew J., Andrew J., Andrew J., Andrew J., Andrew Jackson, Andrew Jackson, Andrew Jackson (Jack), Andrew Justin, Andrew Lester (Andy), Andrew M., Andrew Richard, Andrew Thomas, Andy, Andy, Andy Gene, Angel, Vinnie, Angela Gayle, Angelina Adalia (Angie), Angeline, Angeline, Anice, Anie, Anis Marie, Anise H., Anita, Anita, Anita Carol, Anita Gail, Anita Marie, Anita Marlene, Ann, Ann, Ann, Ann, Ann, Ann Eliza, Ann Fern, Terry Oldfield, Sarah and Seth, Anna, Anna, Anna B., Anna Barbara, Anna Bell, Anna Bell (Annie), Anna Elizabeth, Anna J., Anna L., Anna Lee, Anna Louise, Anna Mae, Anna Mae, Anna Marie, Susie Phelps, The Sandersons, Irene Murtha and Marguerite Sater, Faye and Ralph Miller, Anna Martha, Anna May, Annabelle, Anne, Anne Marie, Annetta, Annetta Marie, Annette Effie, Annette Kristine, Annie, Annie, Annie, Annie, Annie, Annie, Annie (?), Annie Alice, Annie Bell, Annie Dee(Ann) Mangum, Annie E., Annie Laura, Annie Love, Annie Lucille, Annie Mae, Annie Mae Arnold, Annie Marie, Annie Maurine, Annie Pearl, Annie Ruth, Annie Viola, Ansley Jo, Anthony, Anthony, Anthony Andrew, Anthony B., Anthony Carey, Anthony Joseph, Anthony Joseph, Anthony Theodore, Anthony Wayne, Antionette Ginette, Anton, Apostolos Harilos, Arcadia F., Arch, Archer Thomas, Archibald, Archibald Joaquin, Archie, Archie Ewell, ardell, Ardis, Ardis Arlene, Ardyth Marie, Aria, Arimenta, arjorie Nell, arjorie Susan, arl D. J., Kevin Hisel, Arlene Lorena, Arley Ray, Arlie Ernest, Arlie M., Arlonzo L., Arminda Fern, Arnold A., arol Elaine, Arta Lynn, Arthor Benton (Benny) (Jr.), Arthor Benton (Sr.), Arthur, Arthur, Arthur, Arthur, Arthur, Arthur, Rob and Mary Lun, Chuck and Jean Origer, Arthur Byron, Arthur Byron (Jr), Steve Scardello, Arthur Elmer, Arthur Hans, Arthur L., Arthur O., Arthur Ray, Arthur Thomas, Arthusa Dillard, Artie, Arvilla, Arzera, Asa, Ashanna Marie, Ashely Renee, Ashlee Maegan, Ashlee Renee, Ashleigh Elizabeth, Ashley Ann, Aubrey, Dick and Linda I., Julie, Aubrey Walter, Audie Gene, Audrey, Audrey, Audrey Flora, Greg Van Der Werf, Aughty H., August, Carol Mahoney, Avis, Avis Totelo, Jim Butterfield, Axel Hyalmar, Baby, Bailey, Barbara, Barbara, Barbara, Barbara, Barbara, Barbara, Barbara, Barbara, Barbara, Jeff, Barbara Aline, Barbara Ann, Barbara Ann, Linda Conners, Barbara Hope, Barbara J., Barbara Jean, Barbara Jean, Barbara Joyce, Barbara Sue, Barbara Sue, Barham H., Baron Howard, Barry, Barry Dean, Barry Ken, Bartholmew, Beatrice, Beatrice, Beatrice , Beatrice, Beatrice, Beatrice, Beatrice, Becky Ann, Beegie, Benjamin, Benjamin, Benjamin, Benjamin, Benjamin, Benjamin, Benjamin, Benjamin, Benjamin, Benjamin Alphus, Benjamin Beacker, Benjamin Everett, Benjamin F., Benjamin Franklin, Benjamin Franklin, Benjamin Franklin, Benjamin Joseph, Benjamin Mathew, Benjamin R., Benjamin Robert, Benjamin Todd, Benjamin Tot, Benjamin Wesley, Benjamin Woods, Bennie, Donnie Lee, Dora , Dora, Dora Belle, Dora Belle, Dora Edna, Dora Etta, and over 8000 more of my closest relatives and friends...

Your Family Tree

Jim Oldfield, Jr.

Abacus

Copyright © 1997   **Abacus**
                          5370 52nd Street SE
                          Grand Rapids, MI 49512

This book is copyrighted. No part of this book may be reproduced, stored in a retrieval system, or transmitted in any form or by any means, electronic, mechanical, photocopying, recording or otherwise without the prior written permission of Abacus Software.

Every effort has been made to ensure complete and accurate information concerning the material presented in this book. However, Abacus Software can neither guarantee nor be held legally responsible for any mistakes in printing or faulty instructions contained in this book. The authors always appreciate receiving notice of any errors or misprints.

This book contains trade names and trademarks of several companies. Any mention of these names or trademarks in this book are not intended to either convey endorsement or other associations with this book

---

Printed in the U.S.A.

ISBN 1-55755-310-6

10 9 8 7 6 5 4 3 2 1

Cover design: Matt Ridgway

Your Family Tree
Contents

1 Before You Begin — 1

Planning Your Research 3
Tools Of The Trade — What You Need To Have With You 4

2 Starting Your Search — 13

Where Do You Start To Research Your Family History 17
    You 19
    Village, town or city and county resources 22
    State and regional resources 24
    National resources 24
    International sources 27
    Other sources 28

Contents

3 Researching Your Family History On-line 31

Accessing Information On-line 33
    Non-commercial BBSs (Bulletin Board Systems) 33
    Online trial periods 34
    Usenet newsgroups and mailing lists 36
    The Internet (more precisely the World Wide Web or simply "the web") 36

E-mail Is The Number One On-line Research Tool 39

America Online (AOL) 42
    AOL Genealogy Forum 42

CompuServe Information Services 48
    CompuServe Genealogy Forum 48
    CompuServe Genealogy Support Forum 49

What Are Usenet Newsgroups? 54
    GeneSplicer 57
    Genealogy Software Distribution System (GSDS) 57

Mailing Lists And List Servers - Keeping Track Of The Jones, Smiths, Moffetts and Thousands more 58
    ROOTS-L 59
    GENMTD-L 59
    GEN-NEWBIE-L 59
    GEDCOM-L 59
    MAUCK, MAUK Family Interest Mail List 59

Contents

Other Important Web Sites 60
    ROOTSWEB 60
    GENSERV 61
    GENWEB 61
Online Electronic Genealogy Newsletters 61
Saving A LOT Of Time On The Web 62
    Using the genealogy bookmarks file 63
My Favorite Web Sites 65

4 Using Photos, Maps And Sound — 81

Putting Photographs Into Your Computer 84
    Using Seattle Filmworks' PhotoWorks 87
    Using EasyPhoto 90
Manipulating Your Photos 92
    Using Paint Shop Pro 92
    Elementary example 102
Using Maps To Tell A Story 102
Putting Sound Into Your Computer 105

Contents

5 Using Other Programs For Your Family History 109

Using Microsoft Word 111
Microsoft Publisher 116

6 Using Genealogy Programs 121

Using Brother's Keeper for MS-DOS 126
Using Family Origins 132
    Adding information 136
    Adding graphics and sound 136
    Reports 139
Building A Family Web Site 142
    Importing and exporting GEDCOM files 145
Using Family Tree Maker for Windows 146
    Adding graphics and sound 149
    Printing reports 151
    Importing and exporting GEDCOM files 154
    Saving a GEDCOM file 155

Contents

7 Using The Companion CD-ROM — 157

What's On The CD-ROM 160
    Select Catalogs 165
Web Site Menu 166
    Directory - WEBSITE 166
    Add the famtree.htm file 171
    Installing the famtree.htm file for Microsoft Internet Explorer .
    174
    Additional demos 176

Appendices 183

    Appendix A: Glossary 185
    Appendix B: Resources 191

Index 237

Before You Begin

Chapter 1

Before You Begin

PLANNING YOUR RESEARCH

Genealogy can quickly become a complicated hobby (yet still enjoyable!). By nature it is a disorganized endeavor, due to the variety of places and documents you'll be investigating. As you explore deeper into your material, you will need to analyze and assemble more and more information. Starting with a plan lets you impose some order on this chaos and allows you to work with manageable pieces of information, instead of trying to swallow it all as one chunk. This will make your work much easier.

Your goal is to write, as I did, a complete history (as best as can be done with the information you have) of your family in a comprehensive book that's easy and enjoyable to read. This process will include making copies of original and photocopied documents, scanning and fixing images, designing graphics and assembling all your ancestor's personal information into a book format, which will tell a family history that's more than just names and dates. As I mentioned earlier, you and your family deserve your place in history.

Family trees can be complex affairs of divergent branches and criss-crossing lines. You should think about what family lines you want to research. Start by choosing one and focusing on it. Whether it's your father's or your mother's ancestry, each of your parents had two parents who also each had two parents, and so on. Decide which one to start on and stick with it. You can focus a family history on the male line (such as your father's last name) of your family, or just the females or even both. (Please note though, that it is usually easier to trace the male's line than the female's because of the tradition of women taking their mate's last name after marriage.) As you become more proficient in your research and knowledge of your family history, you will soon be working on several lines at once. When I began my work, I started with my father's ancestors

1 Before You Begin

of the same last name. This is usually the easiest starting point. Later, I began to fill in my mother's side. I soon saw that I could easily get information confused. So, and I say this from experience, start focused and then branch out. Beginning with too wide of a focus will lead to confusion and frustration from the opening.

When I began I traced my direct male ancestors as far back in history as I could, gathering all the information I could find on each. I then went back and entered their siblings, spouses, offspring and so on. The family history I began with just my father and his ancestors soon included aunts, uncles and cousins (several times removed) that I had never known existed. As I worked on each family, inputting the children's spouses and their children and their children's children, I soon saw my database of relatives increase dramatically. Remembering to plan your work and work your plan will help you keep your data organized as your family's history becomes more complex.

TOOLS OF THE TRADE — WHAT YOU NEED TO HAVE WITH YOU

Having the proper tools is important for any undertaking. The implements discussed here will make researching your family tree both easier and more successful. They will also help you to organize and document your findings. As you get deeper into this hobby of genealogy and family history and learn more about your family, the pains you take now to document your findings will pay for themselves many times over as you near completion. If you need to double-check some information or can't remember exactly where Aunt Sadie said Ted and June were married, it will be much easier to locate those bits and pieces of information tucked into a notebook or folder if you have detailed notations.

Though some of the items listed here may seem obvious, I've included everything you'll need. It's always a good idea to review what you'll need ahead of time. Even simple items may be hard to find once you're far from home and familiar areas. These tools will help you record your family's history in an organized manner.

Back pack

Get a good, sturdy one. You can use it to hold many of the items listed below. Otherwise, you'll be dropping things.

Before You Begin 1

2 ink pens

For writing down your information and notes.

2 pencils

If your pens don't work (like getting wet).

1 pencil sharpener

For sharpening the pencils.

Highlighter

I prefer yellow, but green, blue, pink or lavender will do. DO NOT use these on original documents, library books or someone else's printed material. Always, always copy the original document, label that copy and then use your marker.

2 (minimum) 3-ring binders

These should be the larger ones, between 2 and 3 inches thick. These notebooks are important because you'll keep most of your notes in these. You'll start with two, but as I have found, you'll probably need more. Don't get the cardboard kind, get the plastic coated ones. You will discover that these survive rainstorms and coffee spills much better.

3-hole paper punch

To put into the binders. College ruled paper is fine, but if you find it too difficult to read because of the narrow lines, use high school paper.

Notebook dividers

These will enable you to quickly locate information in your carefully sorted notebook. A dozen is a good start.

3 x 5 index Cards

Use these to write miscellaneous notes that can be shuffled and organized later. I've found that having these cards forces me to use them rather than scraps of paper, such as magazine page corners or even napkins.

1 Before You Begin

1 paper clip dispenser and paper clips

You will find that even in this high tech world, you'll need to use them.

1 stapler with staples

The same reason as the paper clips.

Paper hole punch

This will let you neatly store collected documents in your three-ring binders. A three-hole punch will be easiest, though a single-hole punch and good coordination may also be used.

Envelopes

You will be sending a lot of letters to people asking for information. You will want to include a self-addressed stamped envelope for each to return the information to you. This small courtesy could be the difference between getting a response or none at all. The standard business size envelopes will do fine.

Stamps

You'll need a LOT of these. Unfortunately, not everyone has a PC and an email address. So, you'll soon be using the US Mail quite a bit to write to your friends, relatives, and historical and genealogical societies. Most people, like me, can't afford a postage meter machine, though it is another option.

Various family history forms

You can send these forms to your relatives to fill out. They are useful as you record your own family history. On the companion CD-ROM I have included several useful forms, including family group sheets and pedigree charts. For more information about printing these forms, see the "What's On The CD-ROM" chapter.

Address book

The old-fashioned way to keep addresses. This is handy when you don't have a portable computer or PDA (Personal Digital Assistant) handy. You will be putting addresses in your PC later and the more care you take now to keep those addresses organized, the better prepared you will be later.

Before You Begin 1

US road atlas

If you don't have one, get a new one. An atlas is great for mapping out your future travels. If you pursue your family history beyond your immediate locale, a good road atlas is indispensable. It also helps you see geographically how and where your family is in relation to others and yourself and how they've moved through the years.

Tape recorder (or dictation machine)

If you don't know short hand, have terrible note-taking skills or simply don't like taking notes while Aunt Jennie is talking about family history, record your conversations (being sure your interviewee doesn't mind). I recommend from experience that a small portable cassette recorder with an external microphone does the best job. Dictation machines and many of the newer recorders have built-in microphones, which can create muddy recordings in some environments. You don't want to record an hour or more of family history only to discover later that you can barely make out the words. Over the years I have collected several recorded interviews and I play them again just to listen and remember.

Camera (and film)

You need a good working camera, preferably a 35 mm. This is the most common format and 35 mm film can be found just about anywhere. 35 mm cameras take sharp pictures, which is important when you learn how to transfer them to your PC later in the book. Whether you are going to scan them in or put them on CD-ROM you will want crisp, clear photos. I recommend using only Kodak film. I'm not getting any money plugging Kodak, but nearly all film processing companies can use this type of film. You will want to transfer your pictures and negatives later and the quicker you get your film processed the better. You can learn more about graphics and photography in a later chapter.

Furniture and space

You should set aside an area in your home or apartment to keep and work on the materials you'll gather. It doesn't have to be a room, or even a large area of a room; just a small desk (with a drawer or two) tucked in the corner of your family room or bedroom is an excellent spot. You will discover over time that you'll need the little bit of privacy it affords while you read and write.

1 Before You Begin

You will also want to have at least a 2 drawer filing cabinet. You don't need a new one. You can purchase cheaper-than-new furniture through used office supply stores. A book shelf is also a necessity. You may not know it now, but you'll find that your genealogy and history books collection will increase dramatically.

Copier machine (optional)

You should be able to find a good personal copy machine at your local office supply store. There are many different brands to choose from. I suggest that you purchase one only after you have a chance to test it with a sample document, preferably a graphic one. You can also find good buys at used office-furniture supply stores. If you don't want to buy a personal copier then you will need to familiarize yourself with the local copy shop. You may have a Kinko's or Sir Speedy near you. Remember though, you'll save yourself a lot of gas money and travel inconveniences by having your own.

Microfiche or microfilm reader (optional)

Having one of these is a luxury. You'll be looking at a lot of records on film, and most of the census work which is on film can be rented or purchased. Libraries and most active historical and genealogical societies will have one or more for you to use. Having your own reader can save you trips back and forth from the library or court house. If you can find one reasonably priced you should purchase it. Used readers range in price based on condition and options from $50 to $500. If the reader can print a copy of the document, that's even better—it'll save you from hand-copying everything you find. You can find used ones at auctions (personal properties, schools or libraries in most medium sized cities) or several of the genealogical supply stores (See Catalogs on the CD-ROM).

PC

Obviously, you'll also need a personal computer. It should be at least an Intel Pentium-based system. I recommend the following: Any brand of a Pentium 120 (or above) based system, 32 Mb of RAM, 1.2 gigabyte hard drive, a CD-ROM drive (4x or above in speed) and a 28.8 baud modem.

Before You Begin 1

The Pentium-based computers offer more speed. You want the fastest PC you can afford because you will be running graphic programs in the near future (see chapter on family photos and graphic presentations later in the book). You will be very discouraged if you must wait several minutes while the computer tries to display your work-in-progress. This speed is also directly related to the amount of RAM you have. The more RAM, the faster the PC can display images.

The 1.2 gigabyte (or larger) hard drive size is important because the graphics, images, newsletters and other related material will take a lot of room.

The CD-ROM drive is important to have. You will be using it to install some genealogy software and accessing the many different genealogical data CDs on the market. For more information about the many CD-ROMs, see the software chapters later in the book.

The modem (modulator demodulator) speed is important when you are ready to use America OnLine (AOL), CompuServe (CIS) or the world wide web (WWW). The faster the modem, the faster information is sent to your computer. Later in the book (Online Genealogy) I discuss the enormous amount of electronic information and the sometimes confusing ways to research your family history on-line.

Computer monitor

The PC you purchase may or may not come with a monitor. If you are able to choose, get one you can afford with a .28 dot pitch display or less (such as .26 to .24). I also recommend a 17" viewing screen. You'll be spending a lot of time in front of that monitor, and a larger viewing screen will be much more comfortable on your eyes.

Printer

Today you have a large variety of printers to choose from. Epson, Citizen, Lexmark, Brother, IBM, Apple and Hewlett-Packard (HP) are all leading companies producing quality PC printers. HP sells basically two types of printers: deskjets and laserjets. The deskjet printers are inexpensive, easy to operate, produce good quality (usually 600 dpi) printouts and will be compatible with virtually all the software you'll be using. The laserjets offer faster printing and sometimes better resolution printouts (from 600 to 1200 dpi). The higher the dpi (dots per inch), the better your printed documents will look.

1 Before You Begin

There are also several printers on the market that print near-photographic images. One in particular is Fargo Electronics' Foto Fun series of printers. These printers let you print excellent quality images, but will not print regular 8 1/2 by 11 sheets of paper.

The best price/performance printers are the HP Deskjet 600 and 800 series. These offer 600 dpi black and white as well as very good color output. You will find these printers the most versatile and the best quality. This quality can be improved even further with a printing kit (such as Kodak's or Fuji Film's), because the printing kits include very high-quality paper on which to print your color documents.

Scanner and/or copier (optional)

You will need access to a copier or, better yet, a scanner connected to your PC. A portable PC with an attached portable hand scanner is very useful. However, I've found that toting this equipment can be a bit much. With a color scanner you'll scan at 256 colors at the least. Many of the newer scanners go upwards of 16 million colors. If your PC has a high resolution display, you can go up to resolutions of 1024 by 768. Be aware, though, that the file sizes increase quickly with the higher scanning resolutions. For black and white images, you should scan at 256 shades of grey. You must make sure that the image size and number of colors doesn't exceed your monitor's screen limits.

There are several models of scanners available to you today. The major brands include Mustek, MicroTek, Hewlett-Packard, Epson, Canon and others. Scanners can be broken down into two basic configurations: hand scanners and desktop flatbeds. Hand scanners are so named because you must use your hand to move the scanner over a document. They are convenient and inexpensive. If portability is important to you, they are a nice accessory. However, the output quality of the hand scanners is usually much less than a flatbed one.

Flatbed scanners come in several configurations, such as 300, 600 and 1200 dpi (dots per inch) scanning resolution and between 8-, 12-, 24- or 32-bit color resolution. Basically, the higher the dpi and color resolution, the better your images will look after they are scanned. The only disadvantage is that they can be very expensive, although today you can get a 600 dpi scanner (the lowest resolution I recommend) for as little as $350 retail. I highly recommend getting the best scanner you can afford. This will directly correlate to better images when you're working with them.

Before You Begin

Another type of flat scanner is the new crop of personal photo scanners sold by several companies, the most popular being Kodak, Polaroid and EZ Photo (from Storm Software). The latter I will show you how to use in the Photography and Graphics chapter. These scanners are designed to scan the most common sized photos: 5 X 7 and smaller. They are an excellent value for those on a budget. They range in price from $179 to $279 and are sold at most major electronics and computer stores.

Software

Aside from the PC, the software you'll be using to record your family's information and history will make the greatest difference between creating a good project or publishing a great one. You will need at least three programs: a word processor, a graphic program and a genealogy program.

The word processor you use will probably depend on what came with your system or what others have recommended to you. I recommend Microsoft's Word (version 6 or the Windows 95 version 7). It is both powerful and easy to use. Word will be used to write your notes and correspondence and prepare your material for publishing. Word allows you to import photographs and other graphics to adorn your family history. Word is also capable of importing all text files that you will encounter from other family members or historians, from WordPerfect to AmiPro to standard ASCII text files.

Another Microsoft product, MS Publisher, is a great program to create family newsletters and other heavily formatted documents you want to write. Publisher has an important feature for beginners called a Wizard. The Wizard leads you step-by-step through creating layouts for cards, letters and newsletters. You can also import text from a variety of sources and "drop in" pictures and graphics. See chapter 5 for examples of how to create a newsletter.

Many graphic and photography programs are available. The dozens of choices range in both price and power, including products from Adobe, Microsoft, Micrografx and JASC, Inc. You will want to use one of these to create and edit images for inclusion into your family history. Later in the book I will show you how to use one of the most powerful and inexpensive graphic programs, Paint Shop Pro.

1 Before You Begin

As powerful and versatile as Microsoft's Word and Publisher are, they're no substitute for a genealogy program. Word is not suited well to tracking text (including descriptive biographies, obituaries, etc.) in your database of relatives and their relationship to you. A genealogy program is designed to keep all your family members in proper relation to each other. They can even tell you if you enter incorrect information, for example, giving a father's birthdate that is more recent than his child's birth.

In the early 1980s, genealogy programs were limited to the Church of Latter Day Saints's Personal Ancestral File (PAF) and a few DOS-based programs. Today there are over 150 genealogy programs and dozens of genealogical software utilities which make the early programs seem primitive. Several of these programs are outstanding, including Roots and Visual Roots, Brother's Keeper, Family Origins, Family Tree Maker, The Master Genealogist, Cumberland Trails, Epicenter Software, Family Tree House, Genius, MatterWare, and Family Reunion.

I detail three genealogy programs in this book. The DOS-based Brother's Keeper by John Steed, Family Origins from Parsons Technology and Family Tree Maker from Broderbund Software. Each has strengths and weaknesses and all are excellent choices to record your family history.

Be as prepared as you can. The most important thing about all of these tools I've discussed is that you'll have a much more enjoyable time working on your family history. The job is half done once you have the proper tools.

As you research your family's history, keep it organized and documented. Write down your sources and how and where you found them. You may want to go back and search more later, and maybe discover something you missed the first time. If you write it down now, you'll have an easier time finding it later. I can't stress enough the importance of organization. You will find that as you get more into this hobby and become more familiar with your own family history, that organizing and documenting your sources are paramount. Whether you do a little now, a little later or let the years go by, the time you spend organizing now will be more rewarding today and tomorrow for you and your family members. You may have thought that you were going to do two or three generations of your family and stop. It is more likely that you'll have a lifelong study ahead of you.

Beginning Your Search

Chapter 2

Using Other Programs For Your Family History

I've been researching my family's history for many years. I am not an expert genealogist, but I have done a lot of work using many methods and sources. This chapter is intended as a guide or possibly a check list that you can refer to when searching for those elusive ancestors. I hope that this chapter will give you some ideas that you haven't thought of yet. Don't be discouraged if you can't find every single one of your ancestors. In all likelihood, you won't. You'll need to focus on what you can find and let the rest take care of itself. You will discover that when you hit a brick wall, working on a series of clues will often lead you around that wall.

Records, records, records—it's said that over 20 government agencies keep current information on you. Although the US government is larger today than it was two-plus centuries ago, you'd be surprised at the depth of information you can find about ancestors if you know where to look. I have included quite a bit of information for you to track. For some I have given addresses, and others you will discover on your own. You will notice that I've put all source addresses in the appendix and on the CD-ROM. The CD-ROM has a file on it called "SOURCES.TXT" that has these addresses and any contacts that I have not listed in this chapter.

As I mentioned at the end of the previous chapter, you've got to document your information—*thoroughly*. You won't be around forever, and someone else will most certainly be interested in doing more family research after they've seen your work. The better you document your sources, the easier it will be for the next family member to continue your work. A common term used is "citing" your sources. What is a citation? A citation is a reference to the source of specific information.

2 Beginning Your Search

There are four levels of citations that are explained in Parson Technology's Family Origins:

Primary (or original)

This would include objects and documentation that was created at the time of the incident and include state or federal census records, courthouse records, church records, passenger lists, military records and interviews with witnesses or participants.

Secondary

Published records including previously printed family histories or genealogies, collections of census or marriage data, family Bible data and other documents.

Questionable

Rumors or unconfirmed family legends. One of the oldest and often-believed is the family history of two brothers that came over from another country and split up. This is one way for many to explain the existence of several linkages of families with the same name. Be aware that you'll need to find out if that is true or not.

Unreliable

Guessing or assuming. There will be times that you simply will not find the solid information you need to confirm an event or a particular person's information. I would call this an "educated guess" at best. You must be careful not to ASSUME anything.

An excellent example of citing your sources is shown below (Wayne Thomas author).

Beginning Your Search 2

> *Example of citing your sources (Wayne Thomas author)*
>
> REFERENCE: Family Search IGI Batch 7614214 Source Call # 1058438 Sheet 71
> CENSUS: 1850—Washington Twp., Hocking Co., Ohio, #27 age 40 Farmer
> CENSUS: 1860—Washington Twp., Hocking Co., Ohio, #231 age 50 Farmer
> REFERENCE: Book 2 Page 5, Certificate #123 Hocking Co. Book of Deaths
> REFERENCE: Family Search IGI Batch M514081 Source Call # 910657
> CENSUS: 1850—Washington Twp., Hocking Co., Ohio, #27 age 40
> CENSUS: 1860—Washington Twp., Hocking Co., Ohio, #231 age 50
> CENSUS: 1870—Washington Twp., Hocking Co., Ohio, #150
> REFERENCE: Book 2 Page 11 Certificate # 176 Hocking Co. Book of Deaths
> CENSUS: 1850—Washington Twp., Hocking Co., Ohio, #37 age 18
> REFERENCE: Family Search IGI Batch 5026679 Source Call # 1553836 Sheet 3
> REFERENCE: Page 172 Certificate #59 Hocking Co Book of Marriages
> TITLE: Index to Birth Records 1867-1882 Hocking Co., Ohio
> REFERENCE: Book 1 Page 334 Hocking County Courthouse
> TITLE: Index to Birth Records 1882-1892 Hocking Co., Ohio
> REFERENCE: Book 2 Page 41 Hocking County Courthouse
> REFERENCE: Certificate #173 Vital Statistics Lancaster, Ohio.
> REFERENCE: Ohio Historical Society Death Index
> TITLE: Index to Birth Records 1882-1892 Hocking Co., Ohio

WHERE DO YOU START TO RESEARCH YOUR FAMILY HISTORY

The following illustration shows how I've outlined this chapter:

2 Beginning Your Search

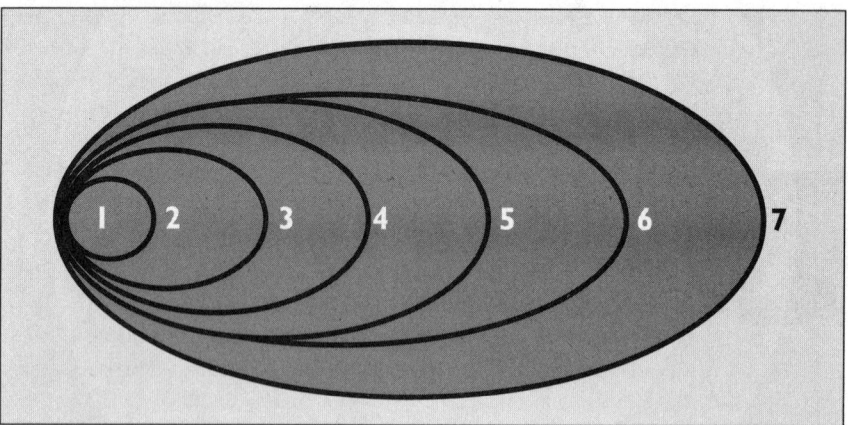

The rings represent the following:

1. You and your family

2. Town (or city) and county sources

3. State sources

4. Regional sources

5. National sources

6. International sources

7. Other sources

You'll likely start constructing your family history by finding and gathering information from sources closest to you and progressively moving outward from there, researching further from yourself and your immediate family members. This isn't the only way to begin. There are literally thousands more methods to find clues to search your family heritage. I couldn't possibly outline them all for this guide. I only hope that this brief outline can at least give you some suggestions and ideas of where to look for clues that you haven't thought of before.

Beginning Your Search 2

You

The center is you and your immediate family members, including your children, spouse, brothers, sisters, parents, aunts, uncles and cousins. Start by gathering the most basic information about each: name, birth date, birth place (be sure to include city, county, state and country), occupation, hobbies and memberships.

You should start with what you know. Start with yourself, your wife, children and possibly their children. There are two things about yourself that you know for certain. You have a name AND someone gave it to you. Your name can give you many clues to your family history. There are surnames—(your last name) and proper (or given) names (given to you at birth). It was (and for some still is) a practice to name your children after your parents and grandparents.

You will find that many of your ancestors used their ancestors to help name their children: for example, David William Smith, where David was his mother's father's name and William was his father's father. These are sometimes good clues to other members of families which you are researching.

Beware of Jr's, Sr's, and Roman Numerals in names given to your relatives after they've gone. They weren't usually used early on. It wasn't all that unusual that more than one son (or daughter) of the same family had a parent's first name. You could have several Johns, Davids, Williams, and others in the same or related families.

If you are interested in how your surname came about there is an excellent article in the November/December issue of *Family Chronicle* magazine titled "The Surname Origin List," by Jeff Chapman. The article gives an excellent explanation on the origins of the majority of last names. You can find out more information about *Family Chronicle* magazine in the Appendix.

Another great source of information about names is the Guild of One-Name Studies (registered as a Charity in England and Wales (no. 802048)) that can be accessed at CompuServe's Genealogy Forum—Societies and Organizations, and also on the world wide web. Mike Spathaky, the Hon. Secretary of the Guild of One-Name Studies, says

2 Beginning Your Search

The Guild of One-Name Studies is a world-wide voluntary organization of people interested in one-name studies. A one-name study involves research into all occurrences of a particular surname on a world-wide basis. Different studies may emphasize different aspects, such as the geographical and historical distribution of the name or the genealogy of different lines bearing the name.

The Guild publishes a quarterly *Journal of One-Name Studies*. Its *Register of One-Name Studies* is published annually in printed and microfiche format. There is also an on-line version which is updated more frequently at the Guild's web-site (http://www.leicester.co.uk/guild/).

The web site also contains further information and joining details. The postal address is: The Guild of One-Name Studies, Box G, 14 Charterhouse Buildings, Goswell Road, London EC1M 7BA, England. Postal inquiries should be accompanied by a large reply-paid envelope or three International Reply Coupons.

You can find more information around your and/or your parents' home. The paper trail you can leave is amazing. Look for the following:

- Birth, death and marriage certificates
- Wedding announcements
- Divorce papers
- Funeral programs
- Church affiliation and membership papers
- Newspaper cutouts (including selected news of family members or obituaries)
- Printed obituaries
- Old family scrap books
- Family Bibles
- Shoe boxes and albums of photos
- Postcards

Beginning Your Search 2

- Letters
- Diaries
- School records (including report cards and year books)
- Military documents
- Certificates and awards
- Real estate papers
- Insurance and medical records
- Final wills
- Membership organizations and affiliations
- Employment documents
- Written family histories
- Stories and traditions.

Remember that all these are going to used as clues to older relatives and can help point you in directions for more research. You will also want to make copies of any original material you have. You should work with the copies and file the originals. For older and more valuable documents, rent a safety deposit box at your bank.

You will be writing to a lot of your relatives for more information about them and what they may know about your family heritage. When writing your relatives, be sure to explain to them what you are doing and don't get too personal with your questions.

I have found that telling a relative what I am doing and giving them a short form (such as a family form) to fill out can be helpful. Don't make the form long. Keep it short and leave lots of room for notes. You'll find that asking direct questions will yield direct answers.

2 Beginning Your Search

Leave room for information they can share without "filling in the blanks." Try to make the letter personal. Your PC is great at mail merge and address labeling, but comes across as impersonal. Instead of sending "Born:_____" as a blank to fill in, you might say something like "When and where were you born?" Always, and I mean always include a self-addressed stamped envelope (SASE) with all of your letters. You will find that it will get you more and quicker results, as well as being a courtesy. Remember though, besides the information about dates and places, your relatives can give you clues to further research. Many family traditions and stories usually have at least a bit of truth to them. Don't write these off—investigate!

Village, town or city and county resources

Location, location, location—find out what city and county your ancestors lived in. You will find valuable information and clues by starting out at the city or town of your ancestors.

The first thing you should look for is a local historical or genealogical society that is located in or near your ancestor's locality. Genealogical societies are a great help. They may have information that can point you directly where to search. You should also join the societies that you frequent. As I said, these are staffed by volunteers and they help because they want to help. The volunteers can save you a lot of time and eliminate a lot of frustration.

The local genealogical societies should be the first place you contact to research an area or family lineage. Many will have other family histories and local biographies available for you to read. An excellent source of information kept there is published county histories. You will find that the majority of county histories were written between the late 1870s and into the early 1900s, when the county was observing a 50- or 100-year birthday of the county.

Many of these include biographies of local citizens (although usually the more wealthy and prominent) and major events that helped shape the county. I have found many of my own ancestors mentioned in them, which has led me to still more research.

Beginning Your Search

You can also stop at the circuit clerk's office, getting copies of birth and death certificates, mortuary records, marriages, divorces, town clerk or city board minutes, land purchases, court records, police records, county census records, orphans court records, Old Folks or Veterans Homes, administration and guardianships and wills. Wills are public property and anyone may acquire a copy of any will (for a copy fee). You can also find more information at the County Health Center, a local hospital or mental health institutions.

Local newspapers are invaluable in helping you find information about your family. The most obvious being published obituaries. But be forewarned; they're not gospel. They should be used as clues for further research. Go to the local newspaper to find out if they have an index of them.

Many libraries have a genealogy room set aside for the local society and are invaluable in providing clues. These rooms can include cemetery and tombstone information, indexed or filed obituary notices, genealogical directories, society newsletters (local and possibly national), city directories, phone books, funeral home information and much more. Larger ones may even include copies of census and immigration records.

It is wise to become familiar with your local library's archives and the types of material they hold. You can also use the library's interlibrary loan system to borrow copies of newspaper archives at historical societies throughout the country. So even though you may not be able to find microfilm copies of old newspapers locally, you can still find them through your own local library.

Church records are another good source. You or your relatives' past and present church records can include: membership records, baptism records, confirmation records, communion records, society, committee or board minutes, Sunday school records, church cemetery records and church archives.

A quick note about cemeteries—although some may feel it's a bit morbid, tombstone photos are important to have. Many of your relatives won't be able to travel to the cemeteries where your ancestors lie and photos can be helpful for them. They are also good to have for yourself when you need to reference birth and death inscriptions.

2 Beginning Your Search

County maps can be found and copied at the county's land office and are an excellent tool to help you research (as well as include in) your family history. Besides local offices, you can find many companies that sell new and antique maps. You can also use many of the current crop of CD-ROM-based electronic maps. These are listed on the CD-ROM for you.

State and regional resources

Your state government has a wealth of information you can use. Much of the information from the local and county level can also be found at your state's capital. This information includes: land grants, state census records, tax lists, military records, the state archives and state genealogical and historical societies. Covering a larger area, the state genealogical societies may not be as convenient to visit but they may provide information not available at the local genealogical society. They usually include general state-wide information as well as material from genealogical societies in the state. For vital information you can write to your state capital and request a list of forms that they provide to help you in your research. In the appendix I have included addresses to which you may write for information. There are also many national organizations with regional groups and societies you can contact, including Daughters of the American Revolution (DAR), Sons of the American Revolution (SAR), and many others. You will find a list of these organizations in the appendix at the back of this book.

Most of you probably have ancestors that landed on the east coast when they arrived in America. One of the oldest and most respected genealogical society is the New England Historical and Genealogical Society. They are very active in research, resources and training and can help give you direction in researching your family history (whether eastward or not). The web site and address of the NEHGS is in chapter three and on the companion CD-ROM.

National resources

You can also research your family history by using the seemingly endless amount of records kept by your US government. The National Archives and Records Administration is the place to go. It's so large that you can buy books just to help you navigate the information available. If you cannot visit the NARA in Washington DC, you can go to a regional branch of the Archives at various locations throughout the country to do your research. The addresses are located on the companion CD-ROM in the RSOURCES file.

Beginning Your Search 2

Some of the other national and government resources include the following:

- The US Census Bureau's archives (taken every ten years beginning in 1790)
- Immigration and naturalization records
- Passenger arrival lists
- Immigration records
- Passport information
- Tax lists
- Land grants
- Bounty land records
- Records of American Indians
- Records of black Americans
- Records of government employees
- Social security indexes
- Military records (all branches from the Revolutionary War to the Gulf War)

This is to name just to list a few.

You can get copies of war pension, military service and disabled veterans records by writing to:

Military Services Branch
National Archives and Records Administration
8th and Pennsylvania Avenue NW
Washington DC 20408

Ask for copies of Form 80. You can also write to the National Personnel Records Center and request NA Form 13043 "Genealogical Statement" of Standard Form 180 "Request Pertaining to Military Records." The address for this is:

25

2 Beginning Your Search

National Personnel Records Center
(Military Personnel Records)
9700 Page Boulevard
St. Louis, MO 63132

For a free list of federal records centers' addresses write to General Service Administration, Washington, DC, USA 20408.

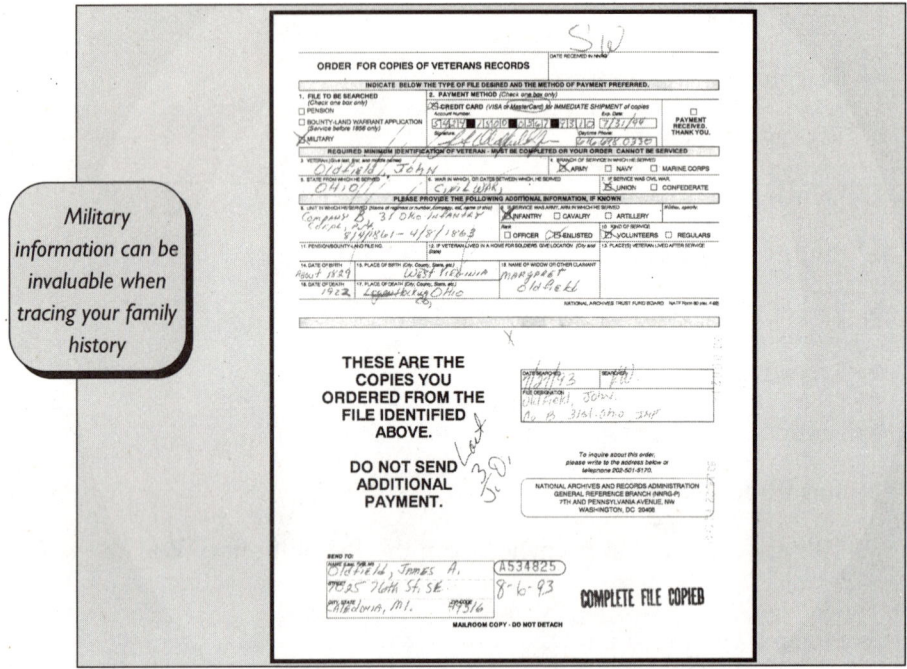

Military information can be invaluable when tracing your family history

The US Census is one of the best ways to research your family heritage. The census information, depending on the year taken, can give you invaluable material to help you find family members and do more research.

The census was taken within township and county and contains the names (first and last after 1830), ages and birth places of the head of the household, wife, children and anyone else living at a location at the time of the census.

Beginning Your Search

In Chapter 7 you will learn how to locate US census information and how to use it more effectively. There are numerous web sites that can help you use the census. You should also check the Catalogs, located on the CD-ROM; these genealogical book publishers have a huge library of books that can help you in your research. There are also national family organizations and publications that you can contact. They are discussed in chapter three.

You can also contact and join the National Genealogical Society. They are the largest genealogical society and have dozens of special interest groups you can contact. They even have a group that covers using your PC for research and recording your family history.

International sources

I have found over the years that this is one area of research in which a computer really helps out. I've written to several organizations in different countries and it takes time for a response. It can be a disappointment to wait weeks for a response and then discover you asked for the wrong information or that the others didn't understand your requests.

When you send requests for information be very specific and always include an international envelope and postage. You should check with your post office for the rates. If you don't get a response, it may be that you didn't include enough postage. The Internet and the use of electronic mail (email) will dramatically improve the turnaround time.

There are hundreds of international organizations that are willing to help, if you can find them. You will discover that most of the countries that helped populate America in its early days have organizations that can help you find that elusive ancestor. I have found that the easiest countries to contact include England, Scotland, Ireland and several other European countries. In the FAMTREE.HTM bookmark file on the CD-ROM there are bookmarks to over fifty foreign countries genealogical organizations.

2 Beginning Your Search

Other sources

There are so many other sources to find information about your family history that it can be overwhelming. You can find information from The Church of Jesus Christ of Latter Day Saints' main library in Salt Lake City, Utah, local LDS Family History Libraries, ethnic organizations, national offices of Methodist, Protestant and Catholic denominations, Native American Indian organizations and professional genealogists.

The Church of Jesus Christ of Latter-Day Saints (LDS) Library has literally millions of records of every type on microfilm. If you have a branch of the library near you, they can be very helpful. I have always found that they are courteous and very helpful, no matter what your religious beliefs are. The depth and breadth of their genealogical information is mind boggling.

The main Family History Library was founded by the Genealogical Society of Utah in 1894 and has the largest collection of genealogical material in the world. The society is dedicated to acquiring and preserving copies of the records of mankind and is financially supported by The Church of Jesus Christ of Latter-Day Saints (LDS), a.k.a. the Mormons. For over fifty years they have been using microfilm as the medium to copy documents around the world. They are also the people who invented Personal Ancestral File (PAF), one of the first nationally recognized methods of exchanging family history.

Besides the main center they have family history centers located in the US and over 50 countries around the world. The local centers give people access to much of the library's resources off-site. Not all of the material in the Family History Library can be accessed through these centers. Some items can only be consulted in the main library in Salt Lake City. These centers and the Family History Library are all open to the public free of charge (except for copying and postage and handling charges). In return, they want you to share your family information so it can be preserved for future generations. You can share your information by submitting a PAF (Personal Ancestral File) or other approved electronic file of your family history database.

Beginning Your Search 2

You will find them indispensable in your research. You should visit the local branch of the LDS Library or write the main library in Salt Lake City, Utah, for a description of their microfilm holdings. You can find a copy of an excellent article written by Conor P. Mac Hale (cmchale@gn.apc.org), one of the best articles about the LDS Libraries, on many of the genealogy web sites mentioned in chapter three.

More excellent sources of genealogical information are the national and international genealogy magazines and newsletters and genealogical book publishers. You will find their electronic addresses and how to contact them in chapter seven. Be sure to use the CD-ROM's Catalog feature to see the huge variety of books and magazines that are available.

If you've come to a point where you've hit a brick wall, you should also consider hiring a professional researcher to help. For lists of researchers, consult the local library in the area you are searching. Also, historical and genealogical societies usually have a list of professional genealogists that you can contact. Professionals are very expensive, but it is an option you should leave open.

Besides all the legal terms, land measurements, old (and oddly named) occupations, weird diseases, and quite possibly a foreign language tossed in, all family historians pick up some history along the way. As you'll find when you share your information with others, history really can be fun.

The next chapter will introduce you to a wealth of resources you can explore without even leaving your home. The world wide web and the Internet host sites devoted to genealogy, discussion groups for genealogists, and databases brimming with ancestral information.

Researching Your Family History On-line

Chapter 3

Researching Your Family History On-line

The World Wide Web is perhaps the best researching tool since the Dewey decimal system, and is much easier to use. It contains a great amount of information from a wealth of sources around the world, from professionals, coorporations, organizations, governments and individuals. Every topic is covered and genealogy is no exception.

To join the online cognosci you need a modem for your PC (see Chapter 1 for selecting a modem). If your modem card came with your PC, you're ready to go. If you recently purchased one, install it and get going. You will find that your PC and the online world will become excellent tools for furthering your research.

Accessing Information On-line

There are 4 ways to access information on-line with your PC and modem. We'll discuss those four methods in this section.

Non-commercial BBSs (Bulletin Board Systems)

Before the internet and the world wide web, FIDOnet connected computer users through bulletin boards. These BBSs are run by volunteers throughout the country. They are still an excellent way to communicate through electronic mail and bulletins from users throughout the country and beyond.

3 Researching Your Family History On-line

Online trial periods

The modem or new PC you have probably included software to try out an online service such as America OnLine or CompuServe (or NetCom, Sprynet, Genie, etc.). These commercial, subscription-based services have many proprietary resources and access to the larger internet. Prodigy is an internet-based service costing $19.95 per month for unlimited usage, including an active genealogy forum you should investigate (www.prodigy.com).

America Online

America Online has become the largest subscription-based service. Its base of more than 7 million users is still growing. I would be surprised if you couldn't find SOMEONE in those millions interested in the same family history as you.

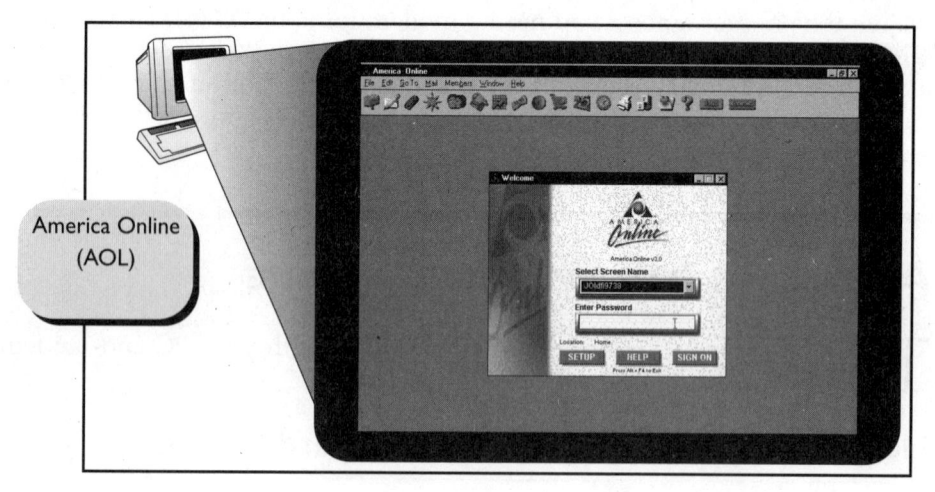

CompuServe

CompuServe, my personal favorite, is the oldest and most "mature" online service. CompuServe has literally thousands of "special interest" groups and forums available for you to join (free with your subscription) and use.

Researching Your Family History On-line 3

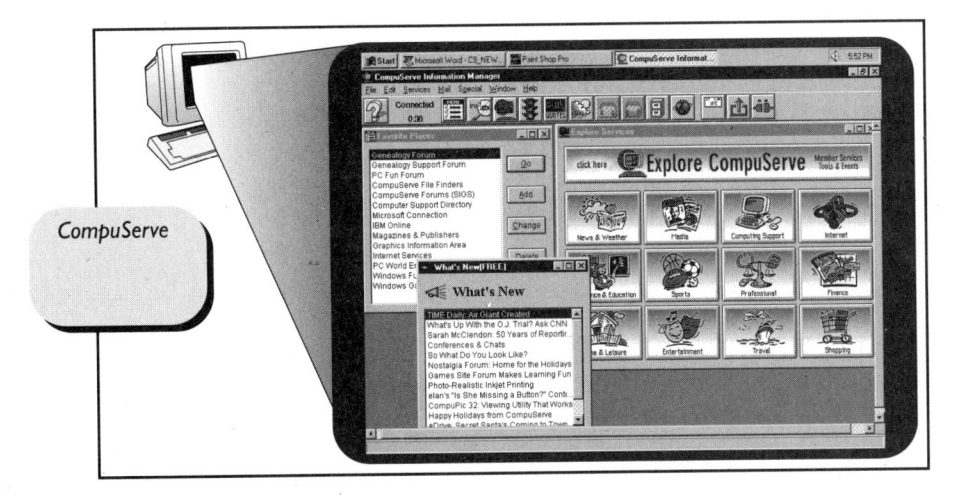

I also feel that Dick Eastman's Roots genealogy forum and the genealogy support forum he is in charge of are excellent sources of information and guidance. Over the years Dick has helped me and I'm sure a thousand others.

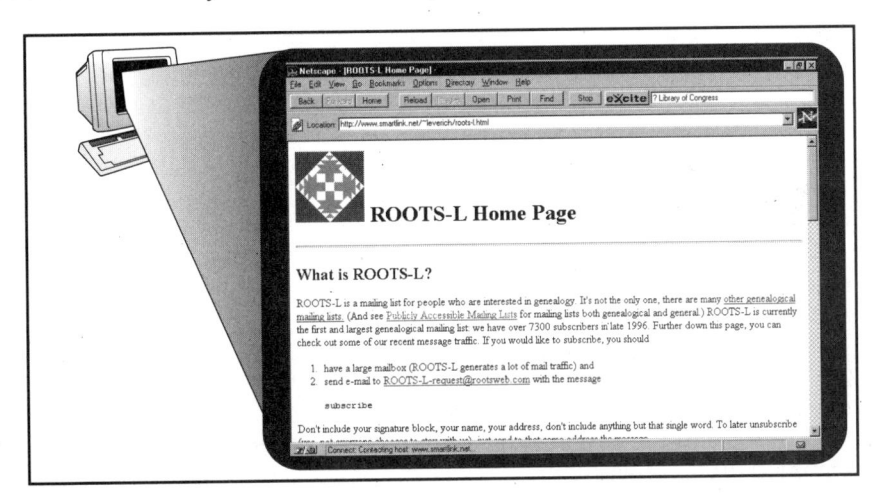

The genealogy forums on these two services feature software libraries, name lists, chat rooms and excellent help from the sysops (system operators) who care for them. You will find several volunteers who may specialize in a particular subject of genealogy or a certain area of the country. Today, one of the great advantages of CompuServe and AOL is that both offer internet "gateways."

35

3 Researching Your Family History On-line

That is, you can use their services and launch to the internet. For most beginners starting out, this is an excellent way to get your feet wet surfing the web. Once you become more proficient with using your PC online, you may want to move on to getting your own local internet service provider.

Usenet newsgroups and mailing lists

Although not as popular as the world wide web, newsgroups can be an excellent source of information. Later in this chapter you can learn more about them and the mailing list sites available. Mailing lists are simple to join and use. All you need to do is send an E-mail to the list's address, where the list administrator resends that message to everyone who is subscribed to that list. This is a great way of discovering others who are researching the same material or family.

The Internet (more precisely the World Wide Web or simply "the web")

The web can be accessed two ways: You can use your commercial on-line service (such as CompuServe and AOL) to go to the web or you can go directly to the web through a local internet service provider (ISP).

The most significant advance in computers today is the internet or, within the confines of this guide, the World Wide Web. The web has changed the way millions of PC owners use their computers. The world wide web seems to be everywhere. You can't help seeing ads on TV or in print displaying a company's online address, like "http://www.webtv.com." You may even have been asked, "What's your 'Email' address?"

The on-line community is growing at an incredible rate and shows no sign of slowing down. In just over two years, the internet (including news groups, mailing groups and the world wide web) have changed the face of computing. An estimated 20- to 30-million PC users are going on-line with their PCs. This internet thing is the beginning of something really big.

Two recent events changed the way we communicate through personal computers. Prior to 1992 the internet was a large network of computers connected through regular phone lines used to share research and data among the academics and the government. The world wide web was developed in 1992 by Tim Berners-Lee to help universities and academics exchange information more consistently with each other throughout the world.

Researching Your Family History On-line

At that time there were only colleges, universities and a few research laboratories on the system. But in 1993 at the University of Illinois' Super Computer Labs, Marc Andreesen and others developed a program called Mosaic. For the first time, anyone with a computer, modem and this "internet browser" could communicate with anyone else anywhere in the world. Although the internet and world wide web mean the same thing to most people, they are different. If you are interested in knowing more about the internet and the world wide web, I recommend visiting your local library or book store. They will have a large selection of books on the subject.

Probably more than anything else, the world wide web has changed the way I research my family history. It can expand your research as well. However, the web is not the "end all" to research. Far from it. It can improve your odds on locating more information about your family. At the very least, the web can take you places you normally wouldn't have time to see.

Let me remind you though, the web is no substitute to going to your local history or genealogy society's meetings. The web can't get you a copy of a birth, marriage or death certificate or even let you research the US Census reports. Many of the documents that I mention in earlier chapters are not available on the web, due either to a desire for personal privacy or just the lack of human resources. You'll find enough to make the web an exciting and valuable new research tool for your family history.

On the world wide web you will discover that your computer can take you to wonderful and exciting places like the following:

- ❖ The National Archives
- ❖ The National Genealogical Society
- ❖ The Library of Congress
- ❖ The New England Historical Society

You can go to virtual stores (electronic storefronts, so to speak) that sell genealogy books and supplies or provide genealogical services (from restoring old photographs to professional genealogical consultations). You can go to the Guild of One Name Studies and research your family name or go to the Heraldry web site to learn about your family's heraldry. You can visit other family historians' web sites and pour over what they have done, discussing their work through E-mail.

3 Researching Your Family History On-line

You can travel from Ireland to Africa to Spain to Australia to Russia and back and the odds are you'll find something that can help you with your family history. You can search for local and national organizations and associations, specialty family name groups, and commercial genealogical services that can locate a professional genealogist, books, maps, restoration supplies and all points in-between.

There are web sites devoted to specialized subjects, from beginner's guides of genealogy to adoptions to finding lost friends and relatives to graveyard tombstone studies to hundreds of subjects in between. The diversity of subjects you can encounter is truly surprising. Despite what you've heard in the press concerning the world wide web's unmitigated freedoms, genealogy is one of the most popular topics on it.

The list of genealogy-related web sites numbers in the tens of thousands and grows literally everyday. It's no wonder all this can be confusing to a newcomer. What I would like to accomplish in the confines of this chapter is to help you sort through it all. If you choose from the recommendations I've listed below, you should have an exciting and rewarding web journey.

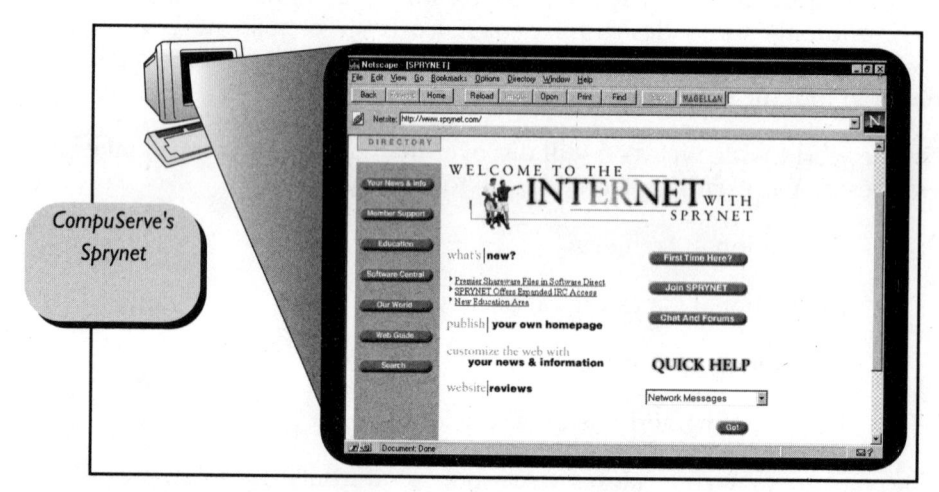

CompuServe's Sprynet

Researching Your Family History On-line   3

E-mail Is The Number One On-line Research Tool

If for no other reason, you should get on the web or one of the commercial subscriber services to use E-mail. Electronic mail is the best tool you have for online research, hands down. With E-mail software and services, you can send messages to others online anywhere in the world. Whether it's to correspond with someone with the same interests, just to ask questions or to keep in touch with your other online relatives, E-mail is quicker, cheaper and more productive than any alternative. You will quickly find that after using E-mail for awhile, you will want to have ALL your relatives online.

As handy as E-mail is, don't forget that this is a person to person transaction. Don't make your E-mail documents impersonal. Use the guidelines mentioned earlier in this guide to correspond with others. And don't forget, E-mail is not a substitute to using the phone for a call by voice. In this high-tech age it's sometimes easy to forget that we are, after all, only human.

There are four distinct ways that you can access E-mail. The simplest is by using the built-in mail service on AOL or CompuServe. If you have Netscape Communications' Navigator web browser program, it has Mail built-in (although you will need to set it up). There is also a wide variety of E-mail programs which you can use in conjunction with your internet connection. The most popular is Eudora, by Qualcomm. Finally, in recent months there has been a surge of web-based free E-mail services. These include companies such as USA.NET and HOTMAIL. The E-mail service is free and is supported by advertisers. If you don't mind the adverts, hotmail is an excellent choice. By using this online service you can access your E-mail from anywhere in the world. And, you have the added bonus of having a permanent E-mail address. I recommend hotmail.

Using a particular E-mail software program or web site service depends on what you want to learn to use. If you are a subscriber to AOL or CIS, their built-in E-mail service will do you well. If you want more sophisticated features and functions and more options and power, you should look over the specialized software and services available.

3 Researching Your Family History On-line

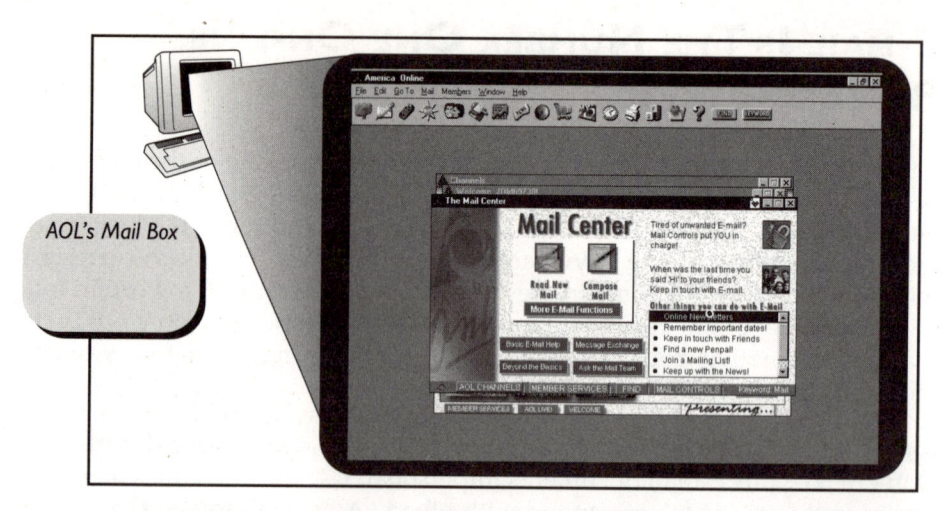

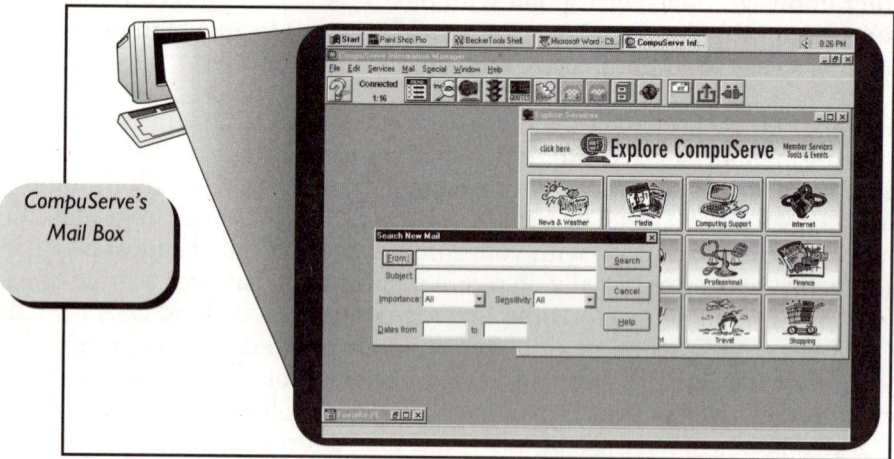

AOL's Mail Box

CompuServe's Mail Box

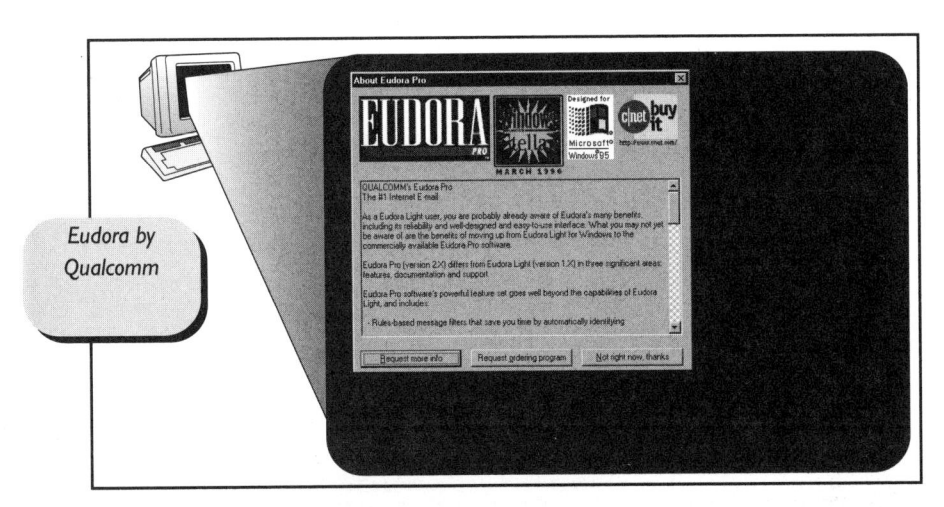

Researching Your Family History On-line 3

Eudora by Qualcomm

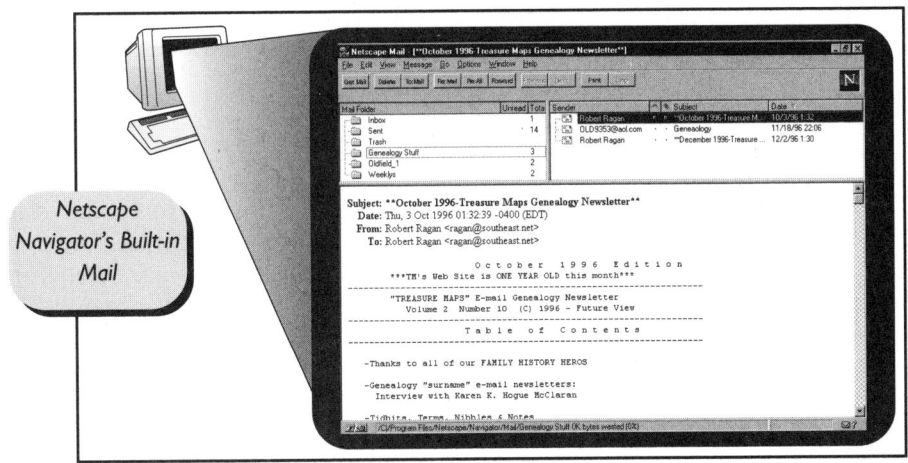

Netscape Navigator's Built-in Mail

41

3 Researching Your Family History On-line

Online Free E-mail Service

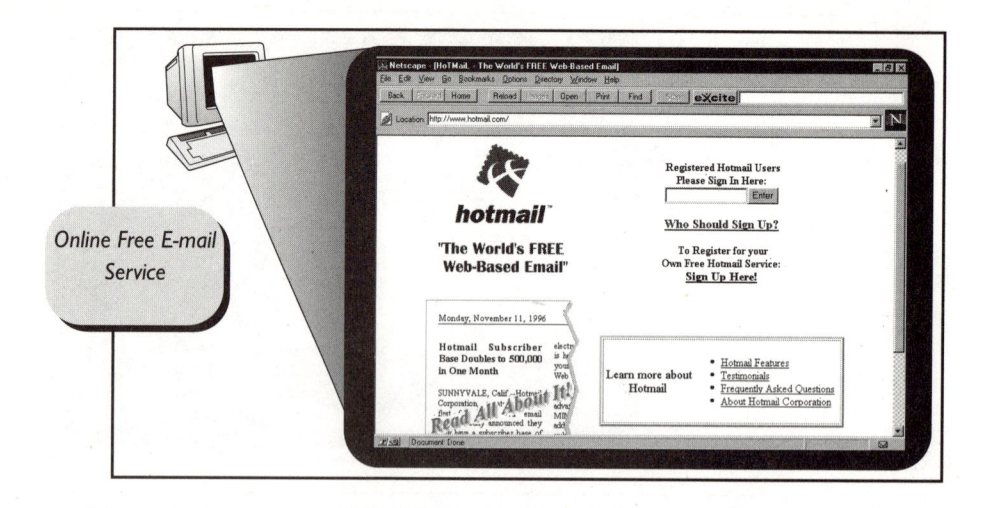

AMERICA ONLINE (AOL)

America Online has an excellent genealogy forum. It features live chat rooms on various topics from New England research, Virginia roots, American Civil War history, Beginning genealogy, the Internet for genealogists and many others. This forum also has "conference rooms," providing a more structured question and answer format than the chat rooms, that include Ancestral Digs, Golden Gates, Family Reunion, Family Tree House and Time Tunnel as subject rubrics. Both the chat and conference rooms are good sources for information and tips to resources.

AOL Genealogy Forum

The Genealogy Forum features Message boards (to read and leave messages to other subscribers), a Software Library (containing thousands of programs and files uploaded by other forum members), Online Genealogy Classes (to learn more about researching using many other genealogy sources), and Adoption Queries (dedicated to finding living people and/or searching adoption records).

Researching Your Family History On-line   3

You can also easily go to the web by just clicking the button for internet access through AOL's service. AOL is priced (as of January, 1997) at $19.95 a month for unlimited usage or $4.95 a month for 4 hours with an additional charge of $2.50 an hour after that.

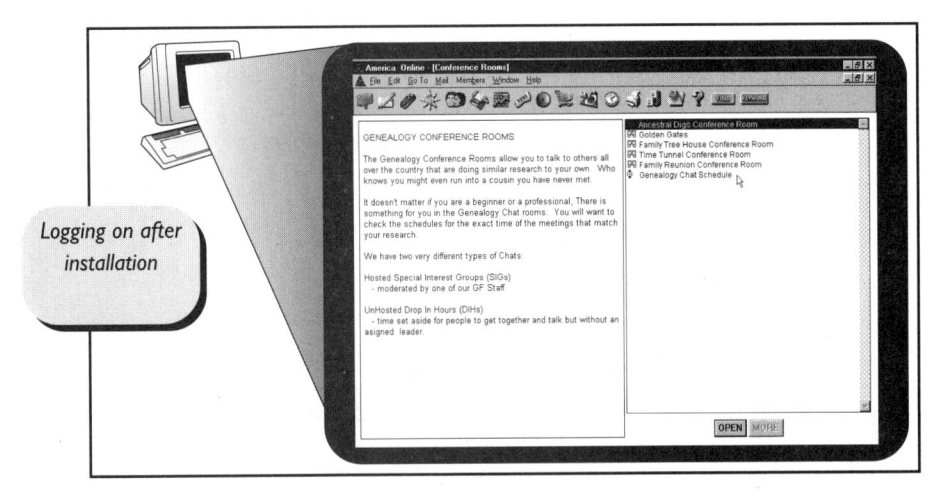

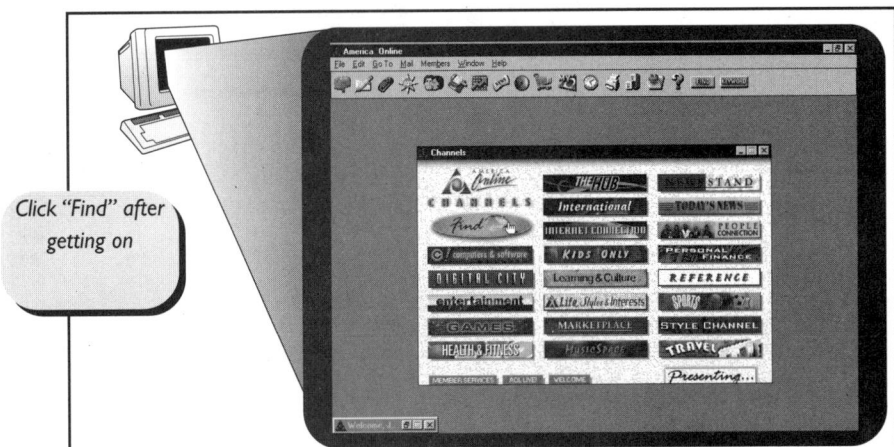

Logging on after installation

Click "Find" after getting on

43

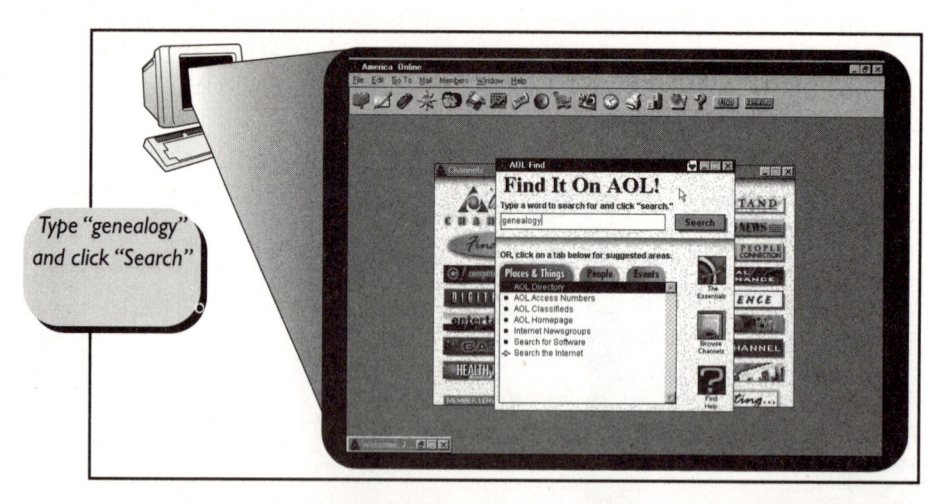

3 Researching Your Family History On-line

Type "genealogy" and click "Search"

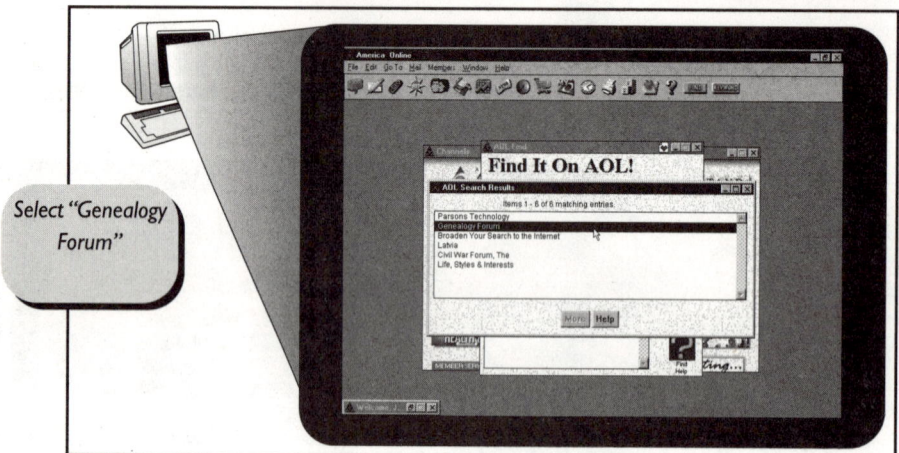

Select "Genealogy Forum"

44

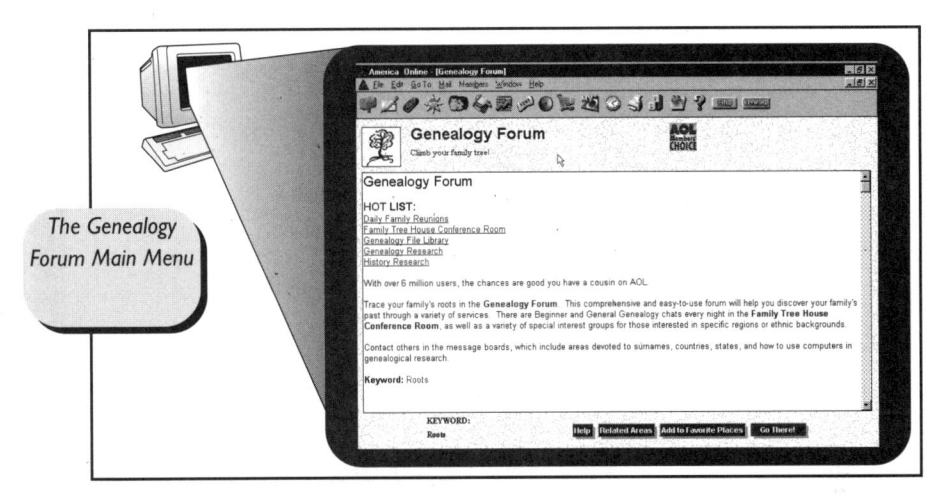

Researching Your Family History On-line 3

The Genealogy Forum Main Menu

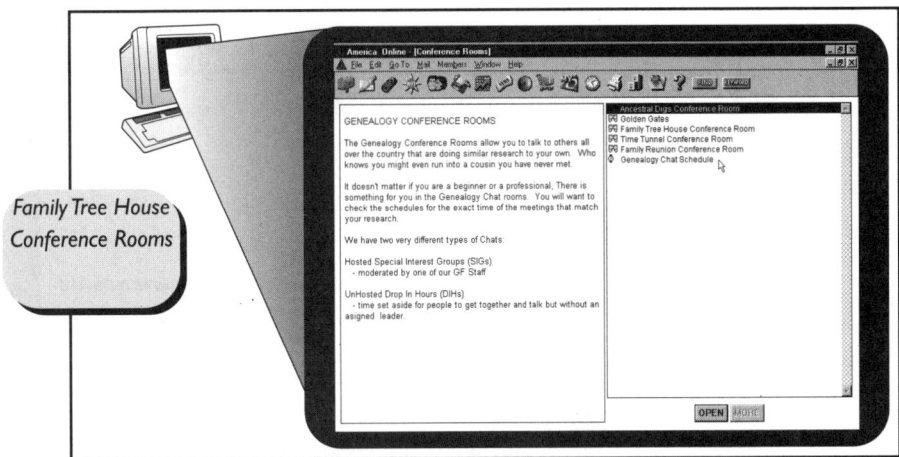

Family Tree House Conference Rooms

45

3 Researching Your Family History On-line

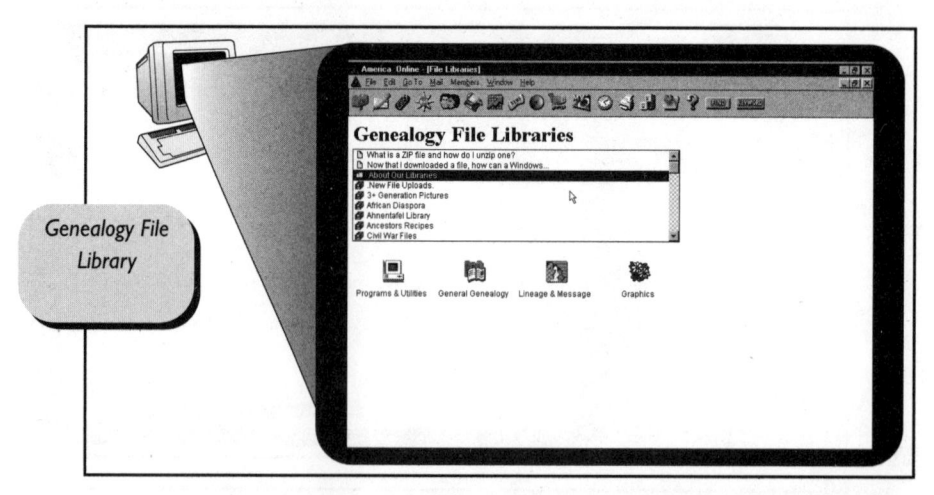

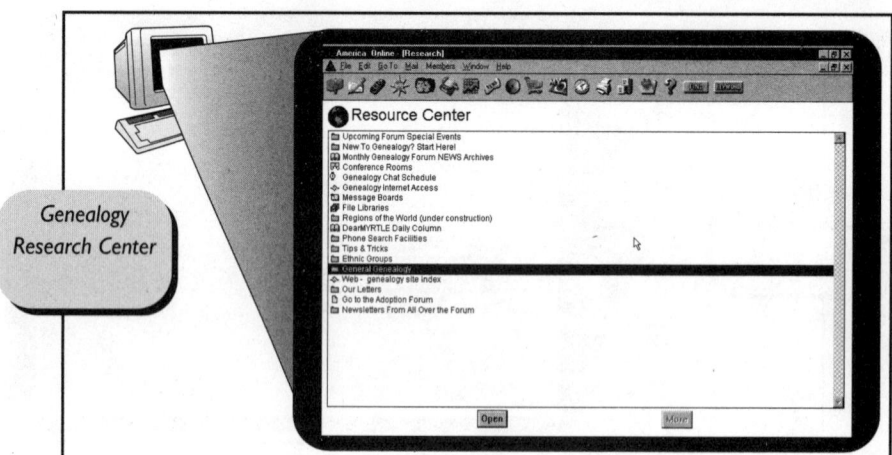

Genealogy File Library

Genealogy Research Center

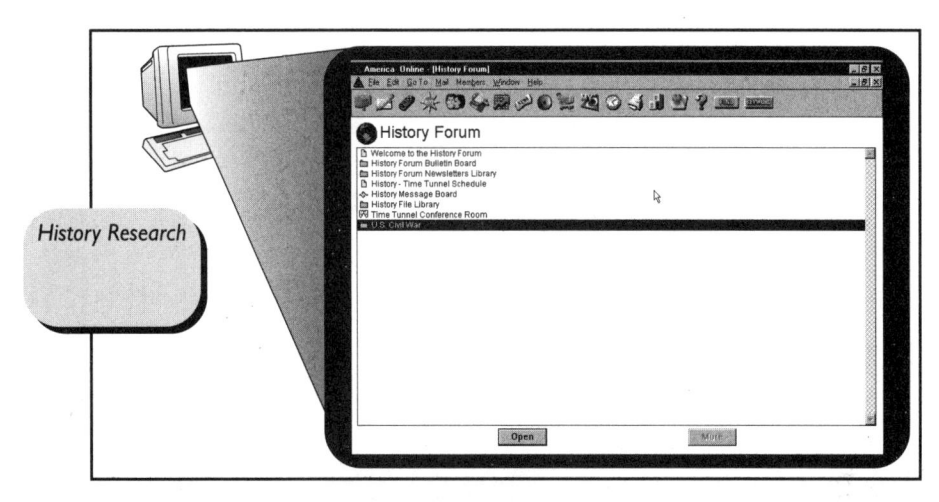

Researching Your Family History On-line   3

History Research

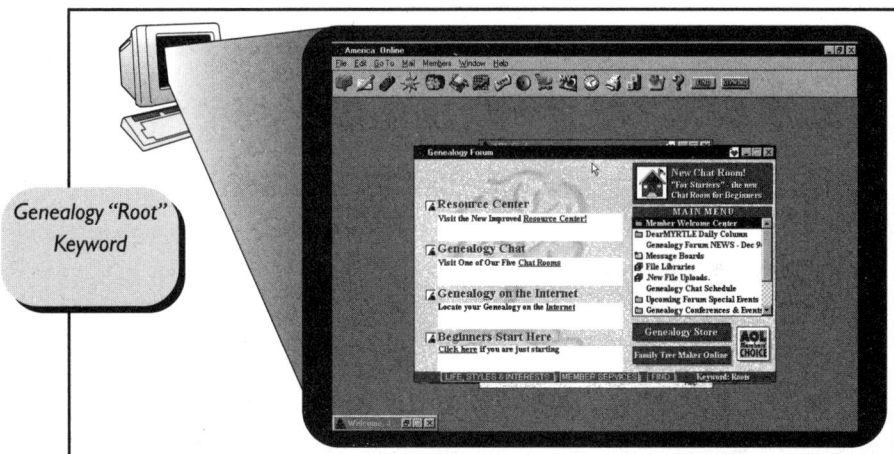

Genealogy "Root" Keyword

3 Researching Your Family History On-line

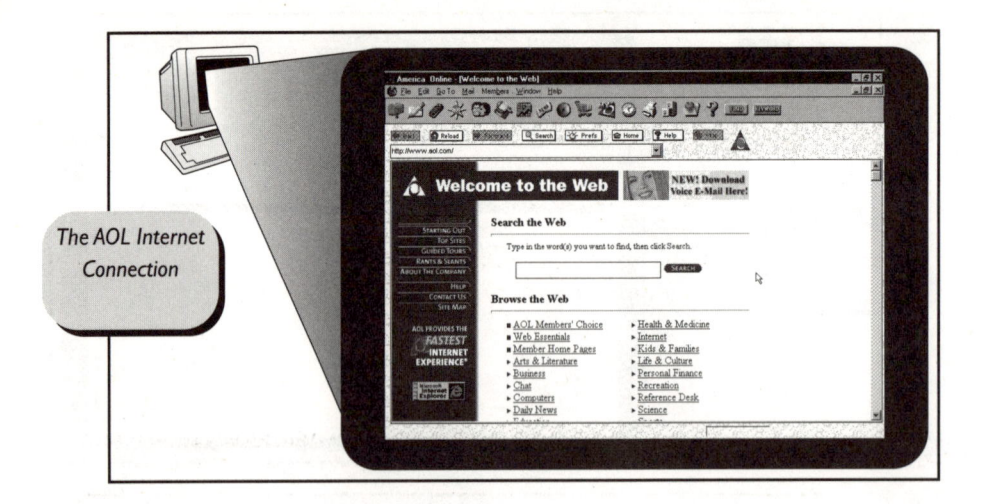

The AOL Internet Connection

CompuServe Information Services

CompuServe has two distinct forums overseen by Richard Eastman, the Genealogy Forum and the Genealogy Support Forum.

CompuServe Genealogy Forum

The information in the Genealogy Forum is massive and quite impressive. There are over 10,000 files and over 2,000 book reviews to download or read. There are also discussion groups, chat rooms (weekly and monthly theme meetings ranging from beginner's help to adoption issues and regional to national subjects), and a message board with segregated subjects including:

General Questions	Search by Locations	US Surnames A-E
US Surnames F-K	US Surnames L-P	US Surnames Q-Z
Native Americans	Canadian Genealogy	Latin America
England/Scott/Wales	Irish Genealogy	European Genealogy
All other countries	Jewish Genealogy	Societies/Libraries
Online Gen. Sources	Genealogy Software	World Family Tree
Adoption Search	Non-Genealogy	

Researching Your Family History On-line

The Genealogy Forum also includes the following directories of programs, text files, reviews and other excellent genealogical information:

Intro to Genealogy	Windows Software	MS-DOS Software
Macintosh Software	Other Software	Eastman's Newsletters
Info About Surnames	Tiny Tafel Files	GEDCOM Files
Societies & Organizations	Public Archives	Book Reviews
Genealogy Magazines	Graphics Files	Information Files
Auto Names Research	Salt Lake City Rec.	World Family Tree
CompuServe Info	Internet Genealogy	

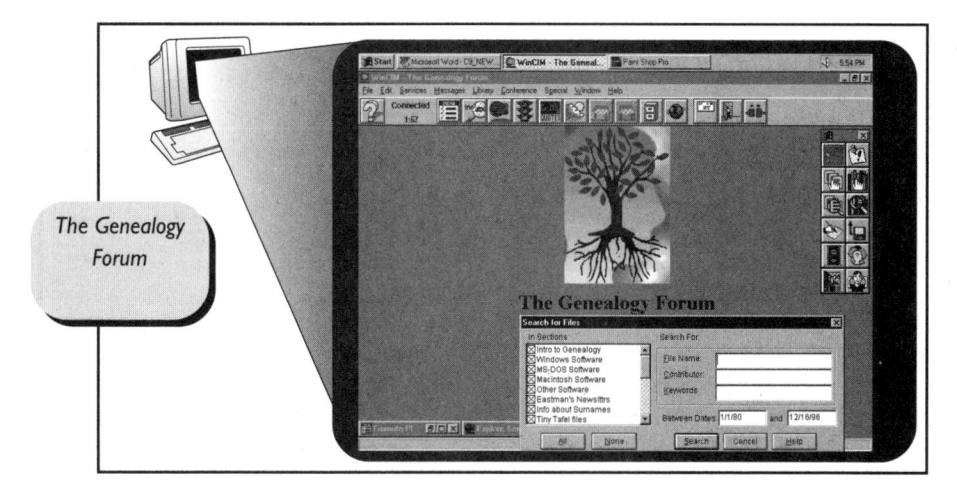

The Genealogy Forum

CompuServe Genealogy Support Forum

The CompuServe Genealogy Support Forum is dedicated to the support teams of the leading providers of genealogy services and products. Each organization listed below has an employee representative online daily to answer your questions:

49

3 Researching Your Family History On-line

The New England Historic Genealogical Society	One of the most respected Societies anywhere
Wholly Genes Software	Producers of "The Master Genealogist"
Leister Productions	Producers of "Reunion" for both Macintosh and Windows
Brothers Keeper	Written and supported by John Steed
CommSoft, Inc.	Producers of "Roots IV" and "Visual Roots" genealogy programs
The Family Edge	Makers of the Family Edge software
Everton Publishers	Leading producers of genealogy books and magazines
National Genealogical Society	The major genealogy society
Schroeder & Fuelling	A major genealogy research firm located in Germany
Automated Research, Inc.	Producers of genealogy products of all types

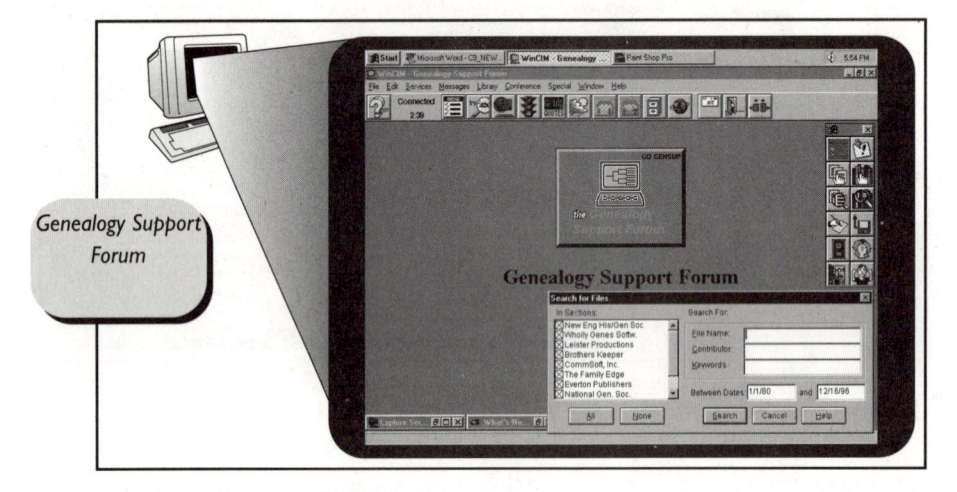

Genealogy Support Forum

Again, hats off to Dick Eastman and the volunteers that work on the Genealogy Forums on CompuServe.

50

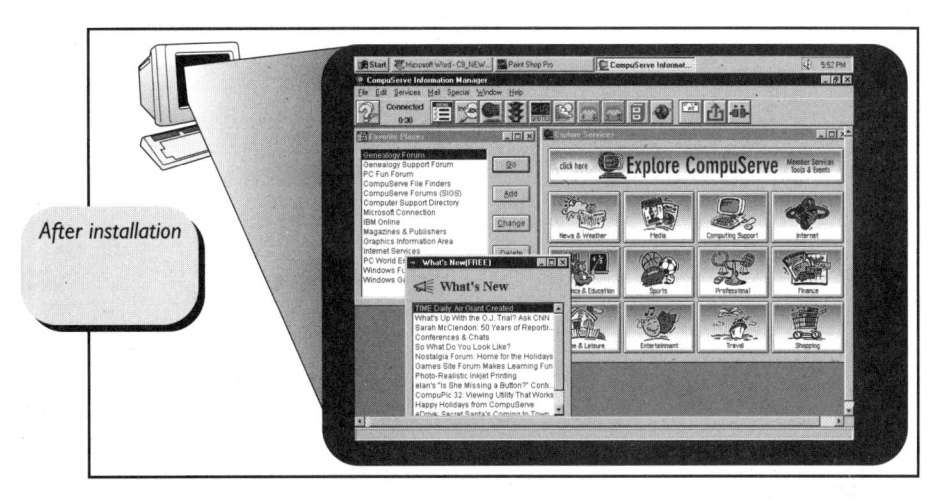

Researching Your Family History On-line 3

After installation

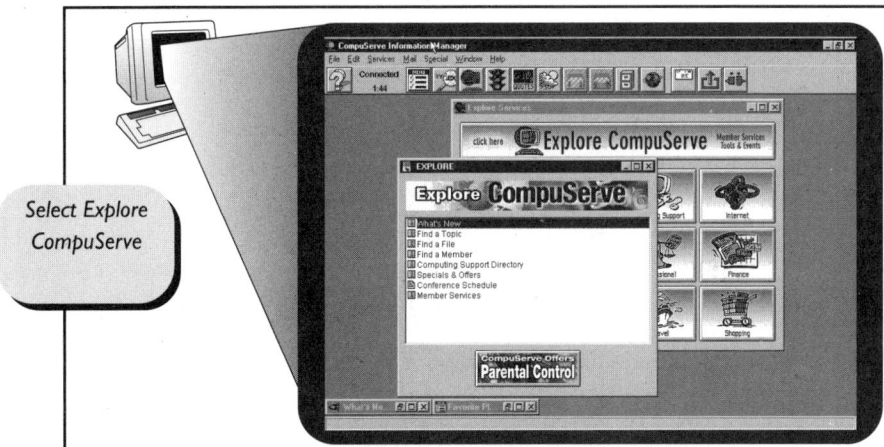

Select Explore CompuServe

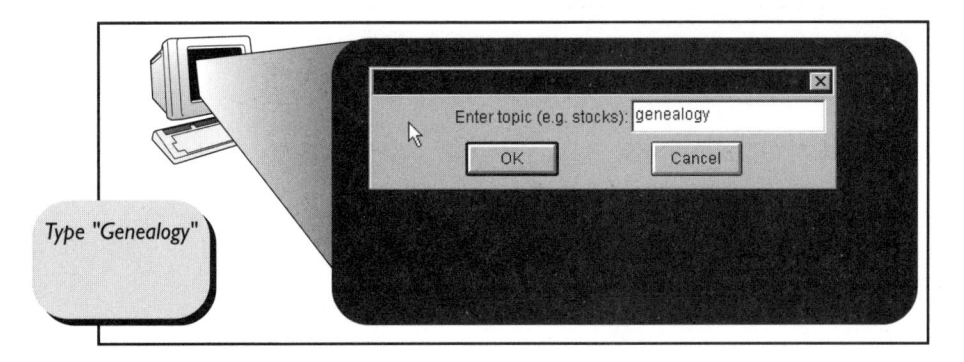

Type "Genealogy"

51

3 Researching Your Family History On-line

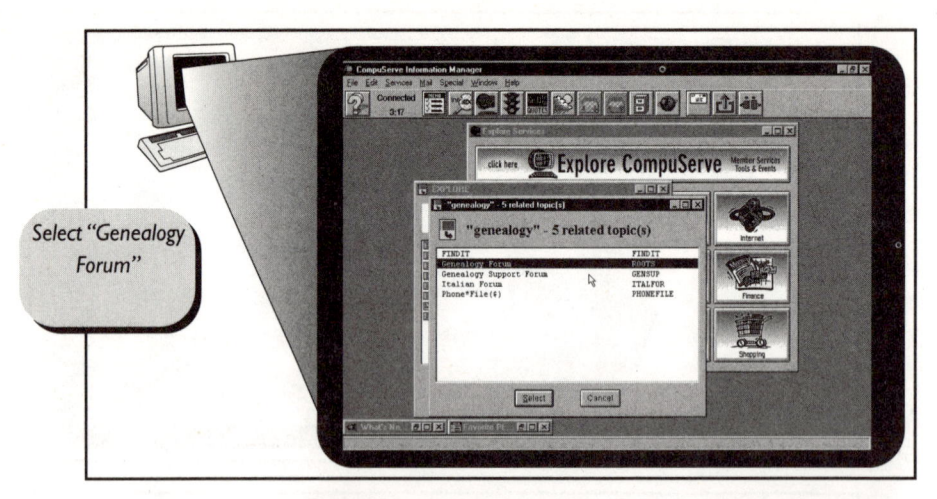

Select "Genealogy Forum"

The Genealogy Forum

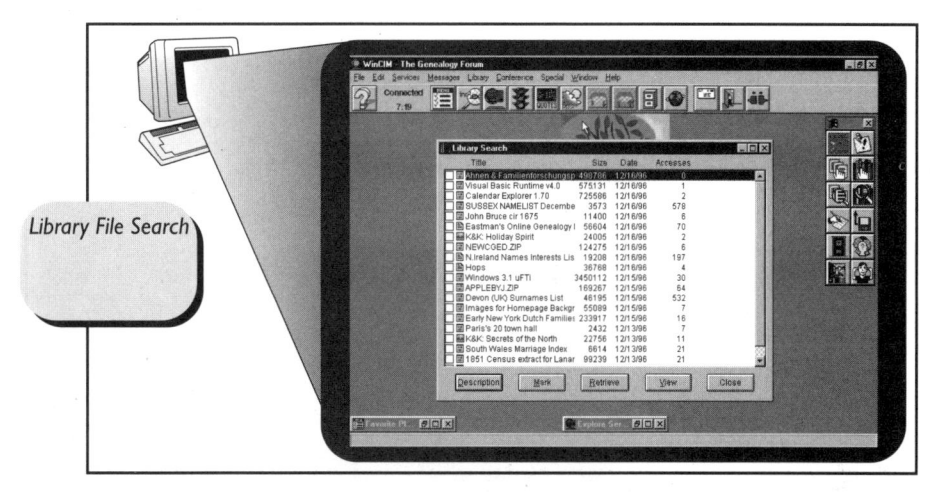

Researching Your Family History On-line 3

Library File Search

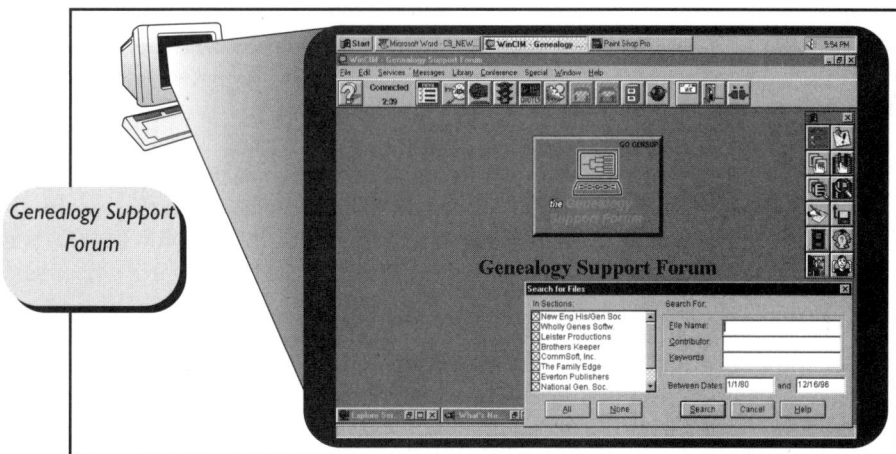

Genealogy Support Forum

53

3 Researching Your Family History On-line

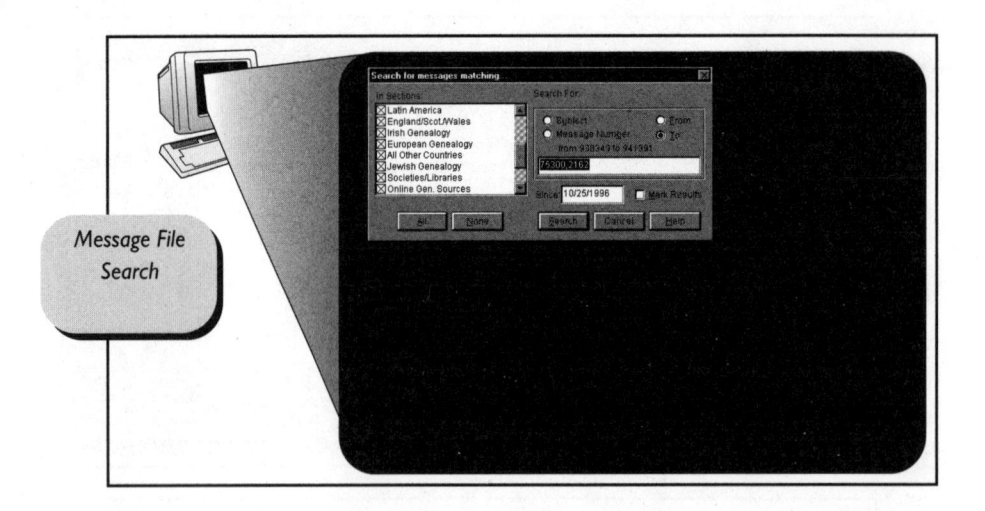

Message File Search

WHAT ARE USENET NEWSGROUPS?

The Usenet, a part of the internet (just as the world wide web is), is a mail message system that's linked to other computers throughout the world. It is made up of a set of moderated newsgroups (estimated to be over 14,000) with names that are classified by their subject matter, including several discussion groups about genealogy.

Some of these groups are free while others charge nominal fees to keep it organized. Usenet is grouped into ALT for alternative topics, COMP for computer-science related topics, SCI for science not related to computers, NEWS for network software topics of interest, REC for recreation, SOC for social interaction and various hobbies, including genealogy and several subsets of special interest, and MISC for miscellaneous items.

Researching Your Family History On-line

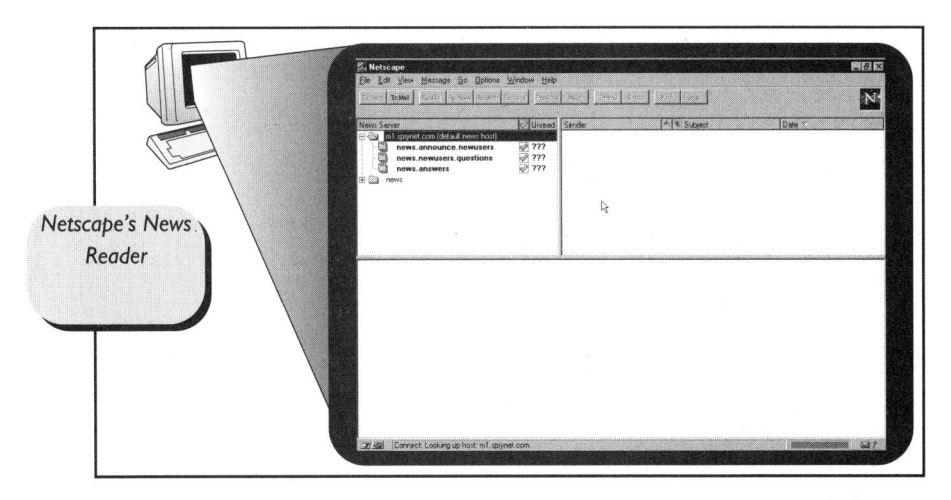

Netscape's News Reader

The web site Deja News (www.dejanews.com) is the largest searchable collection of archived Usenet news available. It is easy-to-use and features a fast search engine. There are other web sites that can steer you into these worldwide discussions as well, though none as comprehensive as Deja News.

Liszt (www.liszt.com) is another useful site for participating in newsgroups, including Roots-L and Gen-L specifically for genealogy and the "SOC" groups more generally. Vicki's Home Page's (www.eskimo.com/~chance) offers you "Genealogy Listservers, News Groups and Special Homepages."

You should also visit www.yahoo.com, www.excite.com, www.lycos.com or www.infoseek.com as well as several of the large genealogy web sites for more information on newsgroups.

3 Researching Your Family History On-line

Some USENET newsgroups	E-mail address to send for information
soc.genealogy.african	
soc.genealogy.australia+nz	
soc.genealogy.benelux	
soc.genealogy.computing	gencmp-l@rootsweb.com
soc.genealogy.french	gen-fr-l@mail.eworld.com
soc.genealogy.german	gen-de-l@mail.eworld.com
soc.genealogy.hispanic	
soc.genealogy.jewish	jewgen@mail.eworld.com
soc.genealogy.marketplace	
soc.genealogy.medieval	
soc.genealogy.methods	genmtd-l@mail.eworld.com
soc.genealogy.misc	genmsc-l@mail.eworld.com
soc.genealogy.nordic	
soc.genealogy.slavic	gen-slavic@mail.eworld.com
soc.genealogy.surnames	gennam-l@mail.eworld.com
soc.genealogy.uk+ireland	genuki-l@mail.eworld.com
soc.genealogy.west-indies	

DejaNews can find a newsgroup on any subject for you

Researching Your Family History On-line

The Directory of Email Newsgroups

For more information about usenet newsgroups (in printed form) and how to find and use them I suggest the excellent book "Genealogy Online: Researching Your Roots," by Elizabeth Power Crowe (Windcrest/McGraw-Hill).

GeneSplicer

The GeneSplicer's Web page (stmp.genesplicer.org) is a function of The GeneSplicer's Bulletin Board in Las Vegas, Nevada. As a member of Fidonet (1:209/720), the BBS has been open for free public access since June first, 1989. The BBS provides the genealogists of southern Nevada access to international genealogy-related conferences from Fidonet, the World Genealogy Association and Usenet; as well as access to genealogy-related text files, programs, and data files distributed via GSDS. The Sysops are John and Jackie Le Duc. While John administrates the networking operations, Jackie oversees the genealogy aspects of the BBS.

Genealogy Software Distribution System (GSDS)

The Genealogy Software Distribution System (GSDS) is a Files Distribution Network which originated within Fidonet in 1990. Through this medium GeneSplicer has distributed several hundred megabytes of genealogy text files, programs, and data files over the years. Files are accepted from the authors (or persons who have rights to the copyright of the file) and distributed to over 16,000 privately operated Bulletin Boards around the world. No fees or charges

3 Researching Your Family History On-line

are made to the authors for this distribution. Futhermore, users who download these files are not charged any fees for the files (although some sysops request a blanket fee for access to their BBS, they may not charge additional fees for access to GSDS files).

The GeneSplicer's BBS maintains a full selection of the current files distributed via GSDS plus many others collected from various other sources. All of these files are shareware, freeware, or public domain.

You may call The GeneSplicer's BBS direct at (702) 736-6819. Or, you may access the same file base on our FTP Site.

Mailing Lists And List Servers - Keeping Track Of The Jones, Smiths, Moffetts and Thousands more

Mailing lists are simple to use. You send the manager of the list (list administrator) an e-mail stating you want to subscribe to the list, and the list administrator in return resends all messages to everyone who is subscribed. This will get you on the mailing list, so to speak. Be prepared to view a lot of messages. To unsubscribe, send another E-mail to the list administrator confirming it. Every mailing list has two addresses: one reaches the list administrator and is used for subscribe/unsubscribe requests and other administrative duties, and the other is where messages for the group are posted. List managers can get testy if you confuse the two and a large uploaded file arrives in his or her administrative mail box.

Mailing lists operate in two modes. In MAIL mode every E-mail message that is posted is sent (or broadcast) to subscribers as a separate piece of e-mail. In DIGEST mode about twenty messages are grouped together and sent as a packet to the mail list subscribers. You still get all the messages, and your E-mail box will be less cluttered, which is important if you subscribe to a number of lists.

The mailing lists presented here should by no means be considered a complete representation. However, they are the BEST when it comes to genealogy.

Researching Your Family History On-line

ROOTS-L

ROOTS-L, the oldest of the lists with over 7,000 subscribers, is a mailing list for people interested in genealogy. If you subscribe, expect to receive a lot of messages each day.

GENMTD-L

This list is linked to the soc.genealogy.methods Usenet newsgroup, and carries messages about research techniques and resources. On it you'll find discussions for beginners and advanced family historians covering genealogical techniques and the best resources around the country. To subscribe to this list, send E-mail to listserv@mail.eworld.com and in the body of the message put SUB GENMTD-L and your full E-mail address. The list manager is Karen Isaacson; her E-mail address is karen@rand.org.

GEN-NEWBIE-L

This is the mail list for beginners to genealogy and is one of the most helpful of the list servers. Don't worry about asking silly questions. Everyone starts as a beginner.

GEDCOM-L

GEDCOM-L is a discussion list for ideas concerning how genealogical data is stored in Genealogical Data Communications (GEDCOM) files. To subscribe to the list, send E-mail to listserv@LISTSERV.NODAK.EDU and in the body of the message, put SUB GEDCOM-L and your exact E-mail address. The list owner and administrator is Marc Nozell at E-mail address nozell@wildcat.mv.com.

MAUCK, MAUK Family Interest Mail List

This site is an excellent example of how to start and run your own archive mailing list dedicated to a surname and its alternative spellings.

3 Researching Your Family History On-line

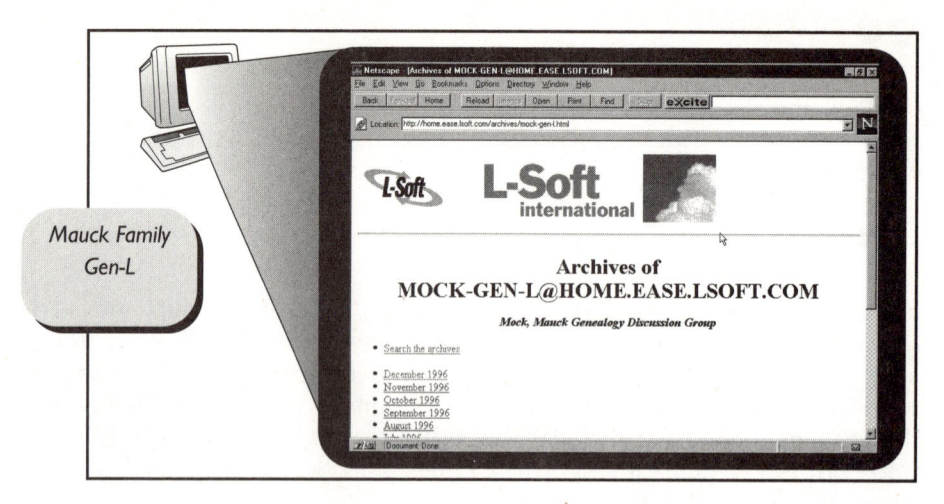

For information about more mail lists, go to Pascal Janssen's Genealogy Page and Mailing list descriptions web site at http://pucky.uia.ac.be/~janssen/genealogy/; or Vicki's Home Page at http://www.eskimo.com/~chance/; or the FAQ (Frequently Asked Questions) about soc.genealogy.misc at http://www.meertech.demon.co.uk/genuki/socgmisc.htm.

OTHER IMPORTANT WEB SITES

ROOTSWEB

The RootsWeb project has two stated missions: "1. To make large volumes of data available to the online genealogical community at minimal cost. 2. To provide support services to online genealogical activities such as USENET newsgroup moderation, mailing list maintenance, surname list generation, etc." This site (www.rootsweb.com) is where you can sign-up to the mailing list. Excellent material and well maintained by some of the best in computer genealogy.

Researching Your Family History On-line

GENSERV

GenServ was conceived and is managed by Cliff Manis. The objective of the GenServ system is "to collect genealogical (family history) data and make that data available on-line to other researchers. GenServ is not an index — it contains actual "family tree" databases with over 3.5 million individuals from around the world (as of 25 April 1996)."

GENWEB

GenWeb is a trademark of The Genweb Foundation first used to describe the system of linked genealogy databases (GEDCOM files) in April 1994. The GenWeb(tm) Project's purpose is to link family researchers' GEDCOM files to each other throughout the world wide web.

The central index to the sites is known as GENDEX and it indexes hundreds of WWW databases containing hundreds of thousands of individuals. The GenWeb project is coordinated by Jeff Murphy, the creator and host of the master page for the Kentucky GenWeb Project. This information came from their home page (www.usgenweb.com) which gives an introduction to the GenWeb project.

ONLINE ELECTRONIC GENEALOGY NEWSLETTERS

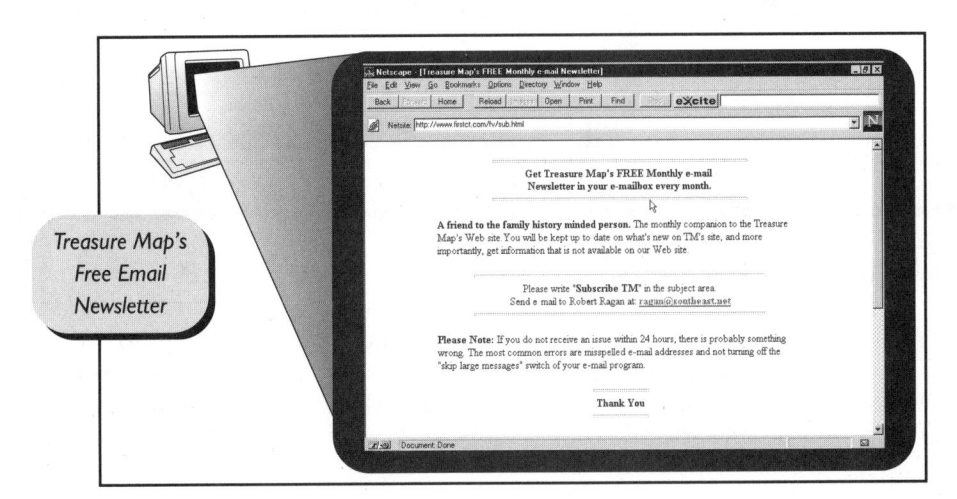

Treasure Map's Free Email Newsletter

3 Researching Your Family History On-line

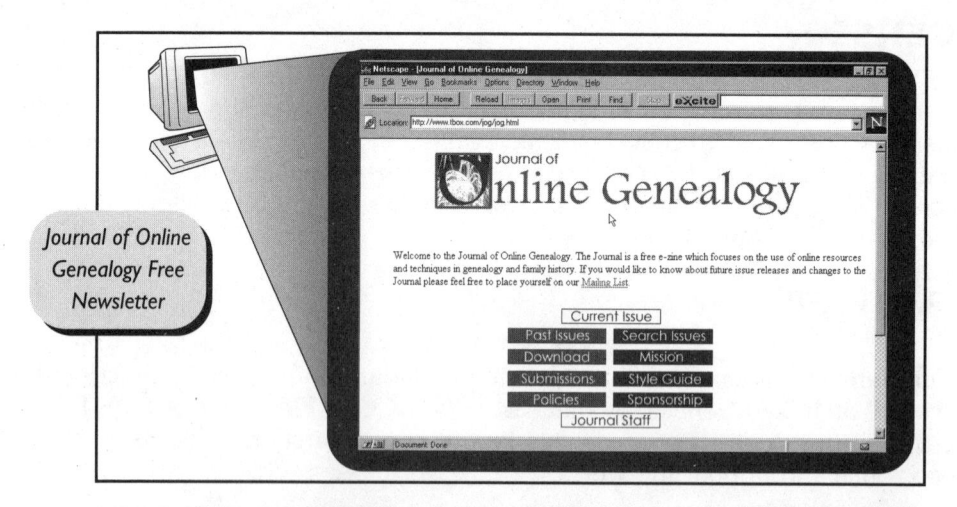

Journal of Online Genealogy Free Newsletter

$24-a-year Online Pioneers Newsletter

SAVING A LOT OF TIME ON THE WEB

As I mentioned earlier in this chapter you need a phone number to call and a "browser" program to maneuver on the web. You also need to know where you'd like to go. The Genealogy Bookmarks File I've included can save you a lot of trial-and-error searching for relevant items. Bookmark files are text

62

Researching Your Family History On-line

files created with Netscape Communications's Navigator web browser that can take you directly to an interesting site. You cannot use this bookmark directly if you are using AOL or CompuServe. However, in the Appendix I have listed the sites and addresses for you to use.

I have included my genealogical bookmark file which I used to help write this book. I have broken them down into alphabetical groups and by various subjects including: Adoption, Book Publishers & Sellers, Magazines-Journals, Commercial Software Co., Finding People, Genealogy Sites With Lists, Government and States Sites, Maps Plus, Online Services Main Pages, War - Conflicts & History.

Using the genealogy bookmarks file

To use the genealogy bookmark file you first need to load it. You can either load it directly into Netscape (or Internet Explorer) or import it into your own bookmark file.

To load it into your Netscape browser, type "d:\genemark.htm" in the Location dialog box and press [Enter] (where "d" is your CD-ROM drive letter). Navigator will load the file and clicking any of the links will send you off to the respective website (make sure you're logged on to an internet service provider). To go back to the bookmark file after you've moved to another site, click the [<Back] button until you see it again.

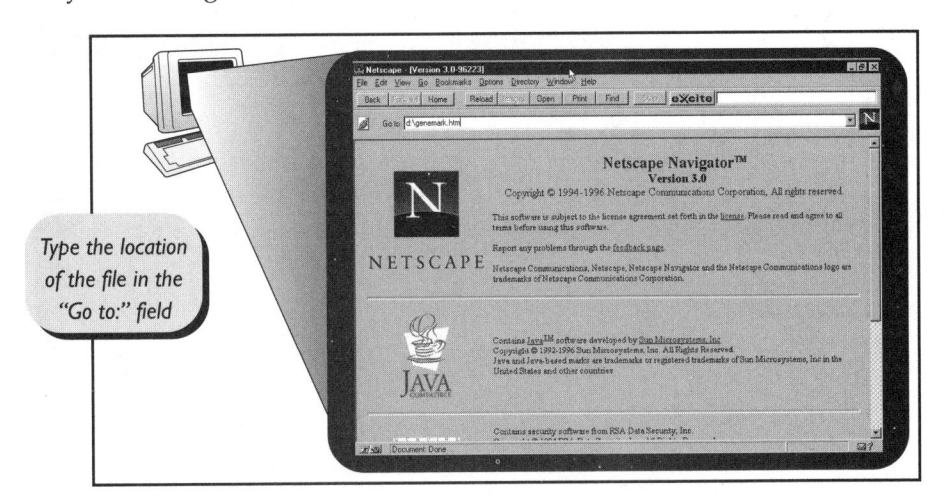

Type the location of the file in the "Go to:" field

3 Researching Your Family History On-line

The bookmark loaded

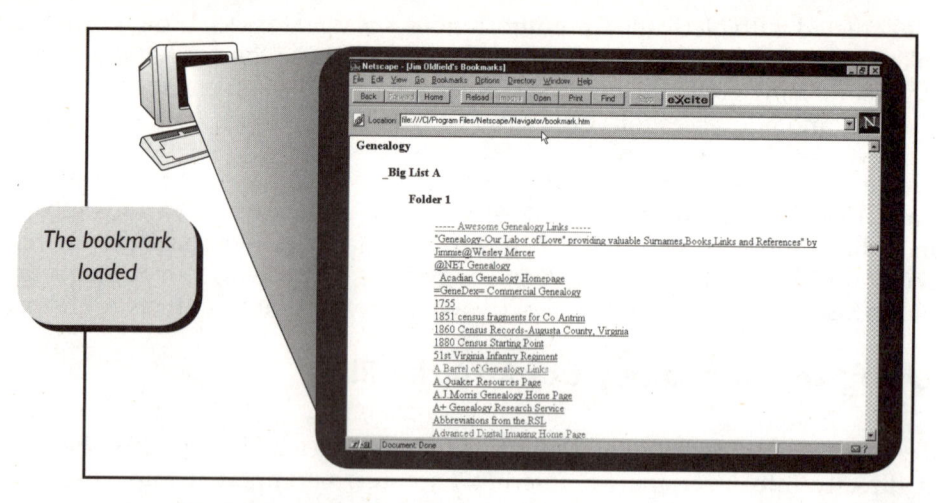

To import the genealogy bookmark file into your own bookmarks, select **Bookmarks/Go to Bookmarks...**. From the bookmarks page select the **File/Import...** command and locate the genemark.htm file on the CD-ROM. Click OK. Be sure you have your bookmark file name highlighted. Otherwise, the genemark.htm will be loaded incorrectly. After you have imported the file, select **File/Close** to go back to Netscape Navigator. Use your new expanded bookmarks as you did before.

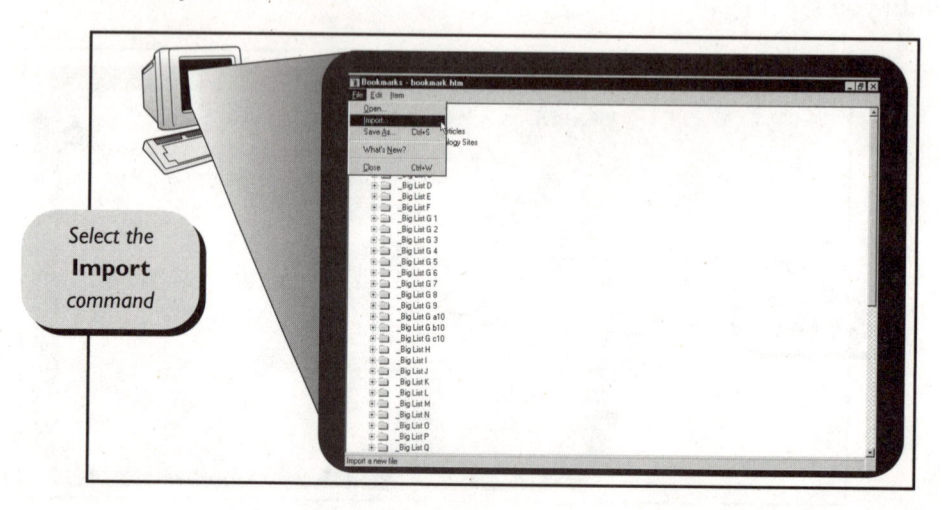

*Select the **Import** command*

64

Researching Your Family History On-line

Locate the "famtree.htm" file

The imported bookmark

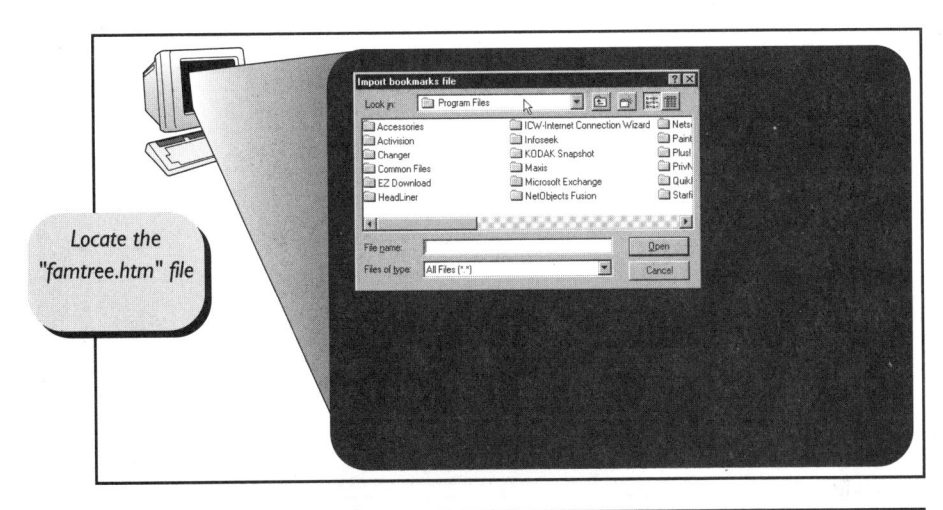

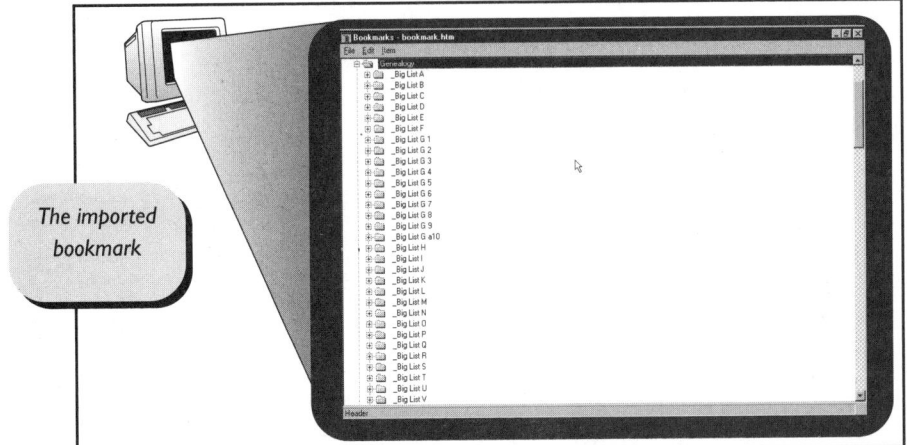

My Favorite Web Sites

I'm aware that the bookmark list discussed earlier might be confusing and just too big. So I would like to share with you my favorite web sites, less than 50 and a little easier to manage. These are just my favorites, yours may vary.

3 Researching Your Family History On-line

AGLL—Genealogy & Family History Products & Services (www.agll.com)

AGLL is a genealogy book, service and supply company. They publish two magazines, Heritage Quest and Genealogical Bulletin. They also sell memberships. Members can purchase or rent microfilm or microfiche to use in their research.

Ancestor Publishers (www.firstct.com/fv/ancpub.html)

Robert Ragan's free E-mail genealogy newsletter is available by signing up here. Ancestor Publishers also have a wide selection of microfiche for genealogists and historians.

66

Researching Your Family History On-line   3

Ancestry (www.ancestry.com)

Ancestry specializes in providing genealogical information, books, techniques, and computer products to help you easily and efficiently find your ancestry. They also publish two genealogy magazines, Ancestry Magazine and Genealogical Computing.

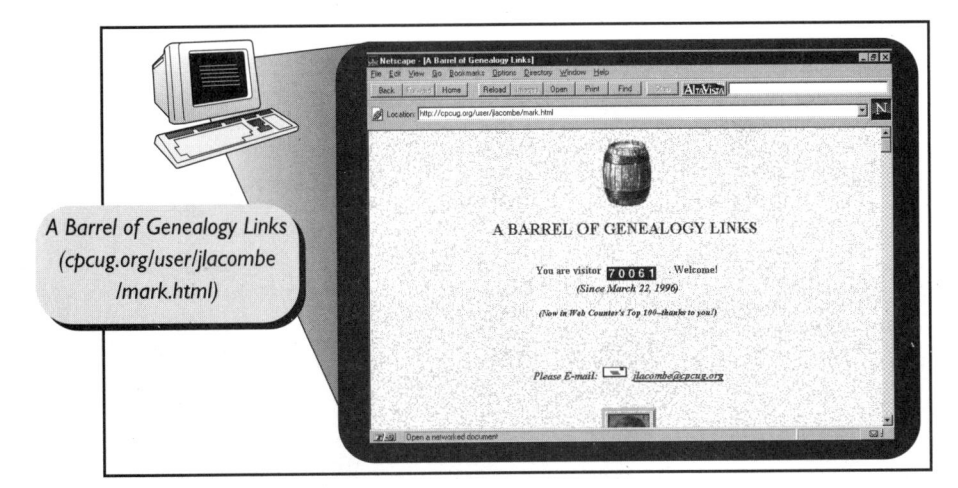

A Barrel of Genealogy Links (cpcug.org/user/jlacombe/mark.html)

A Barrel of Genealogy Links is produced by John J. Lacombe and is an excellent and easy-to-use web site linking to many other genealogy web pages.

3 Researching Your Family History On-line

COMMSOFT, Inc. Home Page (www.sonic.net:80/~commsoft/)

COMMSOFT is the publisher of Roots IV, Roots V for Windows, Visual Roots, Family Gathering and other leading genealogy software. Begun in 1980, they are the oldest publishers of genealogy programs and one of the most respected in their field. I urge you to explore this site of one of the most respected names in genealogy software.

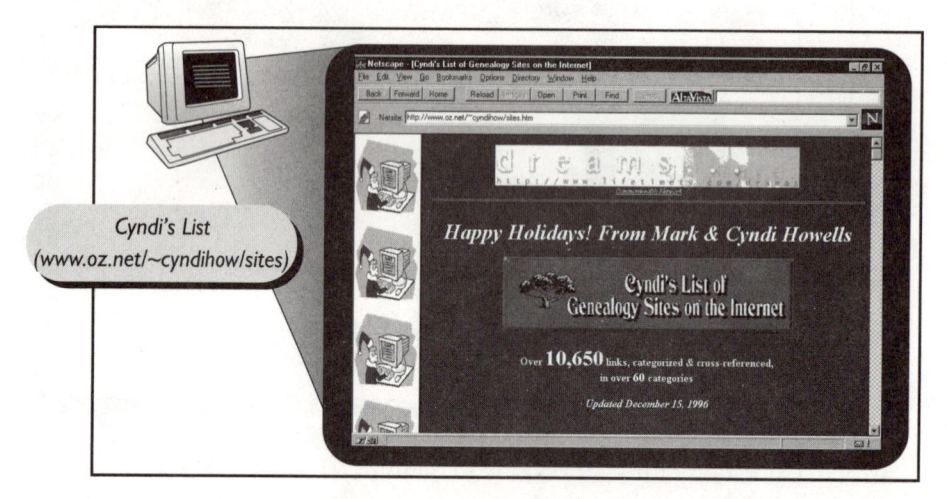

Cyndi's List (www.oz.net/~cyndihow/sites)

68

Researching Your Family History On-line 3

Cyndi's List of Genealogy Sites on the Internet is hands-down the place to go for information about genealogy on the web. She has spent countless hours to save others even more. There are currently over 10,750 links, categorized & cross-referenced in over 60 categories. It's a super web site and a required place to go for online genealogy research.

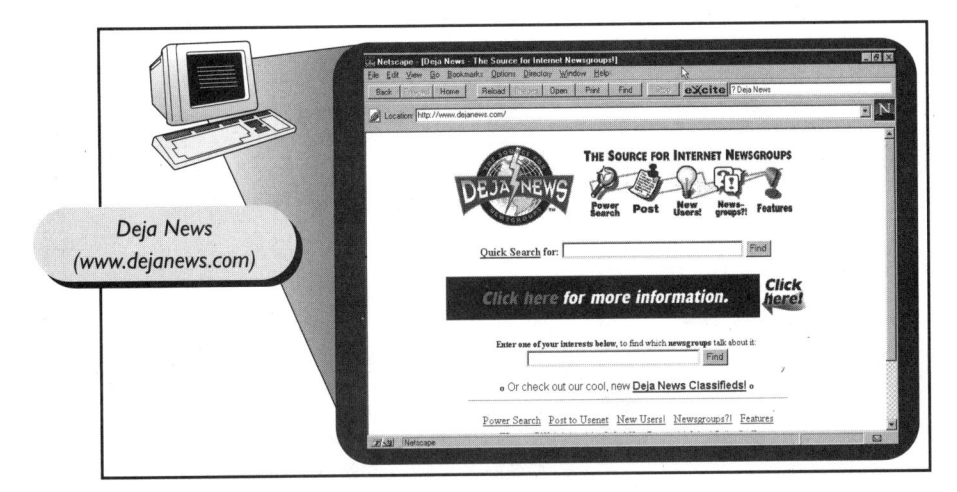

Deja News
(www.dejanews.com)

Deja News is THE source for internet newsgroups. Their only business is Usenet and their web site features powerful, easy-to-use searches to help you find what you're looking for. If you are remotely interested in Usenet newsgroups, visit here first.

Everton's
(www.everton.com)

69

3 Researching Your Family History On-line

Everton's publishes one of the most popular magazines in its field, "Genealogical Helper," and many books including the *Handy Book for Genealogists*. Everton's is an excellent source for everything genealogy. At their web site you can join their online genealogy classes or Chat room or peruse their large collection of genealogical material. This is one of the best.

Family Tree Maker Home Page (www.familytreemaker.com/index)

First-class and a HUGE resource for everything regarding Family Tree Maker and genealogy, it is possibly the best commercial genealogy web site around. Even if you don't have Family Tree Maker, you owe it to yourself to visit. Expect to spend a lot of time browsing and reading.

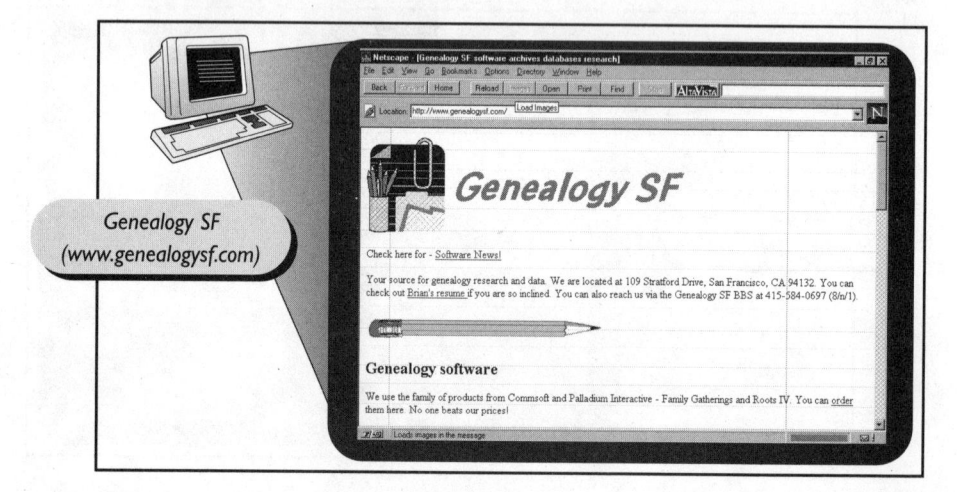

Genealogy SF (www.genealogysf.com)

Researching Your Family History On-line 3

Genealogy SF software has databases for research and links to other genealogy sites. Be sure to visit their FTP site that contains tons of software to evaluate.

Helm's Genealogy Toolbox (genealogy.tbox.com/genealogy)

Matthew Helm's Genealogy Toolbox was one of the first genealogy web sites I ever visited and is one of the more popular genealogy sites on the internet. His web site is an excellent source for software, books, articles and just about everything in between.

USGenWeb Project (www.usgenweb.com)

Whether you have created your own GEDCOM files of your family history or want to access the huge database of others' GEDCOM files, this is the site.

71

3 Researching Your Family History On-line

Genealogy Home Page
(www.genhomepage.com)

This is one of the premier sources of genealogical information on the world wide web. One of my favorites is the What's New section. Updated frequently, it's a great source of what's new online.

Genealogical Publishing Company
(www.genealogical.com)

Genealogical Publishing Co., Inc. is the largest commercial publisher of genealogical reference books, textbooks, and how-to books in the world. Over the years, GPC and its subsidiaries, Clearfield Company and Gateway Press, have published more than 5000 titles in genealogy and related fields. Their extensive catalog is on the companion CD-ROM.

72

Researching Your Family History On-line

Genealogical Journeys in Time
(ourworld.compuserve.com /homepages/Strawn)

This genealogical web site is HUGE. If you can't find it here, you probably won't find it! It is maintained by Curt and Bonnie Strawn-Miller.

Hearthstone Bookshop
(www.hearthstonebooks.com)

As Hearthstone Bookshop says, "We stock more titles from more publishers than any other genealogical dealer." They also carry software, CDs, charts, forms, and other items of interest to family historians. It's a good shop.

73

3 Researching Your Family History On-line

Heritage Books (www.heritagebooks.com)

One of the larger genealogy publishers and book sellers anywhere. They publish and sell books on history and Americana as well as genealogy. Be sure to look at their electronic catalog on the companion CD-ROM. I've shopped with Heritage Books and I recommend them highly.

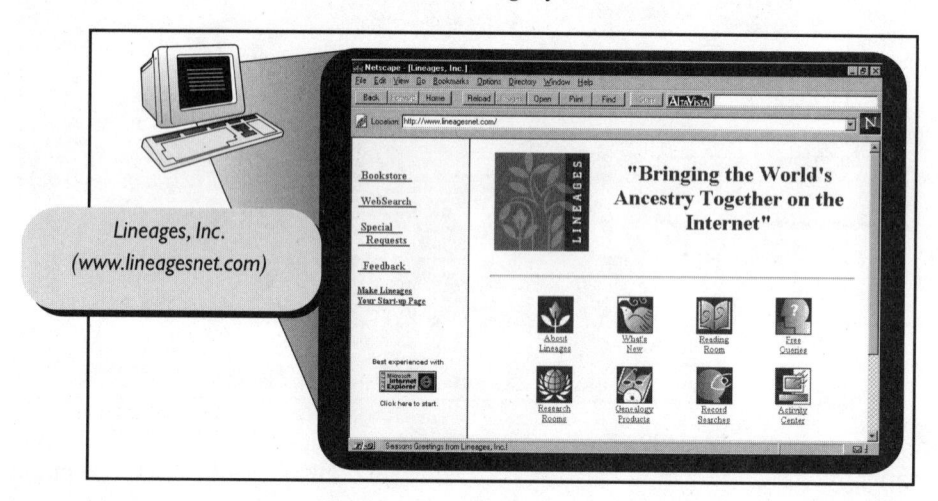

Lineages, Inc. (www.lineagesnet.com)

Designed to guide you to various electronic rooms, Lineages has a first-class web site featuring a wide range of genealogical services and publications. It's an exceptional place to visit.

74

Researching Your Family History On-line

Library of Congress World Wide Web (LC Web) (www.loc.gov)

The Library of Congress is the world's largest library. Their World Wide Web Home Page can help you in your family research. Be sure to follow the pointers for searching family histories and more.

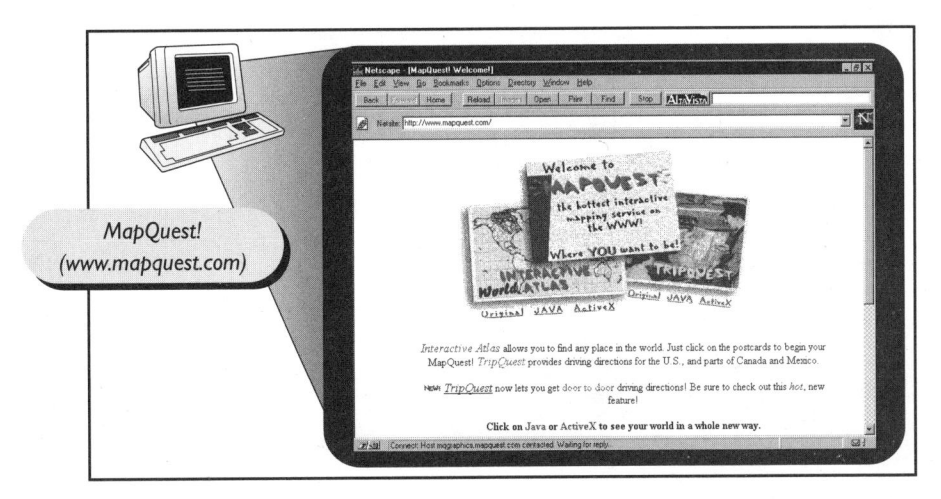

MapQuest! (www.mapquest.com)

I think this is just about the coolest site on the web. You can locate and view on your screen ANY street in the US. You can use this site to research localities with which your ancestors were associated.

3 Researching Your Family History On-line

National Archives and Records Administration (www.nara.gov)

Your tax dollars are hard at work. Be sure to follow the links to genealogical information and also the forms and pamphlets available.

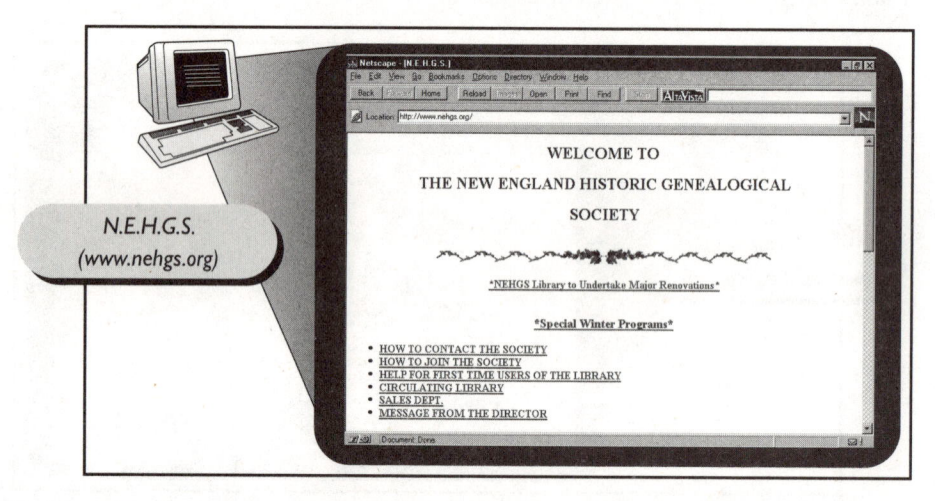

N.E.H.G.S. (www.nehgs.org)

The New England Historical Genealogical Society is one of the most revered genealogical societies in the country. They have a slight slant to the New England area of historical information and their web site is first-class.

Researching Your Family History On-line

*National Genealogical Society
(www.genealogy.org/~ngs)*

The National Genealogical Society's home page is THE place on the web to begin your research. Other web sites may have more links, prettier graphics and such, but this is the web site that will give you the best start.

*Journal of Online Genealogy
(www.tbox.com/jog/jog.html)*

The Journal is a free electronic magazine that focuses on the use of online resources and techniques in genealogy and family history. The mission of the Journal of Online Genealogy (JOG) is to aid the genealogy community in promoting and developing online projects, technologies, and methods of research.

3 Researching Your Family History On-line

The target audience for the Journal are genealogists that are interested in researching family history by way of online resources. I highly recommend joining up and contributing.

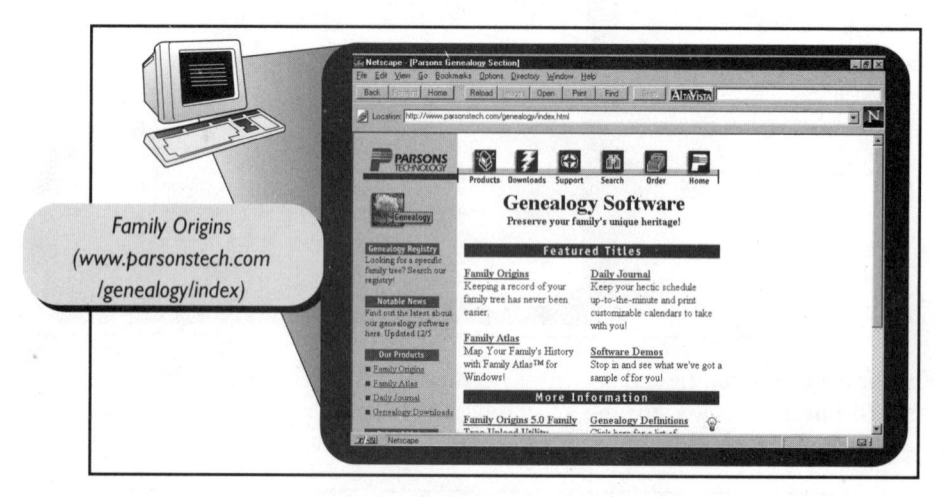

Family Origins (www.parsonstech.com /genealogy/index)

Parsons Genealogy Section is from the publishers of Family Origins for Windows (discussed in an earlier chapter). Their web site is organized very well and Family Origins users can find out more about their product.

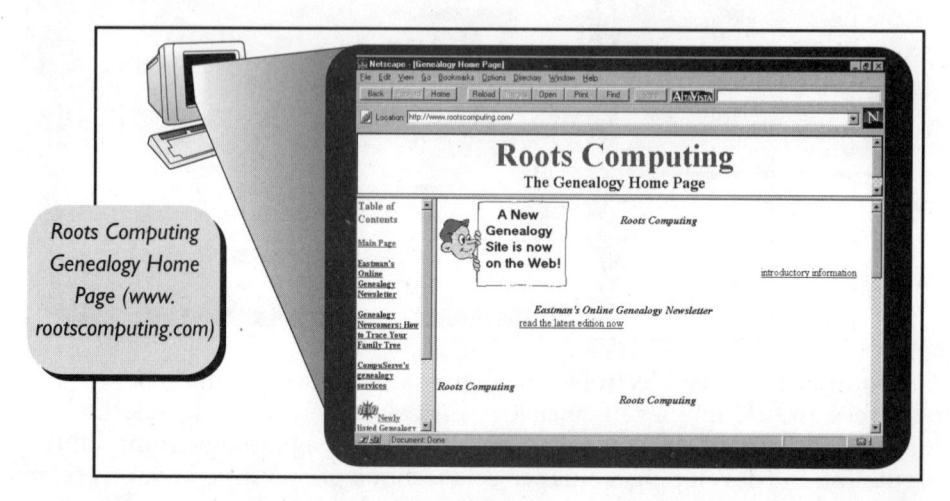

Roots Computing Genealogy Home Page (www. rootscomputing.com)

This is Richard Eastman's Roots genealogy web site, with excellent information and resources to read. I recommend it highly.

78

Researching Your Family History On-line

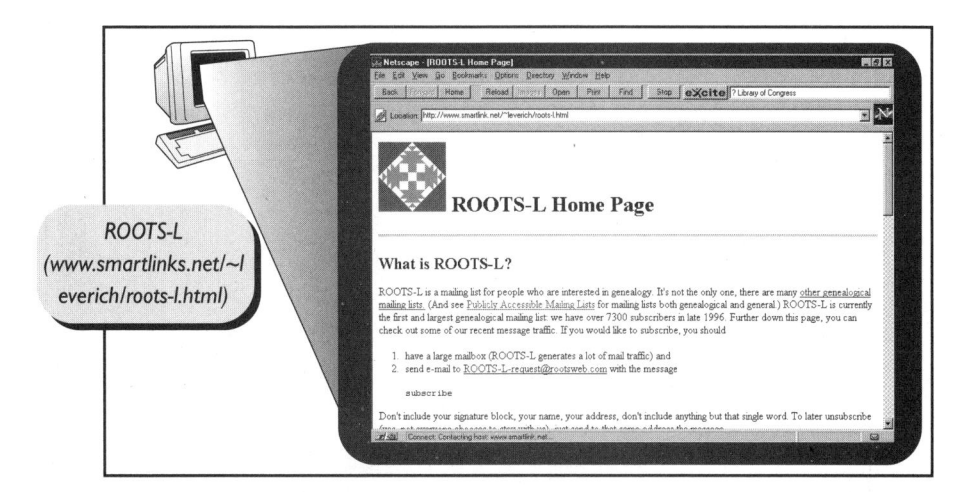

ROOTS-L (www.smartlinks.net/~leverich/roots-l.html)

This is the ROOTS-L mailing list home page. ROOTS-L is the first and largest genealogical mailing list on the world wide web, with over 7300 subscribers. If you subscribe, better make sure your electronic mailbox is BIG.

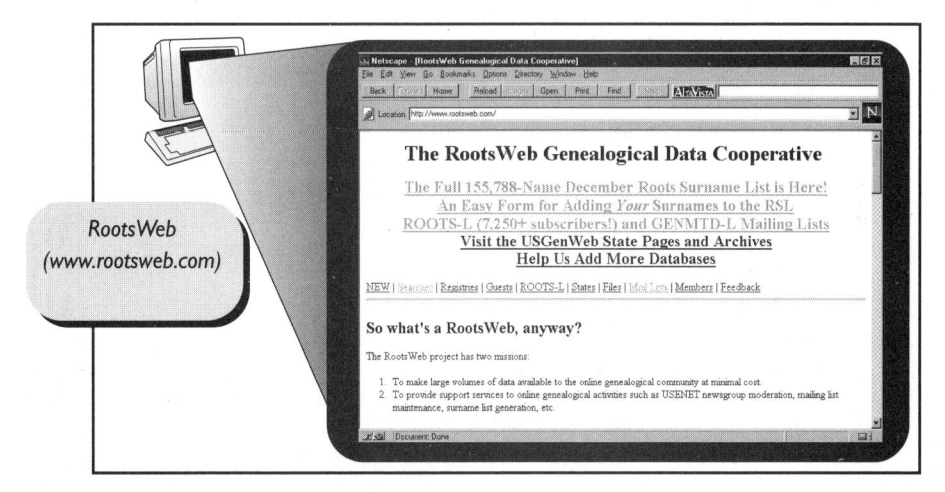

RootsWeb (www.rootsweb.com)

RootsWeb Genealogical Data Cooperative home page is where you can sign-up for the mailing list. It has excellent material and is well maintained by some of the best in computer genealogy.

3 Researching Your Family History On-line

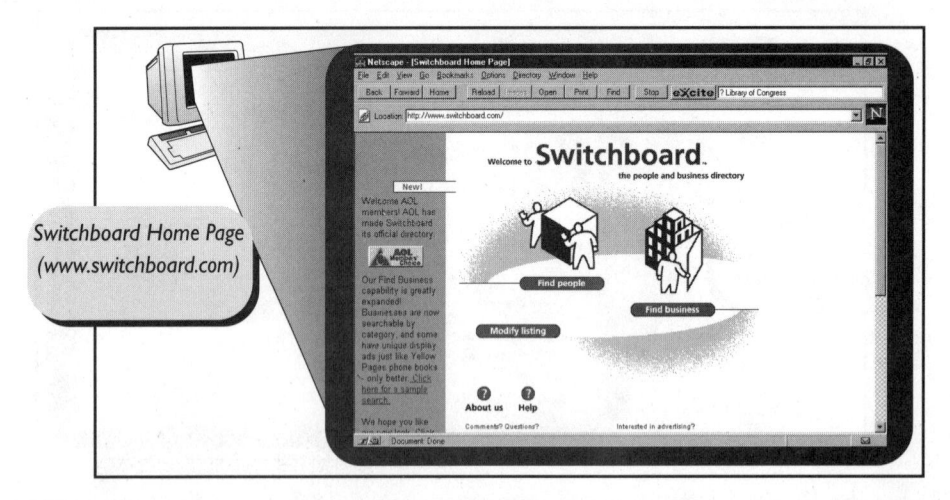

Switchboard Home Page (www.switchboard.com)

This is THE phone book directory on the world wide web. Whether you are looking for a phone number and address for an individual or a business, this is it. It's very easy to use.

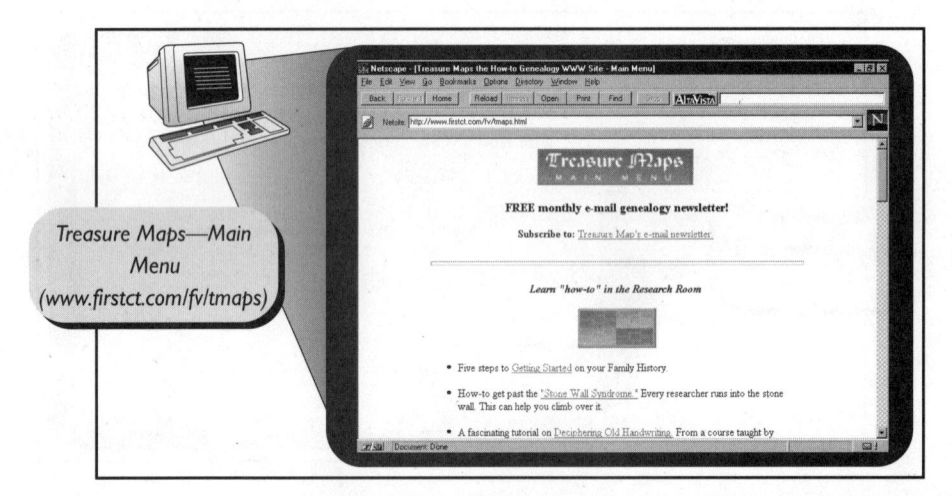

Treasure Maps—Main Menu (www.firstct.com/fv/tmaps)

They publish the electronic newsletter "Treasure Maps," a great "e-zine" and a MUST for web surfing family historians. They also keep their back issues available to download. They do a great job.

Using Photos, Maps And Sound

Chapter 4

Using Photos, Maps And Sound

In the previous chapters I discussed where to find some of your family history. Invariably, you'll discover old photographs that have been passed down through generations of family, or maybe you're lucky enough to have a collection of your own. These family heirlooms are precious and irreplaceable. Old photos are some of the best evidence left behind by your ancestors. You must handle them with care.

Preserving old photographs, copying them, and using high-tech procedures to physically restore them, has fast become a science. If you want to research the techniques of restoring old photos, you will find several articles by leading experts in the genealogy forums of CompuServe and AOL. You can also find several companies on the world wide web that will restore them for a fee. The restoration of photographs, from tin-types to those of the early 1900s, should be left to experts. Handle these photos with care.

The purpose of this chapter is to show how easy it can be to digitize your photographs into your computer and therefore help preserve them. The added bonus is that once your photos are digitized it will be much easier for you to work with them, without worrying about damaging them. They will also be much easier to share with others who may have a computer. If they don't, you can still use your printer or a print/copy shop's printer to send copies to them inexpensively. Whether your photos are of family and friends or places of personal interest, you can easily use them to tell more vividly and vibrantly your family's story. These graphic glimpses into your family's past can tell a more complete story, making your family history come alive. In later chapters I'll show you how to put them into your programs, braiding text and images. But before you can use them, you'll need to load or scan them into your computer.

4 Using Photos, Maps And Sound

PUTTING PHOTOGRAPHS INTO YOUR COMPUTER

There are several ways to put your photographs into your computer. They include:

1. **Use a Photo CD (TM) service company, such as a Kodak film processing center**
   Any authorized Kodak film developing service can send your film to be developed onto paper and to a CD-ROM. The cost is approximately $20 for a roll of 24 exposures and takes 4 to 5 days to receive your pictures and a Photo CD-ROM with the images transferred onto it. This is the easiest way to put them on a medium your computer and software can read and also gives you the best resolution (thus higher quality images) by using Kodak's proprietary image software. Several of the larger film developing companies can transfer older photos as well. However, I've found many people (including myself) don't want to send their only picture of a relative to be handled by too many people.

2. **Local copy and print shops**
   Many Kinko's, Sir Speedys and local business copying centers have scanners. Their scanners are usually capable of high commercial quality scans and are usually out of reach in price for the average consumer. You may also find that some of the larger chains of photography stores (Wolf Camera, ADI, etc.) can do this for you as well. Your costs can range from $3.00 to $20.00 for just a few photographs. If you have dozens or more to scan, you may want to invest in a scanner yourself.

3. **Digital cameras**
   Only in the last year has the cost of owning a digital camera come within reach of most users. Digital cameras are great for taking pictures while you're out on location doing your research. You can take photographs of homes or cemetery headstones or anything else, just like a regular film-based camera.

Using Photos, Maps And Sound

The greatest feature of digital cameras appears when you plug the camera (using the included software program and adapter) into your computer and "download" the pictures directly to your PC. The cost of these cameras range from $299 to $999, depending on the features and memory configurations of the unit. I have had good experience with the Chinon 3000 camera and recommend it highly.

Using the Chinon digital camera to bring images into your PC is very easy. The Chinon package includes the ES-3000 camera, four AA batteries, a connecting cable to plug into your PC's port and the elementary software to enhance and copy the pictures that you've taken. You'll probably also want to buy two options: the AC adapter and a 8 or 16 Meg memory card. The more memory the camera has, the higher the resolution of the images will be, resulting in clearer, cleaner pictures. The camera features two buttons for zooming in and out on the subject and a viewfinder that shows you your subject just as other cameras do.

The 24-bit color images taken by the Chinon camera provide excellent results. The software included with the package is OK for transferring the pictures. However, you should use other software to manipulate the images, such as Paint Shop Pro or other commercial photography and graphic programs on the market.

Chinon ES-3000 digital camera

4 Using Photos, Maps And Sound

4. **Photos on Disk Services**
   There are several service companies that will take your developed film and place the photographs on to a diskette. The disks contain software (as well as the pictures) that let you view and/or transfer the photographs quickly and easily to your computer, converting and copying the photos at will. One of the oldest companies also boasts excellent service and high quality results: Seattle FilmWorks's PhotoWorks photos on disk. They can take your developed rolls of film and digitize them for you. You can also specify how you want the pictures returned to you. They even have an Internet web site from where you can download your pictures quickly (Please see the chapter about Using the World Wide Web). Konica and Floppyshots have recently introduced similar products. Floppyshots can be ordered nationwide at most camera supply stores. This chapter will explain how to view and edit pictures with PhotoWorks.

   Seattle Filmworks Web site (www.filmworks.com)

5. **Scanning your photographs with a desktop scanner.**
   This is the most popular method of putting photos into your computer. In chapter one I gave a cursory view of scanners. In this chapter I will scan a photograph into the computer, showing you how to use a simple scanner produced by Storm Technologies and how to touch up or fix the photograph.

Using Photos, Maps And Sound 4

Storm's Hugely Successful Scanner

6. **Use on-line services to develop or copy your photographs**
   America Online's (AOL) PictureWeb Forum or CompuServe's many Photography Forums are good examples of these. There are also dozens of Internet web sites around the country that can process your film as well. For more information about finding and using these on-line services, please refer to the On-line Research chapter earlier in this guide.

Using Seattle Filmworks' PhotoWorks

You can use your own film or purchase Seattle Filmworks film to take pictures. After you have had your film developed by Seattle Filmworks, you will receive a diskette containing your pictures as well as software to view and convert them.

Loading the software

87

4 Using Photos, Maps And Sound

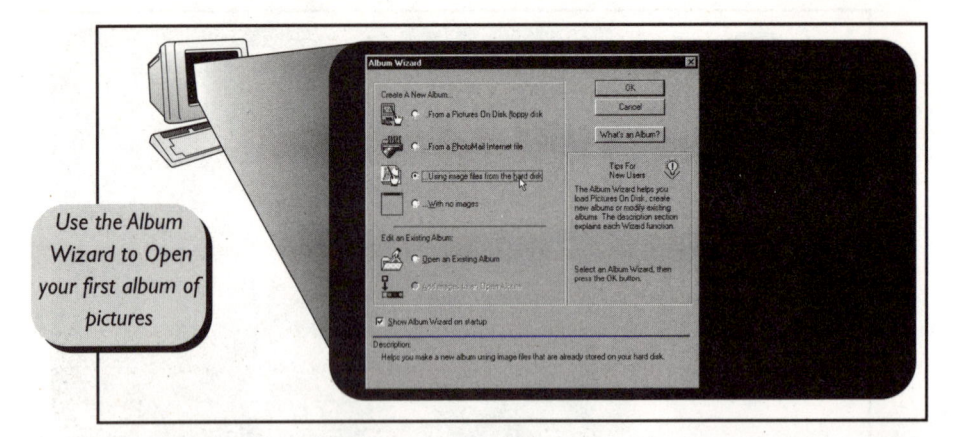

Use the Album Wizard to Open your first album of pictures

You need to follow along with the Album Wizard to easily view your photos.

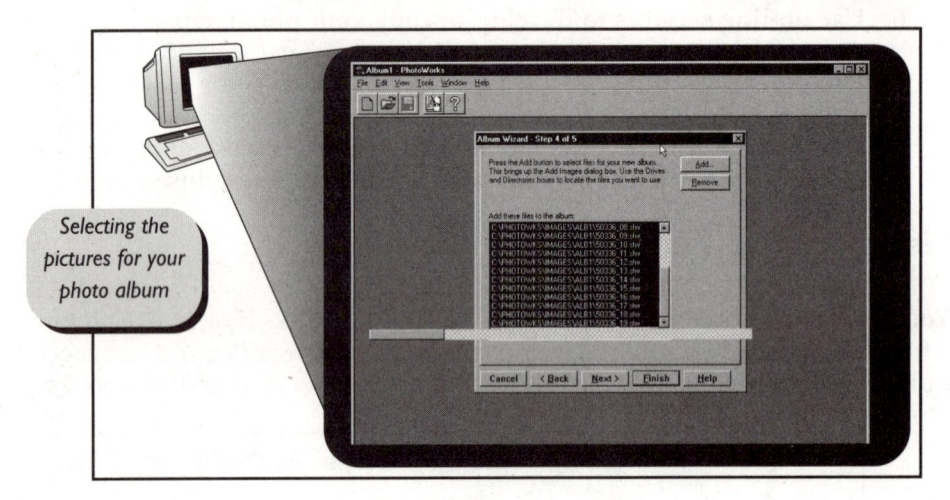

Selecting the pictures for your photo album

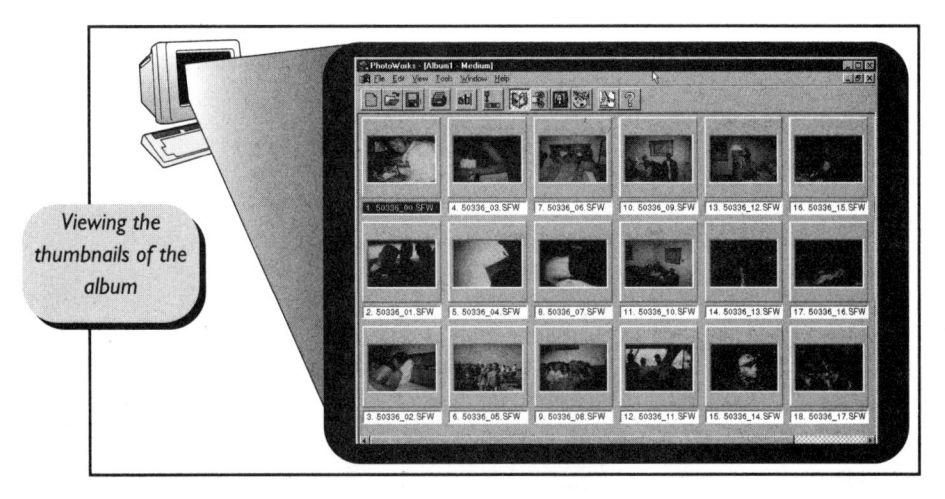

Using Photos, Maps And Sound   4

Viewing the thumbnails of the album

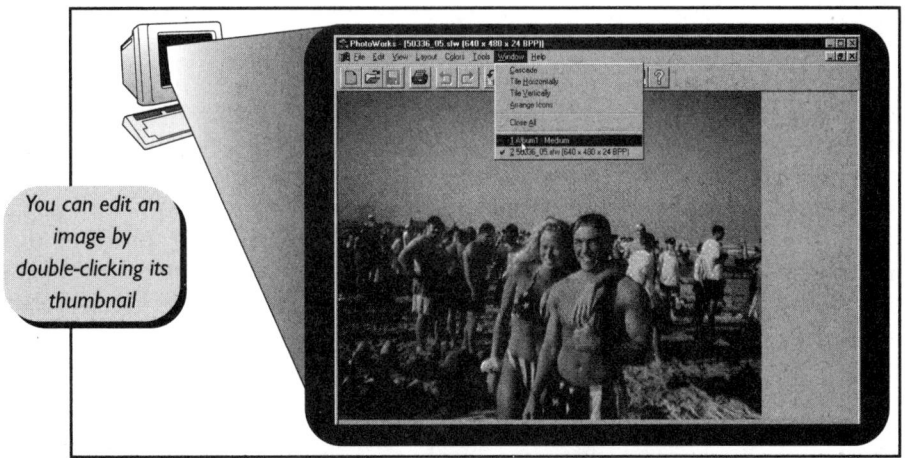

You can edit an image by double-clicking its thumbnail

89

4 Using Photos, Maps And Sound

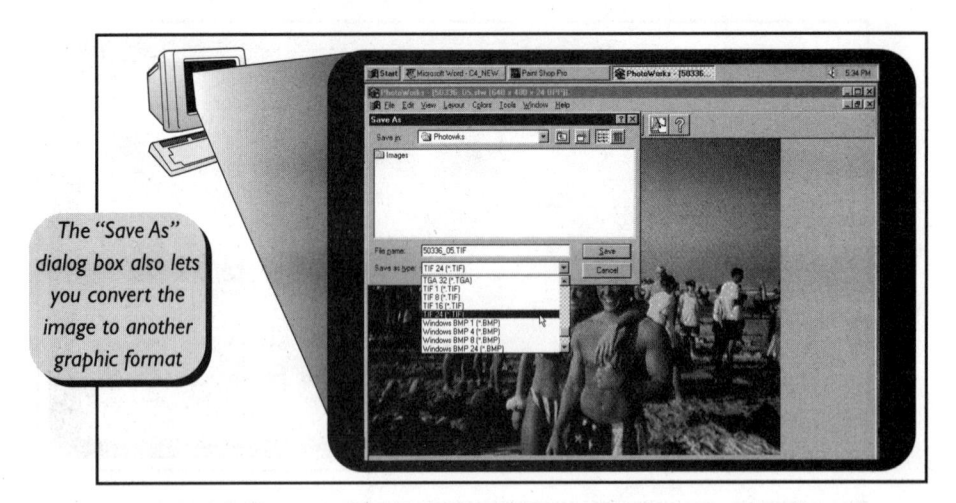

The "Save As" dialog box also lets you convert the image to another graphic format

Using EasyPhoto

Storm Technologies's EasyPhoto Scanner hardware and software package comes in two configurations. The first is a desktop model that will scan pictures up to 6" x 5". The second, and newer, is the EasyPhoto scanner "drive." This unit has the same features and functions as its desktop counterpart and can be installed into one of your computer's drive bays. This frees up precious desk space, making for a cleaner working environment. Unless you're technically inclined, I highly recommend that you have it installed wherever you purchase this drive.

EasyPhoto loads its Gallery

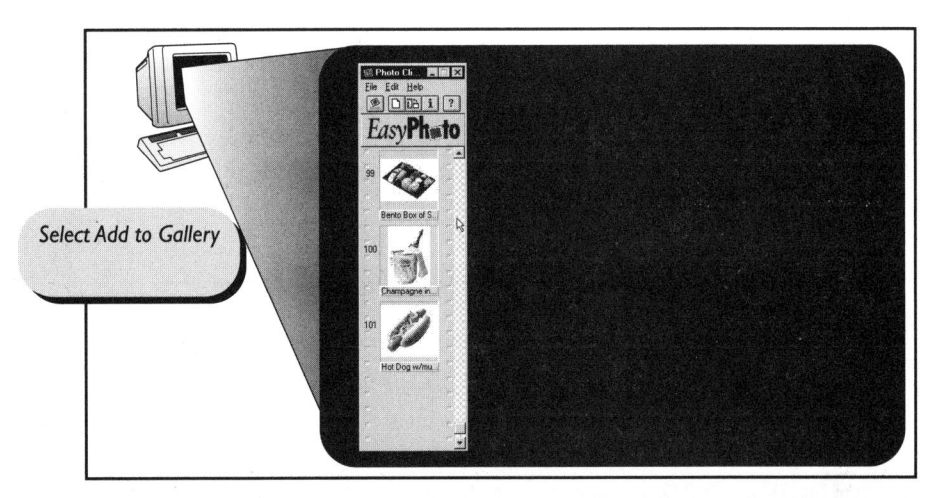

Using Photos, Maps And Sound 4

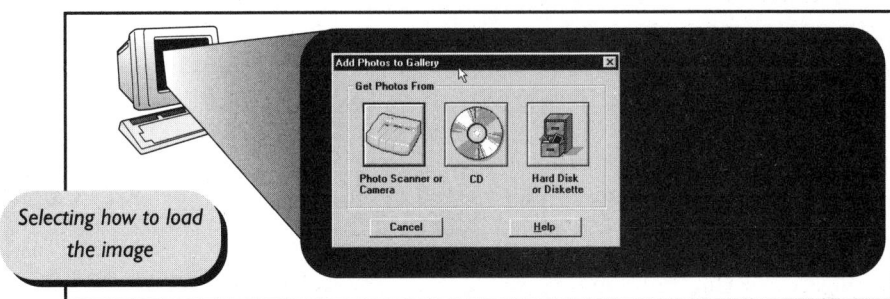

Select Add to Gallery

Selecting how to load the image

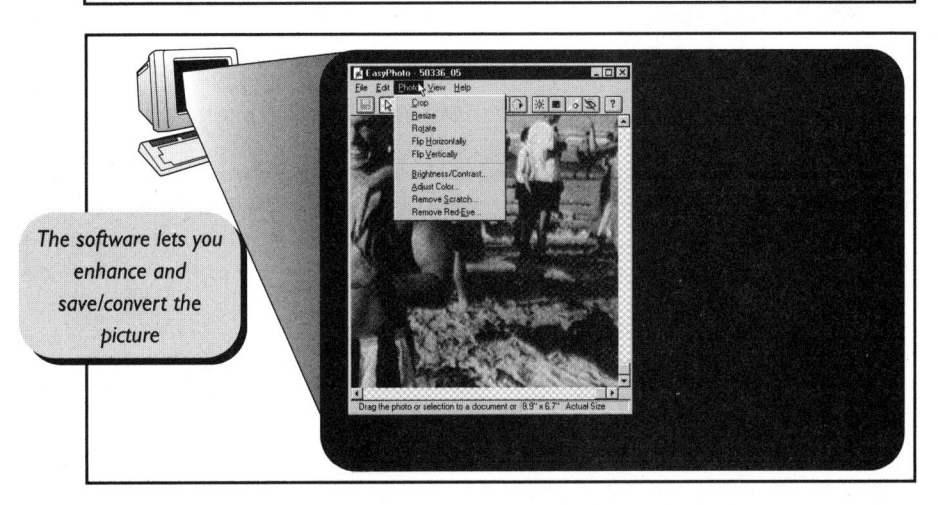

The software lets you enhance and save/convert the picture

91

4 Using Photos, Maps And Sound

MANIPULATING YOUR PHOTOS

By whatever method your photographs are digitized, they may need to be touched up or repaired before you put them into your genealogy software. I'll discuss four progressively more difficult examples of manipulating your photos, each using Paint Shop Pro:

Example 1	Fixing photograph angle and cropping
Example 2	Fixing minor blemishes
Example 3	Fixing a scanned photograph that was torn
Example 4	Advanced cut and paste

Using Paint Shop Pro

Paint Shop Pro (from JASC, Inc.) is the only photo retouching, painting, image format conversion and screen capturing program you'll need. It is both inexpensive ($69 retail) and easy to master. Using Paint Shop Pro you can display, convert, edit and print images. Paint Shop Pro supports the most popular image file formats that you'll need, including BMP, TIF, PCD, GIF and JPG.

Paint Shop Pro displays images up to full-screen, and includes a feature for zooming in and out. Editing tools let you alter the image by flipping, mirroring, rotating in one-degree increments, resizing, resampling, cropping, adding a border and using 19 standard filters. It also supports user-defined filters, which allows you to create, edit, delete and apply your own filters to the images.

You will find that some of the photographs you scan or have digitized by someone else have been damaged in some way, either by bad handling of the pictures over time or by exposure to the elements. Depending on the degree of damage, you can improve many of them by learning a few simple procedures with a graphic program.

The following images show how you can use Paint Shop Pro to touch up older photos and images.

Using Photos, Maps And Sound 4

Example 1 - Fixing photograph angle and cropping

There will be times when you scan a photograph into your computer that it becomes crooked. This is hard to avoid and easily fixed. You may also want to remove the white border of the photograph to make it a cleaner image. Here is a simple technique to accomplish each.

A crooked scanned image

*Select **Image\Rotate...** from PSP's menu bar*

93

4 Using Photos, Maps And Sound

Type in the degree of slant that is needed to straighten the picture. If you get it wrong the first time, don't worry. Select **Edit/Undo** from the menu bar to undo what you've just done and try again. Keep at it until it looks right to you.

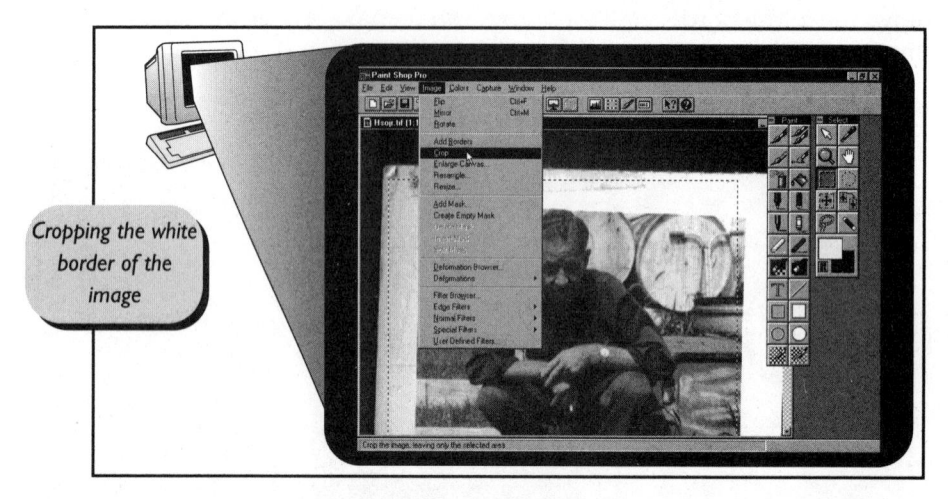

Cropping the white border of the image

Select the dotted rectangular selection tool (from the Select palette) and delineate the image borders by clicking the top left corner of the image, then "dragging" the dotted frame to the bottom right corner and releasing the mouse button. Now select **Image/Crop** from the top menu.

A properly aligned and cropped image

Using Photos, Maps And Sound   4

Example 2 - Fixing minor blemishes

You may notice that some of your photographs have minor blemishes. In this example they seem to be water spots. These can be fixed using Paint Shop Pro's Clone Brush.

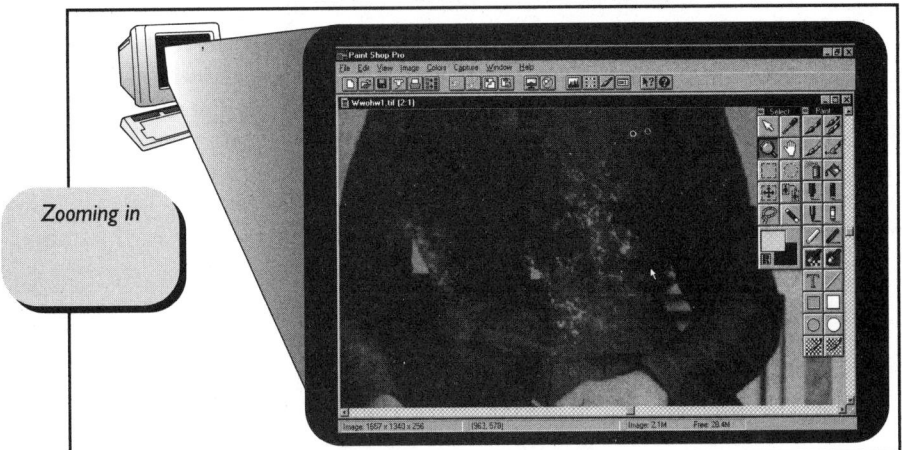

The damaged image

Zooming in

95

4 Using Photos, Maps And Sound

Zoom into the affected area by clicking **View/Zoom In** from the menu bar. Although you can use several PSP tools to fix the damaged area, the two most efficient are the Clone Brush and the Pushbrush. These are the best tools because the missing area contains colors and patterns similar to the area around it, which you want to "clone" into the affected area.

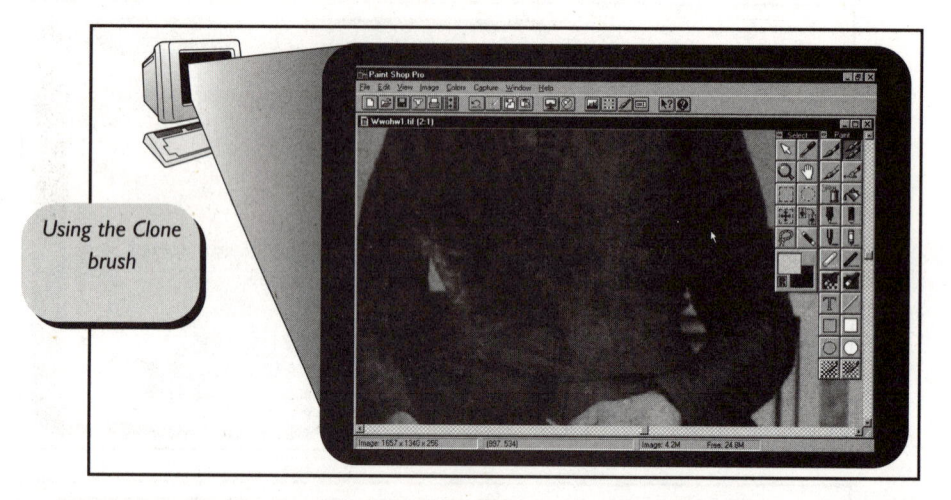

Using the Clone brush

Use the Clone Brush options (double-click the Clone Brush tool in the upper-right corner of the Paint palette). By dragging the cursor through the damaged area and resetting the source point whenever needed, the area around the blemish is copied into the stain. Repeat this process using the Clone Brush throughout the area. Don't forget to change the source point of the clone as needed. You'll have to use your best judgment by looking at the image close up and at regular resolution. Repeat these steps as necessary to repair the image. In short order the image should appear similar to the following:

Using Photos, Maps And Sound 4

With patience and care you'll never know it was there

Example 3 - Fixing a scanned photograph that is torn

Torn or cut photographs are a little more difficult to repair. You will use the Clone Brush from the previous example to "fix" the tear. Again, by dragging the cursor through the torn area and resetting the source point whenever needed, the area around the tear is copied into the tear. Repeat this process using the Clone Brush throughout the area

Note the tear that appears across this photo

4 Using Photos, Maps And Sound

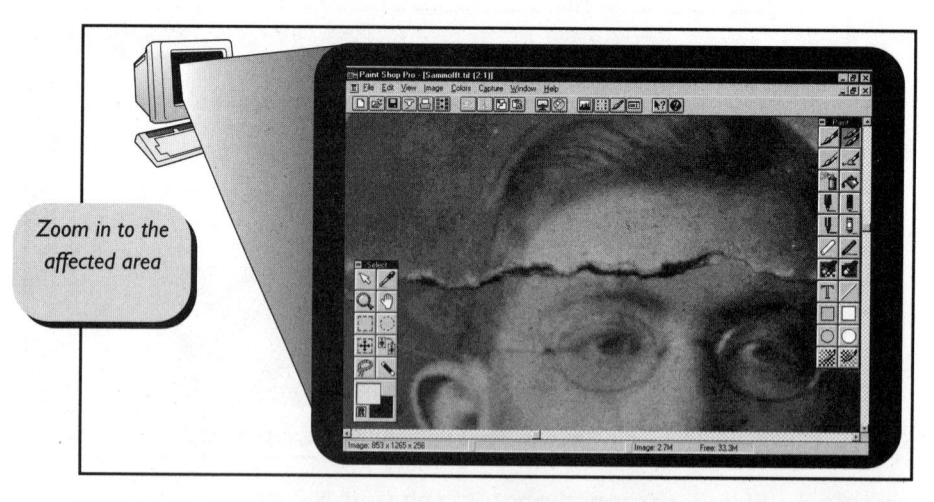

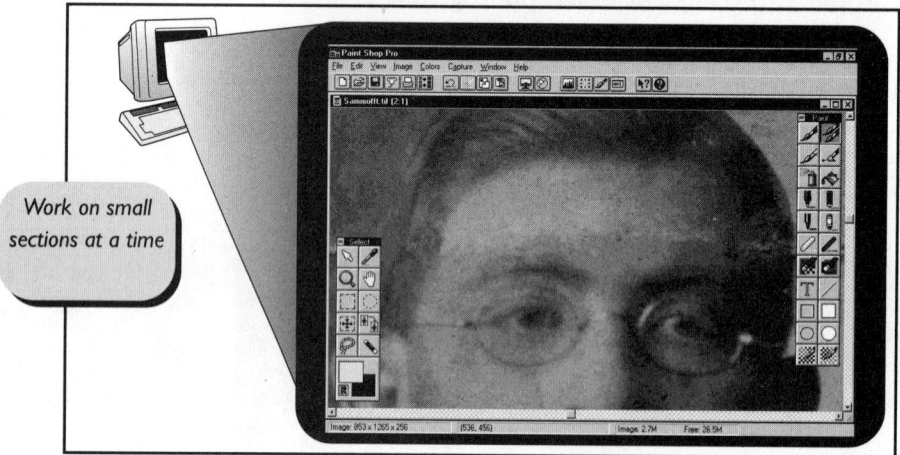

Zoom in to the affected area

Work on small sections at a time

Using Photos, Maps And Sound

> *In a short time you have a great new-old family heirloom*

Example 4 - Advanced cut and paste

One of the many marvels of digital photography and software is that you can do things that would have cost hundreds of dollars to accomplish just a few years ago. Recently, I wanted to present a picture to my father that would have been impossible to take. I wanted to merge a photo of my grandfather with his parents. Eventually, I added several other relatives and I created a photo that featured 5 generations—all in one photo. Here is how to re-size, copy, cut and place any part of one photo into another to get the same effect.

4 Using Photos, Maps And Sound

A scanned family photo

Loading the second picture

Using Photos, Maps And Sound 4

*Resize the picture proportionately to the first one with the **Image/Resize...** command*

Use the "lasso" tool on the second image

The lasso tool (located on the Select tool bar) is a freehand selecting tool. Place and hold down your left mouse button and outline the portion of the image you want to transfer. After you have completely gone around the subject, select **Edit/Copy** from the menu bar. Close the picture you just copied from. Finally, select **Copy/Paste/As New Selection** and move the outline to the area where you want to place it. Don't worry. If you don't like the location select **Edit/Undo** and try again.

101

4 Using Photos, Maps And Sound

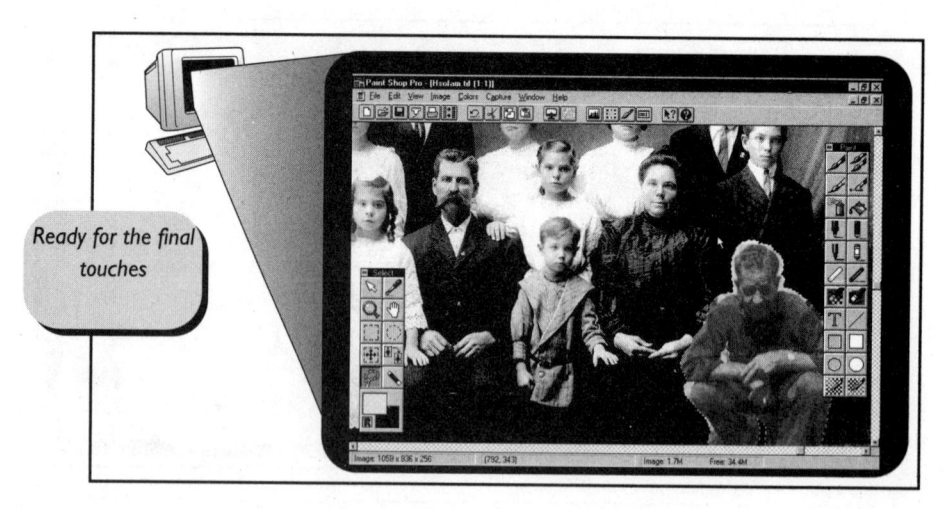

Ready for the final touches

Elementary example

Here's a list of images that are included on the CD-ROM in the directory \PIX:

- ❖ BARNONE .TIF
- ❖ BENTNTWP.TIF
- ❖ CDR_1.TIF
- ❖ DECATRIN.TIF
- ❖ ECOLD2 .TIF
- ❖ ECOLD3.TIF
- ❖ ECOLDF .TIF
- ❖ HSOFAM .TIF
- ❖ HSOJR .TIF
- ❖ JULIES .TIF
- ❖ SAMMOFFT.TIF
- ❖ WWOHW1. TIF
- ❖ WWOLDF .TIF
- ❖ WWO_F.TIF

These images are meant to be used for practicing before you begin tackling your own photographs. Don't worry, these are digitized copies. I have more.

USING MAPS TO TELL A STORY

Maps can add another great dimension to your family history. They can help others reading your book more easily see the geographic localities and how they relate to and influenced your ancestors.

Using Photos, Maps And Sound 4

In the last two years there has been an explosion of software available for mapping information. The most popular are DeLorme's Street Atlas USA line of products, Microsoft's map programs and MapQuest, which is on the world wide web (www). When you are viewing maps of locations (right down to the street level), you can crop and paste them into other applications to be used later. In the two examples below, I am using DeLorme's Street Atlas USA and Paint Shop Pro to create a map for a family history. The location is a small town, South Bloomingville, Ohio, population: about 100.

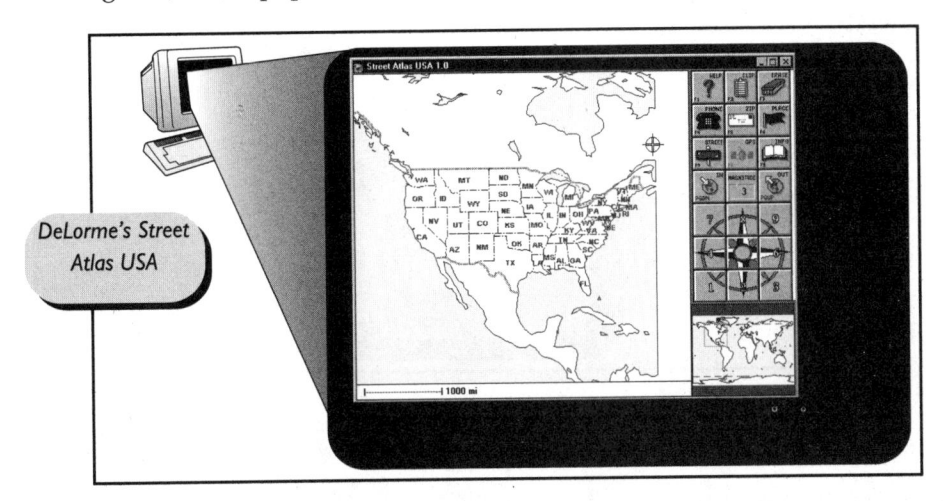

DeLorme's Street Atlas USA

Click the [Place] button located on the right control panel and type your city and state. Click the [Locate] button when the program finds a match.

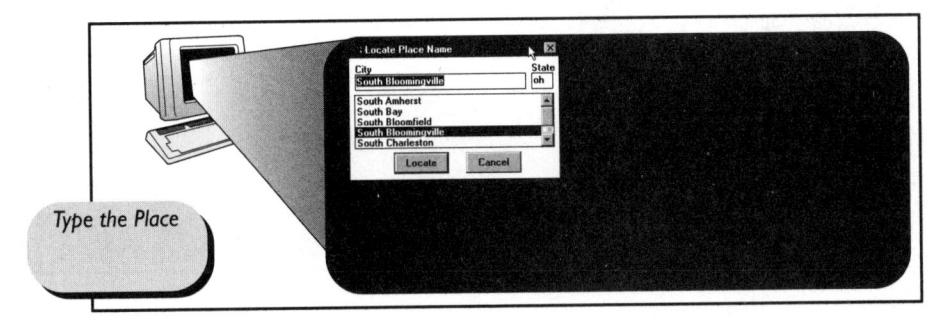

Type the Place

The map will put the location in the middle of the map screen. Use the In (pgdn) and Out (pgup) buttons to zoom in and out on your city. Once you have the map as you want it displayed, press the [Clip] button to save it to your Windows Clipboard.

103

4 Using Photos, Maps And Sound

After you have clicked the [Clip] button hold the [Alt] key down and press the [Tab] key until you see the icon for Paint Shop Pro. When you see the icon, release the keys and you will have PSP on your screen. Choose the **Edit/Paste/As New Image** from the menu bar and release.

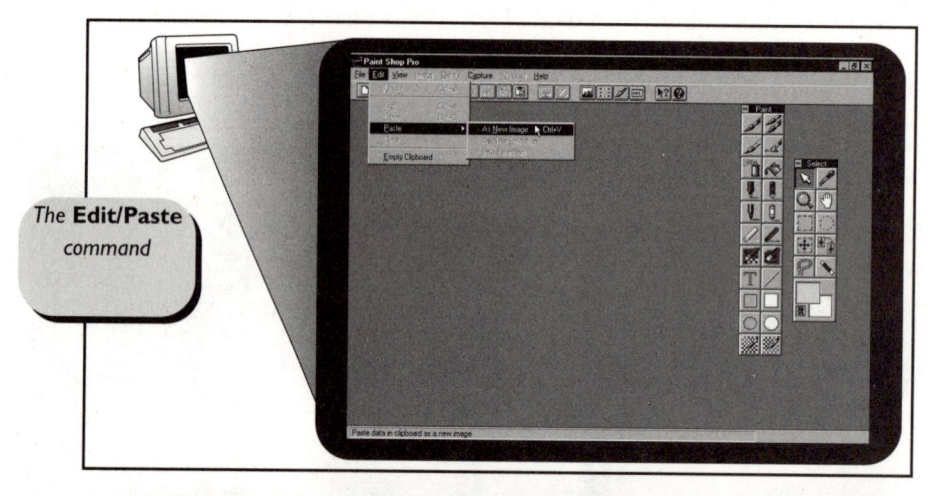

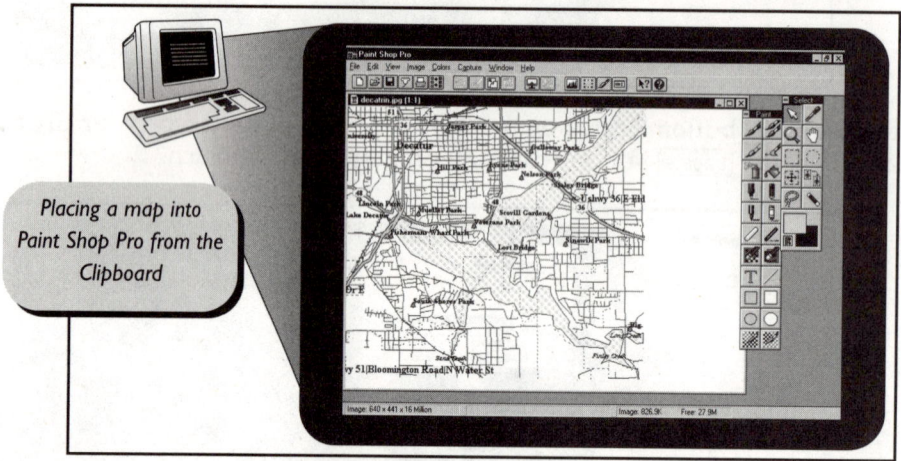

*The **Edit/Paste** command*

Placing a map into Paint Shop Pro from the Clipboard

104

Using Photos, Maps And Sound

After the map is in PSP you can touch it up and/or add text to it to help others understand what the map represents. One quick tip: If you can, use progressively detailed maps to help readers understand where the map's location is in reference to the rest of the country. In this example, another map of Ohio highlighting the county where South Bloomingville is located would be helpful in showing readers exactly where this town is located.

Although I discuss how to get on and use the world wide web later in this guide, I want to show you a screen from MapQuest's Website. It works similar to the other mapping program, except that you use it on a remote server computer instead of your own. It features street level maps of the complete USA and it can even help you locate an address. It's an outstanding example of what can be done on the web.

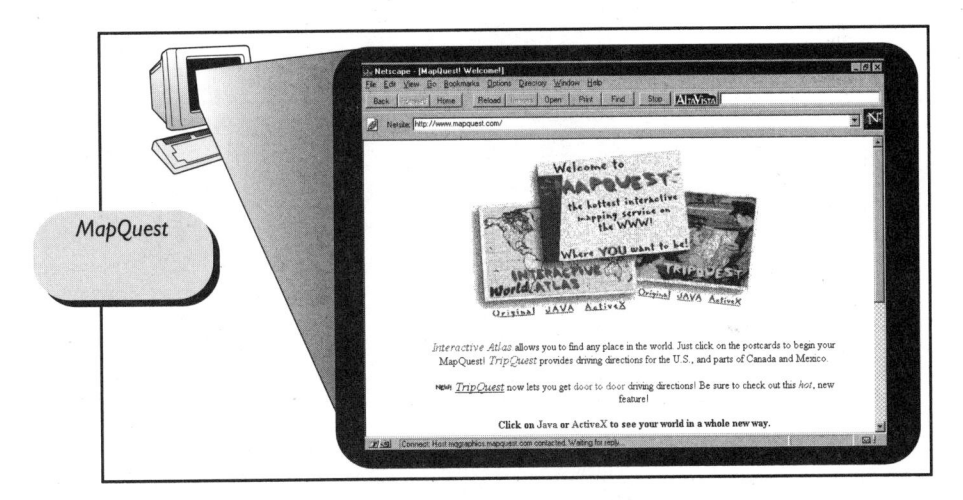

PUTTING SOUND INTO YOUR COMPUTER

A little known yet powerful application that is included with Windows 3.x and Win 95 is the Media Player. It is located in your Accessories Folder or, in Windows 95, in the Multimedia Folder under Accessories. Windows uses the Media Player to play sound wave (WAV) files.

105

4 Using Photos, Maps And Sound

It can also play digitized video in the form of AVI files. If you are interested in learning more about putting sound and video into your computer, we published a book called PC VIDEO which teaches you how to do it. For this guide, I want to show you how easy it is to put audio into your PC.

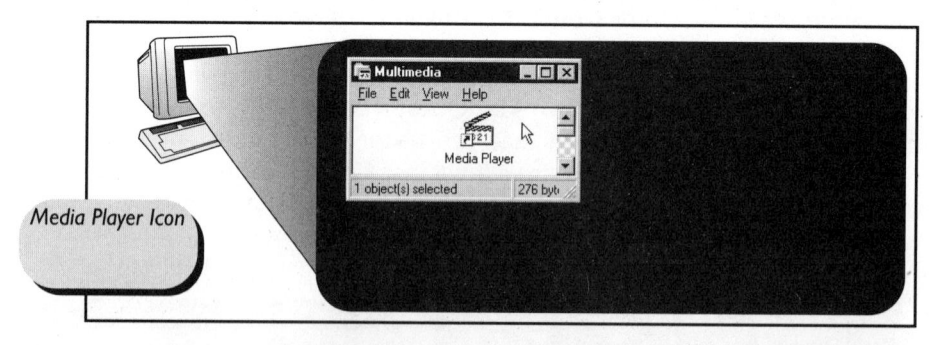

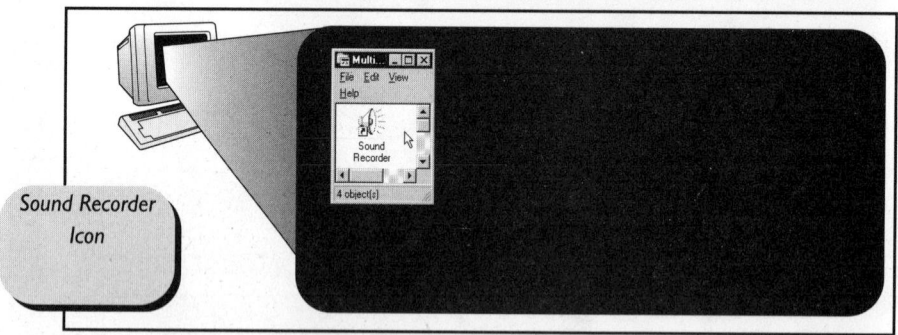

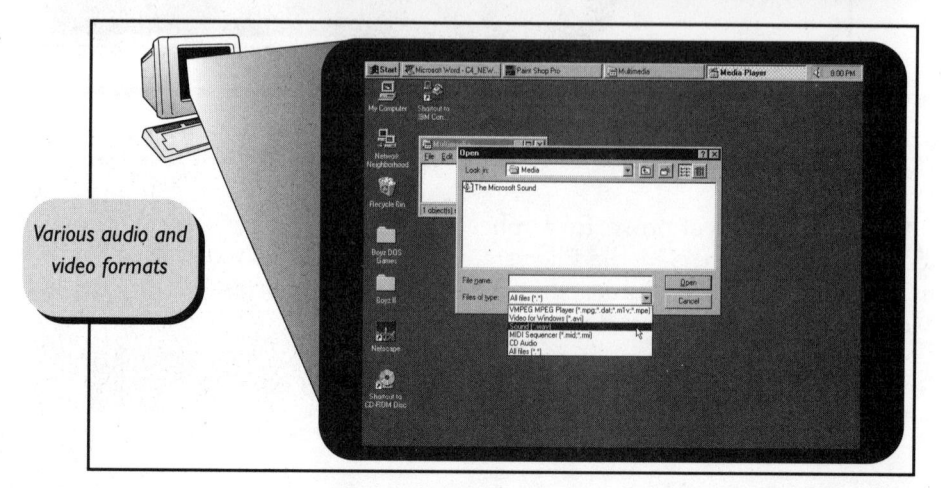

Media Player Icon

Sound Recorder Icon

Various audio and video formats

106

Using Photos, Maps And Sound   4

You can digitize sound two ways: directly from a microphone plugged into your sound board or by plugging an audio player into the sound board. If, as I mentioned in an earlier chapter, you recorded a relative talking about your family history, you can connect the recorder/player directly into the sound card in your PC.

Nearly all PC sound cards are Sound Blaster compatible. This is because Creative Labs's Sound Blaster brand sound boards have become the *de facto* standard for playing sounds on your PC. If you do not have a sound card, make sure the one you buy is Sound Blaster compatible and you will have many fewer compatibility problems in the future.

When you plug the microphone into the MIC jack of your sound card you are going to sample and digitize the sounds. The higher the sampling rate, the larger the sound file size. Therefore, if you want to record a .WAV sound file sampled at 44.100 kHz, stereo, and 16 bit, you must have enough hard disk space to handle the larger file size. The default settings should be fine for you however.

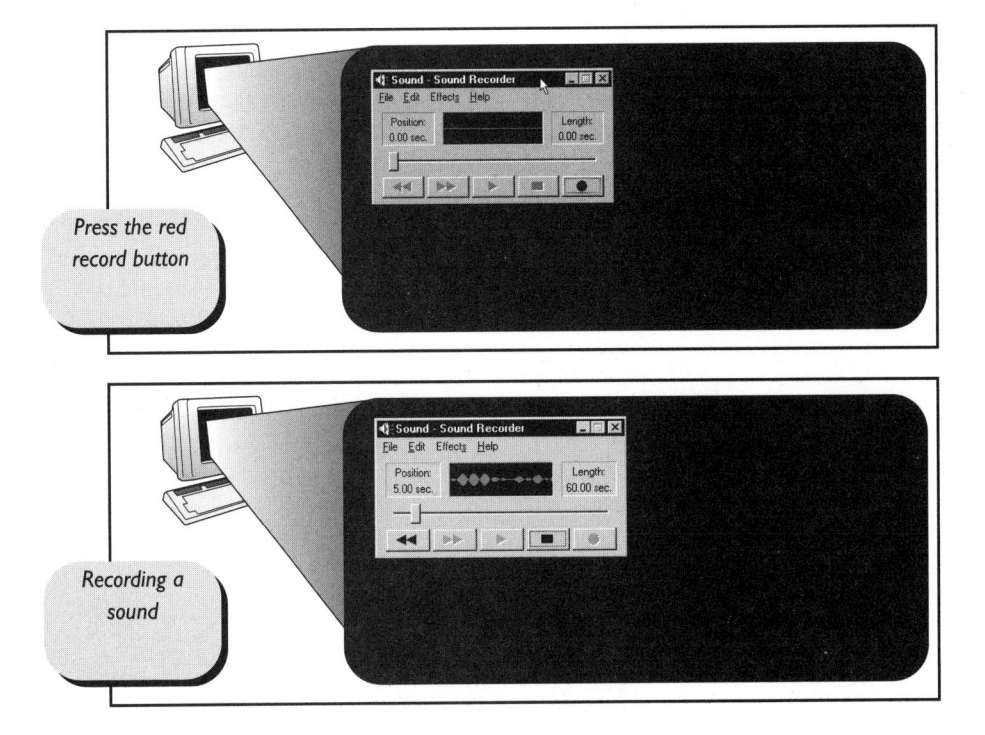

Press the red record button

Recording a sound

107

4 Using Photos, Maps And Sound

You should practice a few times using the Sound Recorder until you get satisfactory results. The better the sound file, the more enjoyable it is to hear later. Don't be afraid to experiment.

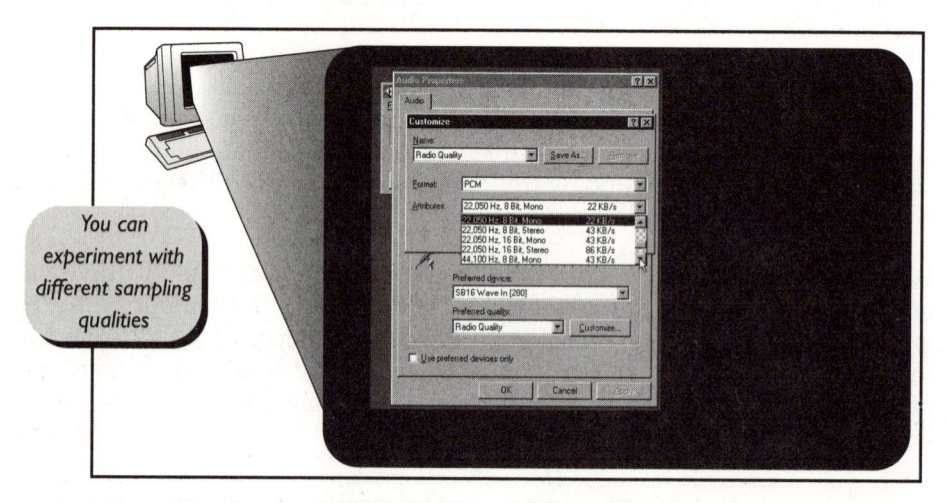

You can experiment with different sampling qualities

Remember, the sound quality is better at higher sampling rates and higher resolution. On the companion CD-ROM I included a recording of the Lord's Prayer. It is a WAV sound file with a good voice recording. Later, I will show you how to put this audio file into your genealogy program.

108

Using Other Programs For Your Family History

Chapter 5

Using Other Programs For Your Family History

Before we begin using a genealogy program to gather all your family information, you can use two other programs to create great looking documents with specialized family material. You should have a word processor and, optionally, a desktop publishing program. Both of these programs offer a variety of ways to share your family history quickly, easily and inexpensively, though these programs are not meant to replace a genealogy program. Genealogy programs feature a relational database of people and events. That is, when you put information into the program, it checks to make certain that the information is correct. You will want to use a word processor in addition to a genealogy program. Although the word processor lacks sophisticated genealogical reports and databases of relationships between people, it is easy to learn and has many graphic and formatting features.

Besides the information you print about your family heritage, nothing else brings it to life like photos and graphics. You can include photos of yourself, your family members, places of interest, old homes, autos, historical events, and any others that help tell your story.

USING MICROSOFT WORD

The examples below will show you how to create a document that includes an obituary and a photograph of the deceased. This can make a nice gift to give to other members of your family.

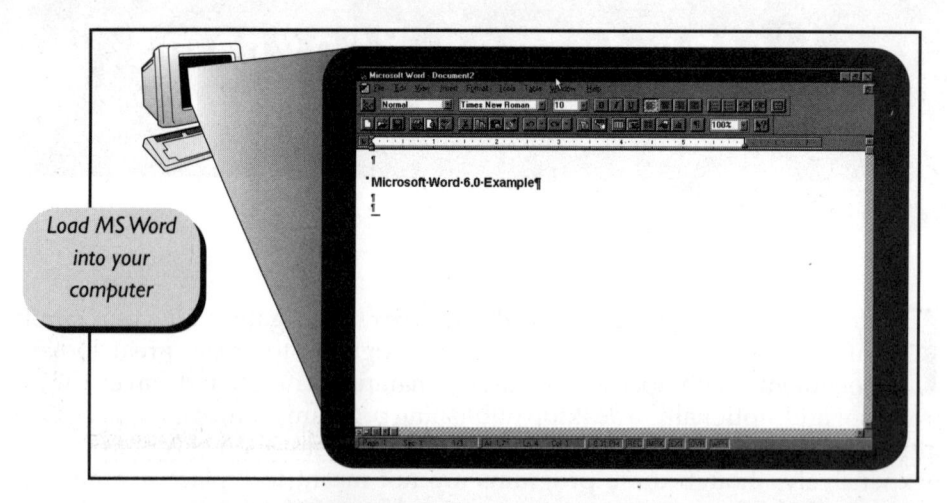

5 Using Other Programs For Your Family History

Load MS Word into your computer

Microsoft Word - Document2

Microsoft Word 6.0 Example

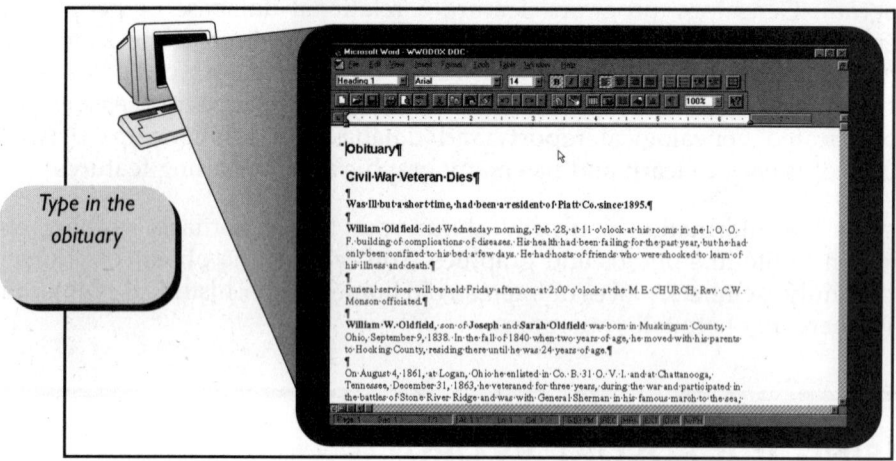

Type in the obituary

Microsoft Word - WW0DOX.DOC

Obituary

Civil War Veteran Dies

Was ill but a short time, had been a resident of Piatt Co. since 1895.

William Oldfield died Wednesday morning, Feb. 28, at 11 o'clock at his rooms in the I.O.O.F. building of complications of diseases. His health had been failing for the past year, but he had only been confined to his bed a few days. He had hosts of friends who were shocked to learn of his illness and death.

Funeral services will be held Friday afternoon at 2:00 o'clock at the M.E. CHURCH, Rev. C.W. Monson officiated.

William W. Oldfield, son of **Joseph** and **Sarah Oldfield** was born in Muskingum County, Ohio, September 9, 1838. In the fall of 1840 when two years of age, he moved with his parents to Hocking County, residing there until he was 24 years of age.

On August 4, 1861, at Logan, Ohio he enlisted in Co. B. 31 O.V.I. and at Chattanooga, Tennessee, December 31, 1863, he veteraned for three years, during the war and participated in the battles of Stone River Ridge and was with General Sherman in his famous march to the sea.

112

Using Other Programs For Your Family History   5

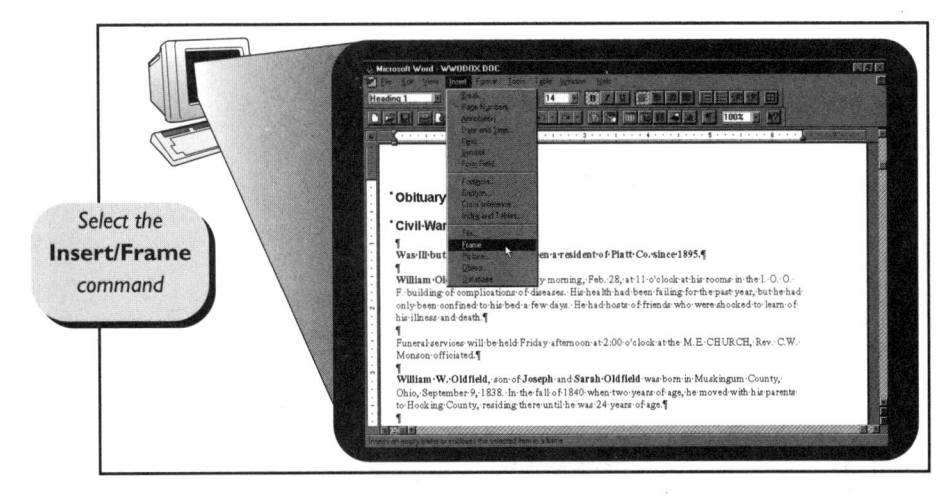

*Select the **Insert/Frame** command*

Word will notify you if you are not in Page Layout format. For Word to insert a frame and place a picture in it, click the [Yes] button.

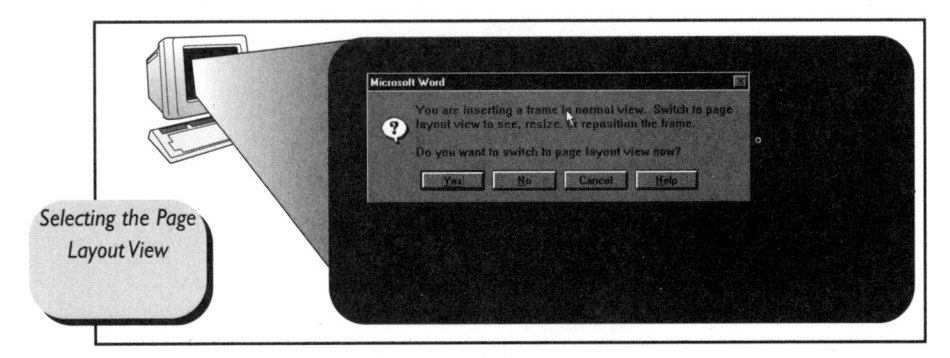

Selecting the Page Layout View

You will see that your mouse pointer has turned into a "+" on the screen. Place this "+" sign where you want the top left corner of the frame to be in your document. Now click and hold the left mouse button. While holding the left mouse button, drag the active frame diagonally from top left to bottom right and then release it. Word will place a blank frame into your document and automatically move text around it. It is now ready to drop in an image. Select **Insert/Picture...** from the menu bar.

5 Using Other Programs For Your Family History

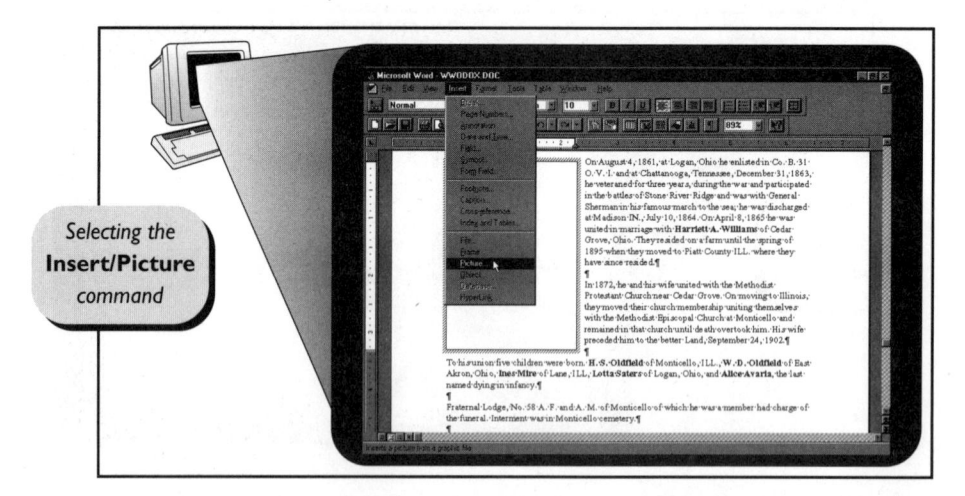

*Selecting the **Insert/Picture** command*

Now locate the picture you want to insert and double-click it.

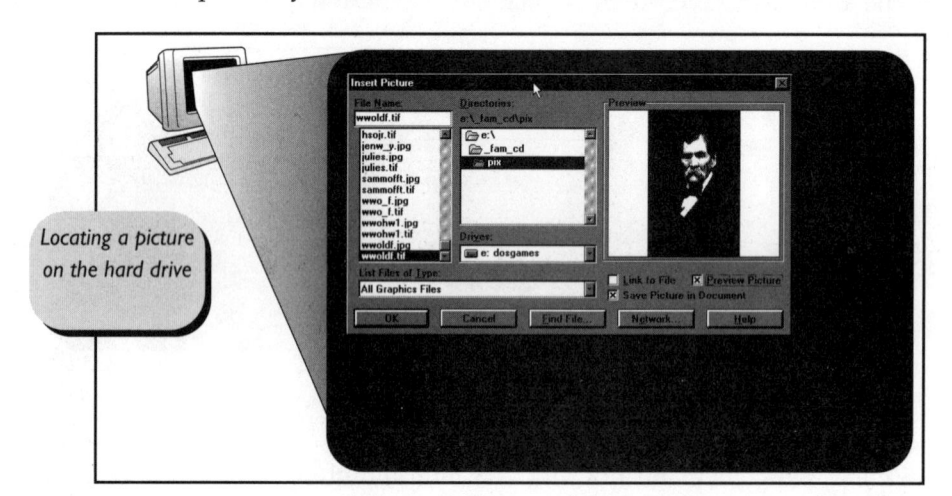

Locating a picture on the hard drive

After you have double-clicked your image's name, Word will place the image into the frame.

114

Using Other Programs For Your Family History 5

The picture and text can now be printed

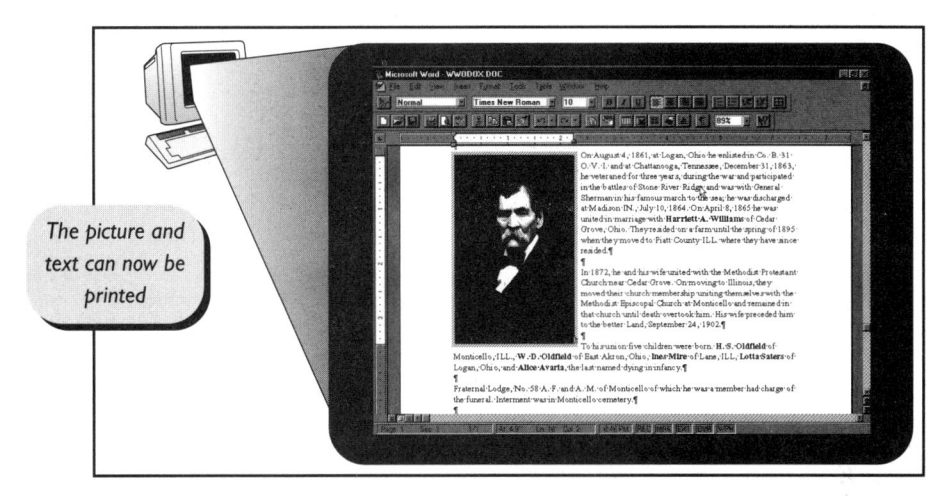

One final note: You can insert images into your Word document without first creating a frame for it. You can do this by simply placing the I-bar anywhere within your document and click your left mouse button to place it there. Select **Insert/Picture...** and find your image. Double-click on the filename and Word will place it into your document.

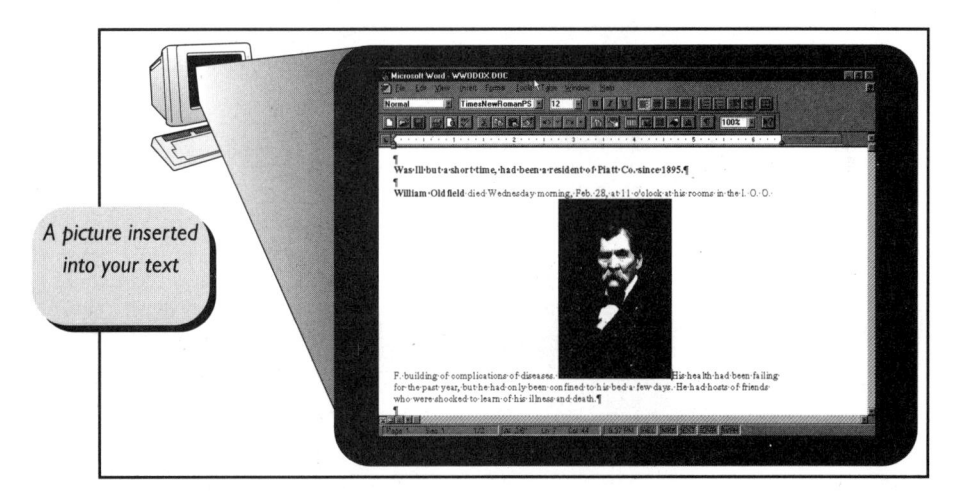

A picture inserted into your text

This is a simpler way of putting an image into your text, but you lose precise control of the placement.

115

5 Using Other Programs For Your Family History

Microsoft Publisher

Creating a family newsletter is one of the best ways to keep in touch with your relatives across the country. It doesn't have to be fancy or elaborate. It's a good way to keep your relatives up to date with the research you are doing, and it shows those from whom you're requesting information that you are a serious family historian.

You can create dynamite family newsletters with Microsoft's Publisher (also available as Publisher 97). Of all its features, the best one for beginners is a handy utility called PageWiz Assistant (also known as a wizard), which can help you create a simple yet effective newsletter.

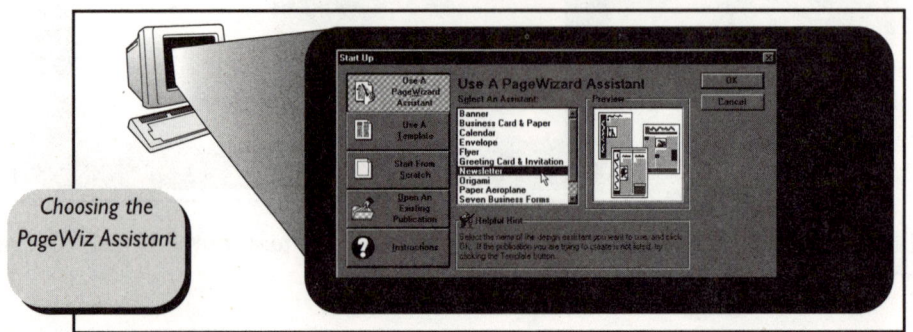

Starting Microsoft Publisher

Choosing the PageWiz Assistant

Using Other Programs For Your Family History

The Assistant will give you choices on how you want to construct your newsletter. For this example I selected the following: classic style, two columns, standard layout and the title: WILLIAM GAZETTE. I also chose Horizontal Title, No Printing on Both Sides, one page and I left all the options checked. After you've moved through these options, click [Create It]. When it's finished click the [OK] button.

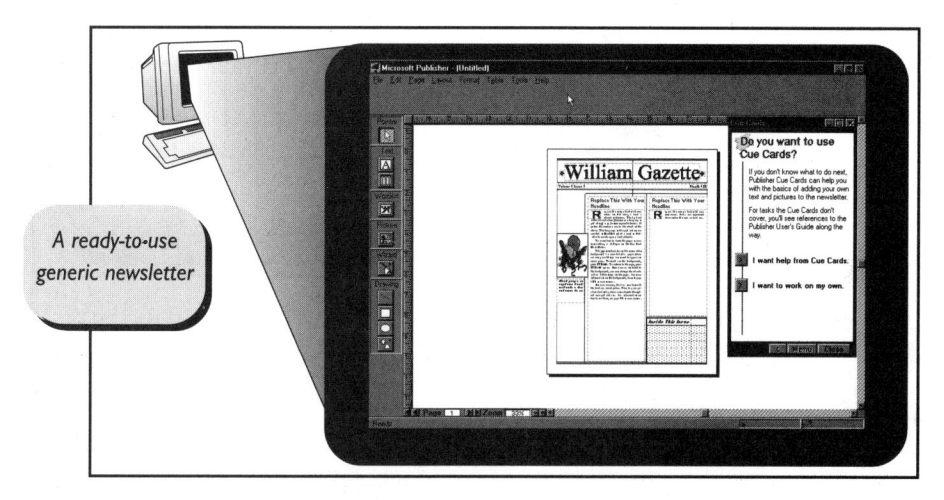

A ready-to-use generic newsletter

To make the newsletter fill the screen so you can see it better, click the "+" button located next to Zoom at the bottom left of the screen.

Click on the column headline and select the text "Replace This With Your Headline" by holding down your left mouse button. When you have all the text highlighted, press the [Del] key. Now type (for this example) "William's Obituary".

5 Using Other Programs For Your Family History

The column headline

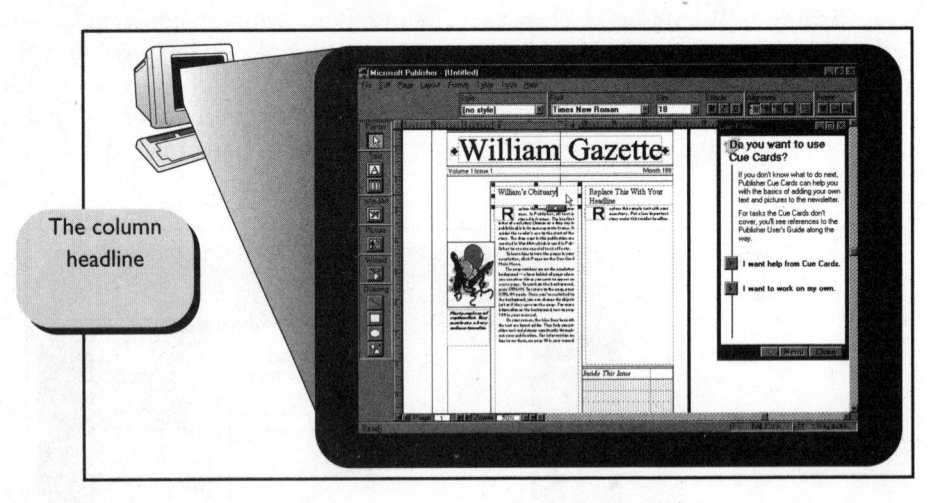

Next, click on the column of text below it and do the same. Click on the large "R" and press the [Del] key again.

Place your mouse pointer in the empty column and click it once. Select **File/Import Text...** from the menu bar. Publisher will then ask you what text file you want to import. Select your text (the CD-ROM has a file called MPSAMPLE.DOC you can use) and click [OK].

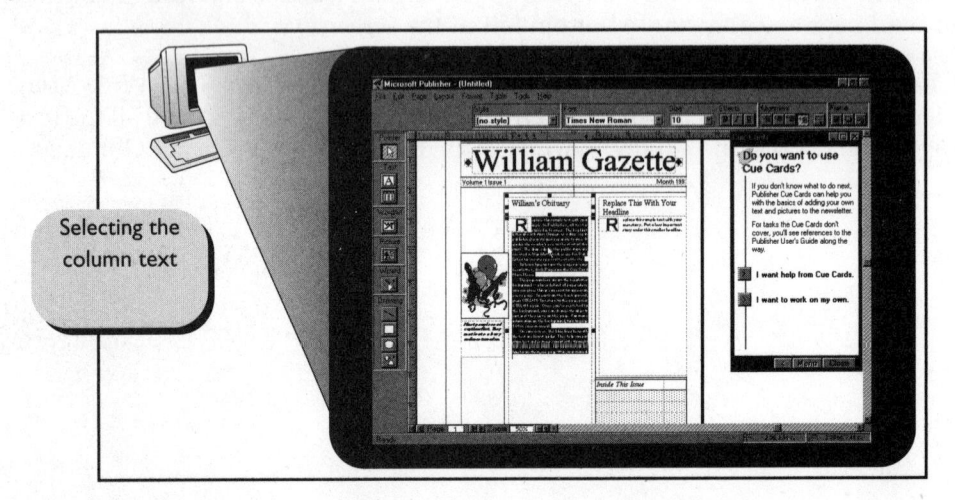

Selecting the column text

118

Using Other Programs For Your Family History 5

To place a photograph on this page, click the graphic to the left of the column. Select **File/Import Picture...** from the menu bar. Publisher will ask you what picture you want to import. Select your picture (the CD-ROM has a file called WWO.TIF you can use) and click OK.

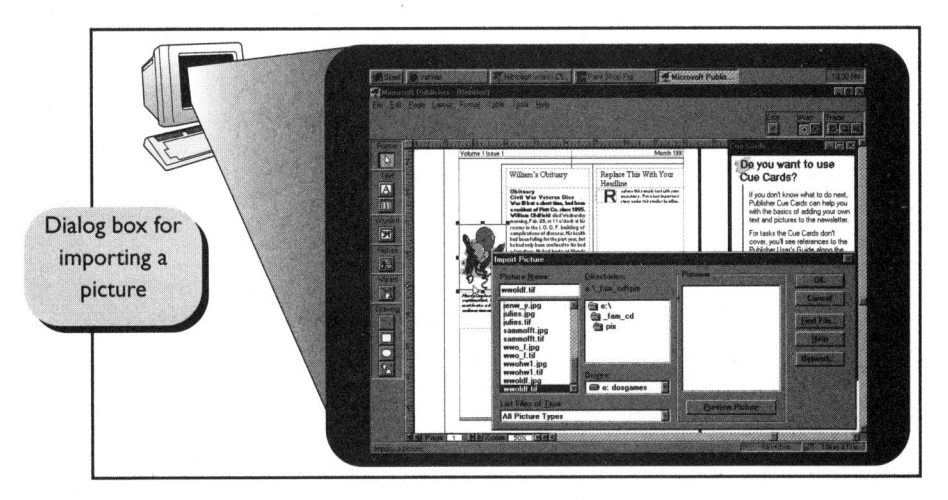

Dialog box for importing a picture

You will be asked to choose how your picture will be displayed on the page. Select "Change The Picture To Fit The Frame" and click OK. You normally want to insert the picture this way because of the space limitations on the page. If you wanted the image to be larger (the same size as the original image) you would select "Change The Frame To Fit The Picture".

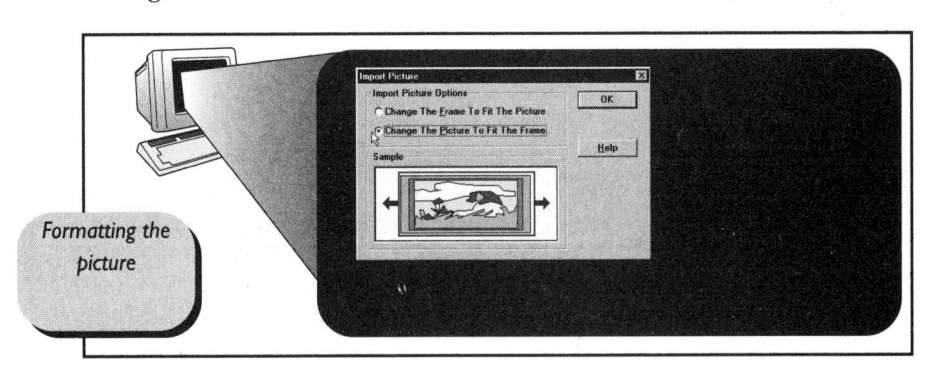

Formatting the picture

119

5 Using Other Programs For Your Family History

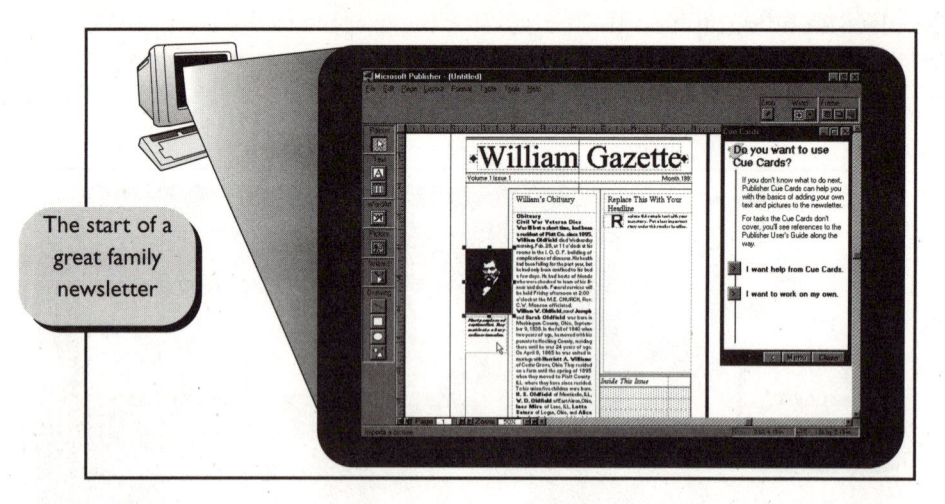

The start of a great family newsletter

You can also change the size of the picture to create a more interesting layout. Publisher is an excellent tool for creating interesting family history newsletters.

A more dramatic layout

120

Using Genealogy Programs

Chapter 6

Using Genealogy Programs

Using a genealogy program can be the fun part of recording and printing your family history on your PC. A genealogy program records your family's past and present. Unlike a wordprocessor or a desktop publishing program, a genealogy program can keep track of your family members and how each is related to another. It will generate family trees and various other reports that are based on the individual family members and their relations to each other, save you countless hours writing your family history by producing modified decendancy reports (or books) for you to share, and can even calculate dates, create calendars, print address labels, and perform other miscellaneous tasks that you use to do by hand. It's also one of the best ways to preserve your family history and store it for the future, adding to it as your family grows.

The following sections are written to show you the basic steps to using a genealogy program. You will quickly learn to use three genealogy programs that I've found useful: Brother's Keeper (DOS version), by John Steed; Family Origins (Ver. 5), from Parsons Technology; and Family Tree Maker Deluxe Edition II (Ver. 3), from Banner Blue Div., Broderbund Software. Each of these genealogy programs will help you organize all the various bits and snippets of information you have gathered (completed or semi-completed pedigrees, family group sheets, treasured copies of documents, scanned family photographs, maps, even precious sound and video files). Wrapping all this information into a single multimedia presentation makes creating the package fun for you, and experiencing it interesting for others. They also make it much easier for you to publish your own professional-quality family history, formatted, indexed and ready to share with others.

There are several other genealogy programs available, including Commsoft's Roots IV and Visual Roots, and a myriad of shareware products from which to choose. You can evaluate the features of these genealogy programs by following the examples in this book and comparing the performance of various programs. Each of the programs has unique features that I and thousands of other family

6 Using Genealogy Programs

historians have used. All have been available for years and are a solid investment in preserving your family history. You may be surprised to know that many family historians use more than one genealogy program for their work (myself included), although I wouldn't recommend you try this until you've become comfortable with genealogy practices and basic features of using genealogical software. It would be confusing trying to learn more than one program at a time and, if you're not careful, you could lose some of the work you've already done on the computer.

Choose your genealogy program based on how easy it is to use, what program other family members use, how thoroughly it keeps track of notes and photos, its flexibility in printing reports and, of course, its cost. Whichever you choose, be sure that the genealogy program you use is GEDCOM compatible.

GEDCOM is an acronym for GEnealogical Data COMmunications data files, introduced by the LDS Church several years ago. GEDCOM set a standard genealogical data file format, making it easy to exchange information between programs. This ability can save you hundreds of hours (and the heartache) of retyping all the information into a second program (I learned this from experience).

GEDCOM files are also easier to manage than the data files of your program, because it compresses all the data into a single file that can be read by any GEDCOM compliant program. An added bonus is that they are great for backing up your data files; you can upload them to an on-line service or submit them to other GEDCOM sites so you have an off-premises backup copy of your work.

When my second database of my family crashed, I was glad to have had the foresight to have uploaded it to CompuServe. All I had to do was re-install the software and import my GEDCOM file to be fully restored. Whew!

Using Genealogy Programs 6

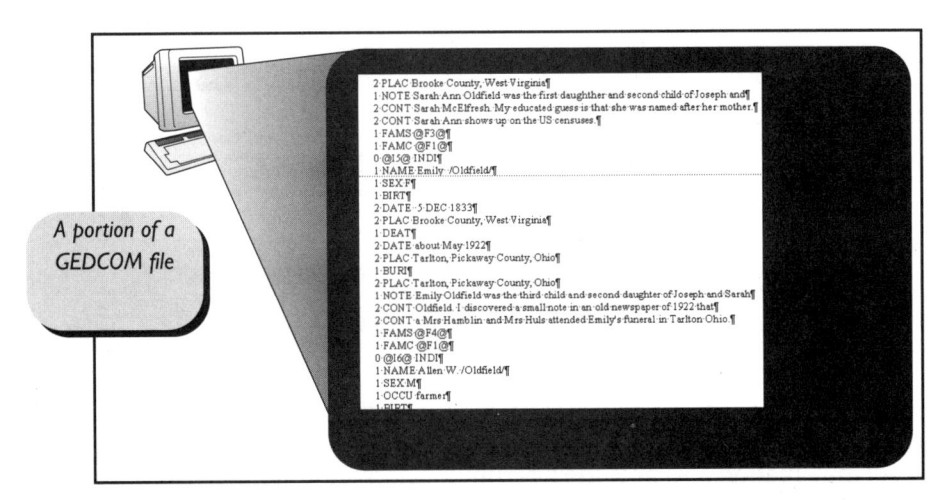

A portion of a GEDCOM file

```
2 PLAC Brooke County, West Virginia
1 NOTE Sarah Ann Oldfield was the first daughter and second child of Joseph and
2 CONT Sarah McElfresh. My educated guess is that she was named after her mother.
2 CONT Sarah Ann shows up on the US censuses.
1 FAMS @F3@
1 FAMC @F1@
0 @I5@ INDI
1 NAME Emily /Oldfield/
1 SEX F
1 BIRT
2 DATE 5 DEC 1833
2 PLAC Brooke County, West Virginia
1 DEAT
2 DATE about May 1922
2 PLAC Tarlton, Pickaway County, Ohio
1 BURI
2 PLAC Tarlton, Pickaway County, Ohio
1 NOTE Emily Oldfield was the third child and second daughter of Joseph and Sarah
2 CONT Oldfield. I discovered a small note in an old newspaper of 1922 that
2 CONT a Mrs Hamblin and Mrs Huls attended Emily's funeral in Tarlton Ohio.
1 FAMS @F4@
1 FAMC @F1@
0 @I6@ INDI
1 NAME Allen W. /Oldfield/
1 SEX M
1 OCCU farmer
1 BIRT
```

Your genealogy program should also be able to save your data into a Tiny Tafel file. The Tiny Tafel format is based on an article titled *Tiny-Tafel for Database Scope Indexing*, by Paul Andereck, in the April-May-June 1986 (vol 5, number 4) issue of Genealogical Computing.

Tiny Tafels provide a compact way of describing your database of family information so that it can be quickly scanned visually or by computer. The file contains the soundex code and each unique last name in each of your family lines. (Soundex converts spelling and phonetic information into computer code that identifies names by pronunciation (e.g., the names Clay, Cley and Claie, sounding the same though spelled differently, would share the same soundex code). This can be very useful for tracking relatives who lived before the standardization of spelling or whose name was changed through clerical errors.)

Tiny Tafel also contains the birth date and place of the first known ancestor in each line, and the birth date and place of the most recent descendant with that last name. By sharing these files with others or getting them from collections on-line or off, you can quickly compare them to see if there are any matches with your family lines.

6 Using Genealogy Programs

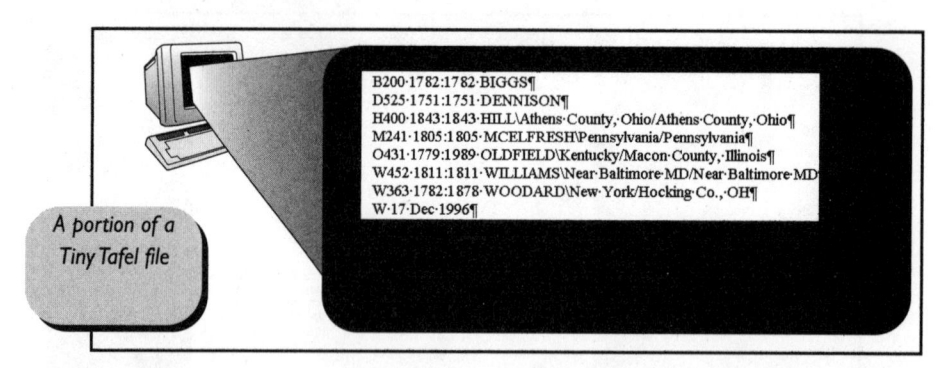

```
B200·1782:1782·BIGGS¶
D525·1751:1751·DENNISON¶
H400·1843:1843·HILL\Athens·County,·Ohio/Athens·County,·Ohio¶
M241·1805:1805·MCELFRESH\Pennsylvania/Pennsylvania¶
O431·1779:1989·OLDFIELD\Kentucky/Macon·County,·Illinois¶
W452·1811:1811·WILLIAMS\Near·Baltimore·MD/Near·Baltimore·MD
W363·1782:1878·WOODARD\New·York/Hocking·Co.,·OH¶
W·17·Dec·1996¶
```

A portion of a Tiny Tafel file

You will find that several genealogy programs are associated with genealogical societies on local and national levels. These user groups can be a great source of helpful information and provide a forum to share mutual interests. Two strong groups include Commsoft's ROOTS and LDS's PAF users groups. You may want to check your local genealogical society to see what most of the members are using. Don't be afraid to ask. What is my favorite? Each has unique strengths; I like Brother's Keeper for inputting family information, I like using Family Tree Maker's CDs, and I think Family Origins's modified reports look the best. All three of these genealogy programs are compatible with the LDS Ancestral File and TempleReady file formats, meaning they can import data from Personal Ancestral File (PAF), one of the most popular genealogy programs in the world.

USING BROTHER'S KEEPER FOR MS-DOS

Brother's Keeper is a shareware package available in a Windows version and a MS-DOS version. While Brother's Keeper for DOS (version 5.2, $49), by John Steed, may not have some of the bells and whistles the other two genealogy programs have (although the Windows version certainly does), it more than makes up for it in speed, simplicity and ease of use.

Brother's Keeper doesn't require you to invest in a faster multimedia machine (such as a Pentium) to run it or a huge hard drive to store it. You can use it on a machine with as little as 2 Meg of RAM and 10 Meg of hard drive space. You can even run this program on a computer that only has floppy drives. It is very compact and fits perfectly into older, less expensive portable computers. If you have or can borrow a portable computer when you go on your next genealogical trip, Brother's Keeper is the program you'll want with you on the road.

Using Genealogy Programs 6

Brother's Keeper has worked with every printer I've hooked up to it and prints all the standard reports you'll need. (Consult the manual for the proper settings for your printer.) It is my favorite for two reasons. One, I like to enter my information in family group forms like Brother's Keeper's, and two, it is super-fast on a Pentium.

The manual included in the shareware files is very well done. When you register your copy with the author, you will receive a printed manual to use as well as technical support through Mr. Steed's BBS or web site. Except for printing some advanced reports or making major modifications to your database, you probably won't read the manual too often.

Before I go into detail on the basic commands and options in Brother's Keeper, I should point out the rules of shareware. Shareware lets you use and evaluate a program for a limited time (usually 30 days). If you decide that the program is one that you'd like to continue using, you are asked to register with the company and pay a registration fee to them. Registering usually gets you more features or updates, a printed manual, technical support and a clean conscience. Shareware benefits both the user and the author as it allows prices to remain low by minimizing distribution, packaging, and advertising costs.

So, gather up your notes, family group forms, pedigree charts and your graphic files to start putting your family history into the computer.

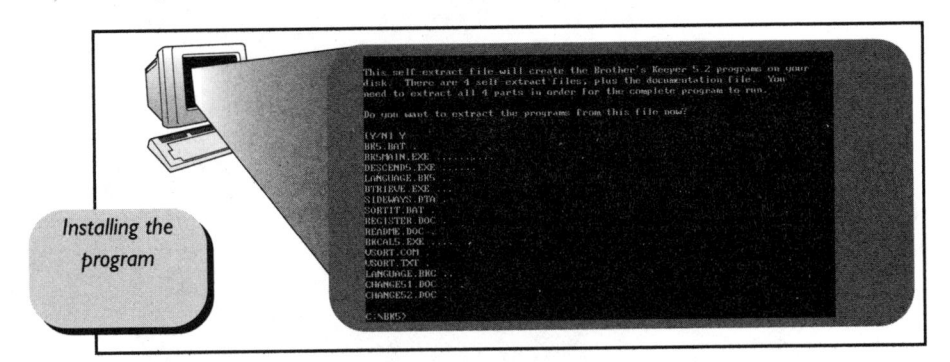

Installing the program

127

6 Using Genealogy Programs

The Main Menu

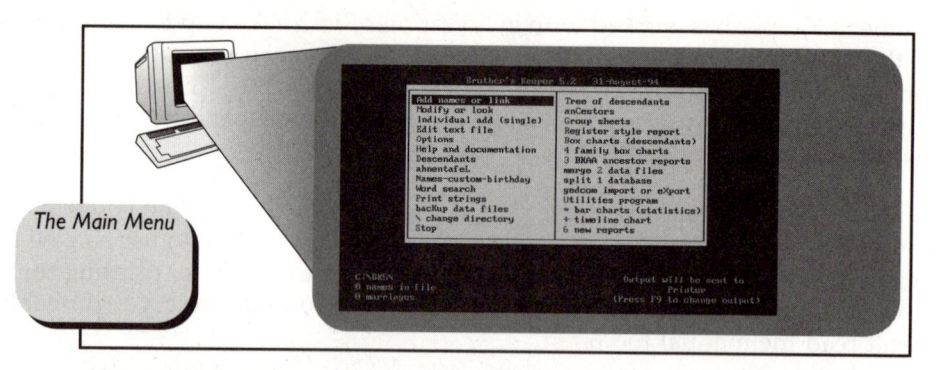

After you've installed Brother's Keeper and setup up the program's options, you can start entering individuals. This main menu is where you'll start all the various functions of the program.

To enter an individual press Ⓐ for "Add". Fill in the blank boxes as much as you can. Don't worry if you don't have all the information you need. You can always return later by pressing Ⓜ for the **Modify Record** command in the main menu.

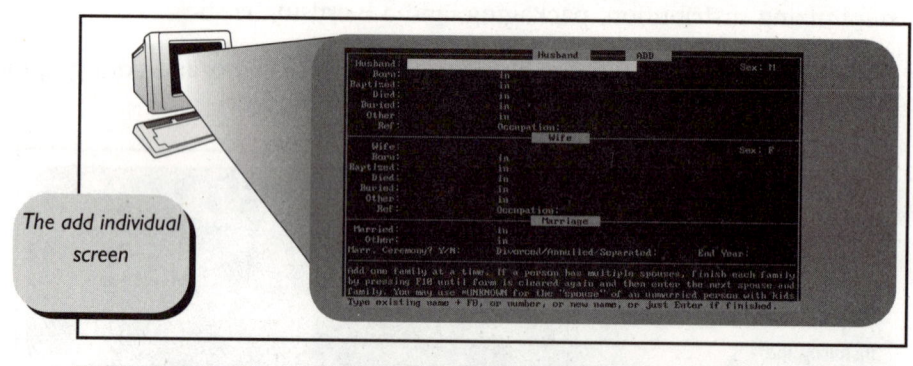

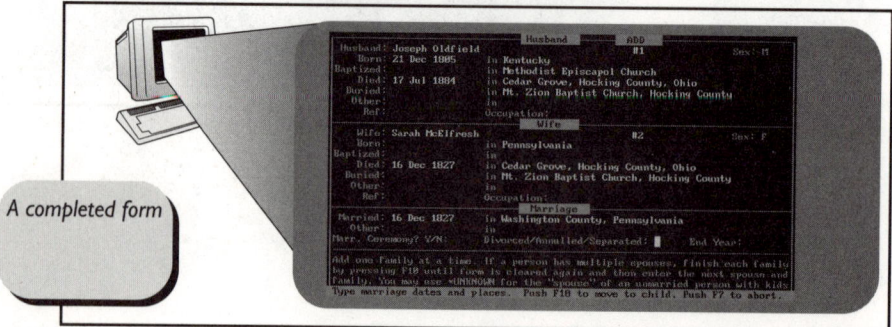

The add individual screen

A completed form

128

Using Genealogy Programs 6

You can add text notes, multiple documents and even graphics to each individual in the database. The illustration below shows how modifying an individual is displayed. To add text to an individual's file select **Modify** from the main menu and type the person's name in the box. When the Modify screen is displayed for the person, press the down arrow on your keyboard to go to the bottom of the screen. Now press the (Cmd22) key. This will open a small blank form at the bottom of the screen.

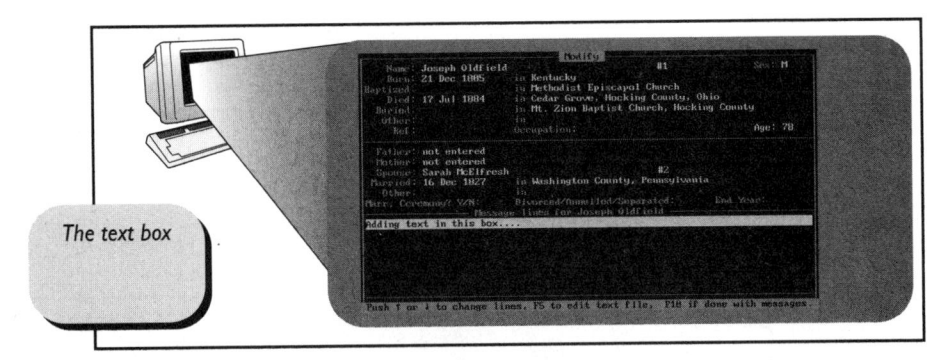

The text box

You can type in a message, a note or other pertinent information. As you type be sure to press (Enter) at the end of each line. If you have text that will be too large for this text box you can tell Brother's Keeper to find the text file located elsewhere on your PC. You will either have had to save a text file before entering Brother's Keeper or, if you press (F5) in the message box, it will take you to its built-in text editor. The example shows that there is an external text file called joe.txt located in the C:\BK5\BKTEXT directory. The dollar signs as the first characters of a line tell the program to load a file while it is printing a report.

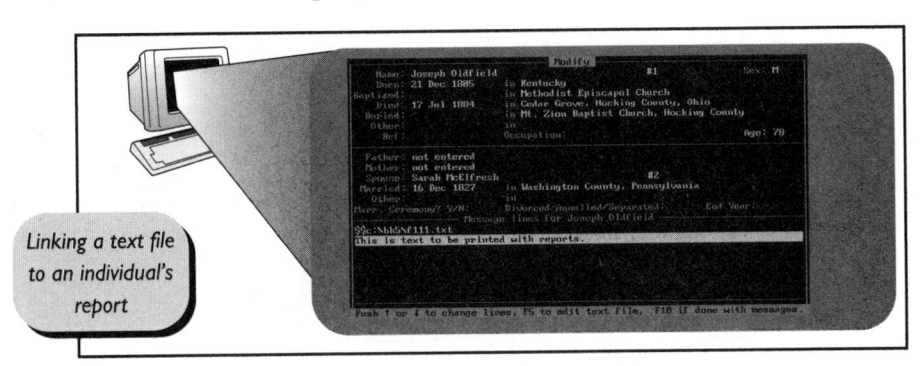

Linking a text file to an individual's report

129

6 Using Genealogy Programs

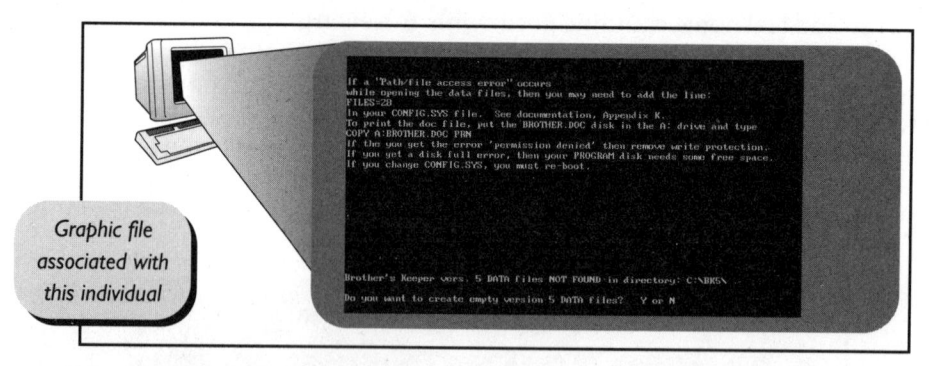

Graphic file associated with this individual

Brother's Keeper has many utilities. To access them, press Ⓤ in the main menu. One of my favorite utilities is the Compute Relationship option. By pressing Ⓧ and typing two family members' names, Brother's Keeper will compute their relationship for you—very handy for those 2nd, 3rd or 4th cousins!

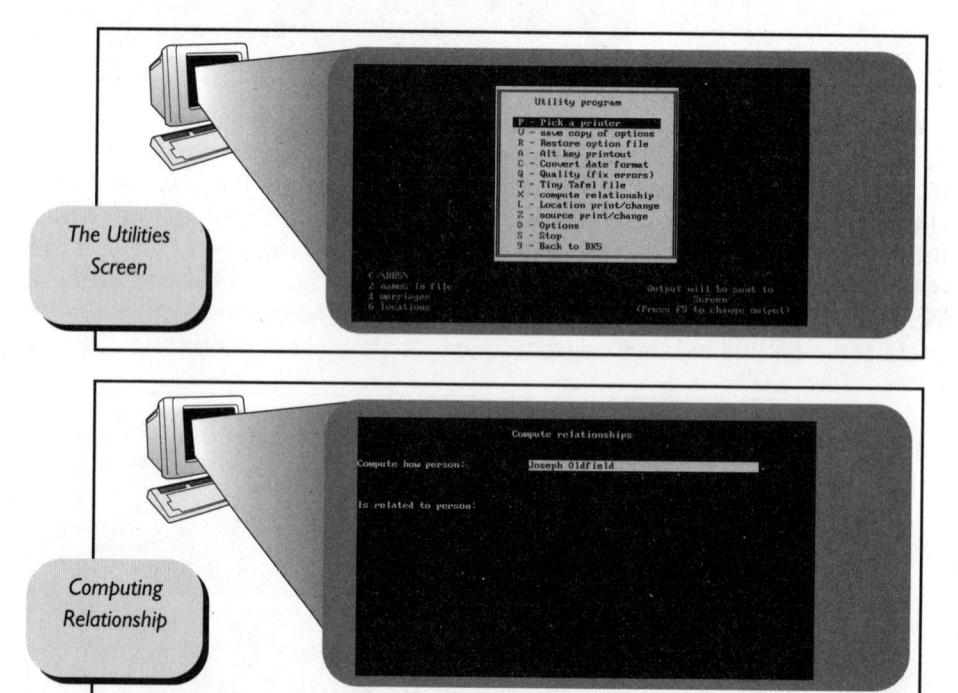

The Utilities Screen

Computing Relationship

As I mentioned earlier, Brother's Keeper can print reports to virtually any printer. It can also create a word-processing file for you to edit later. The supported file formats include WordPerfect for DOS, WordPerfect for Windows

130

Using Genealogy Programs 6

6.0 and 6.1, AmiPro, Microsoft Word, Works or Publisher and a standard ASCII text file. You can also print to the screen to review the report before you print it.

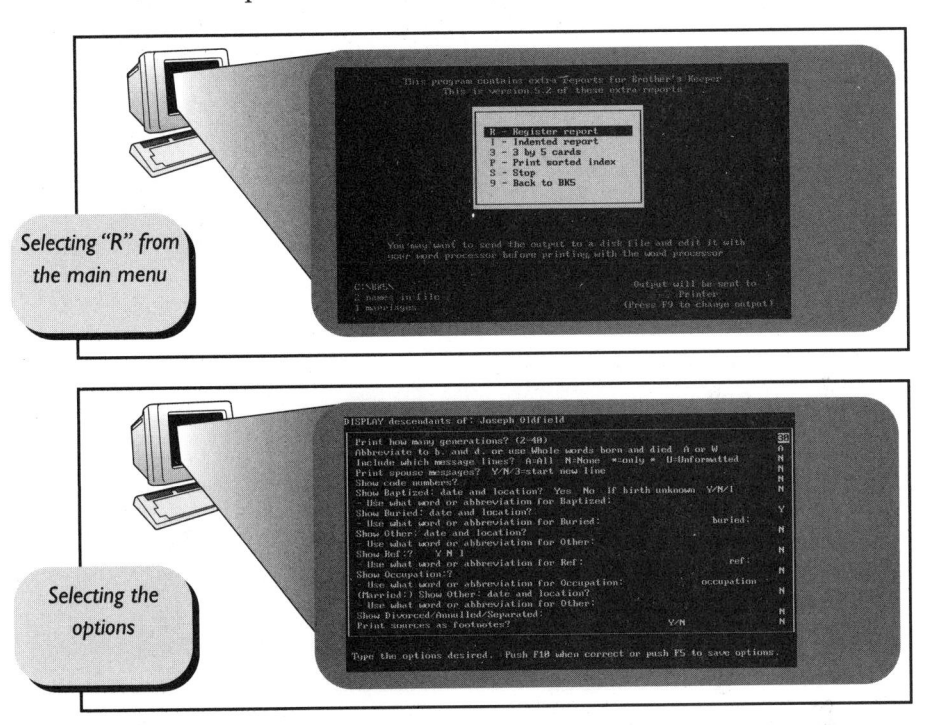

Selecting "R" from the main menu

Selecting the options

The one report that I like to use is the Register Report. It lets me print a decendancy report with all my notes attached to each family member. I also use it to create an RTF (rich text format) file. I then use Microsoft Word to polish it up and print. You can import and export all or selected individuals to GEDCOM files from other genealogy programs by selecting "X" from the main menu.

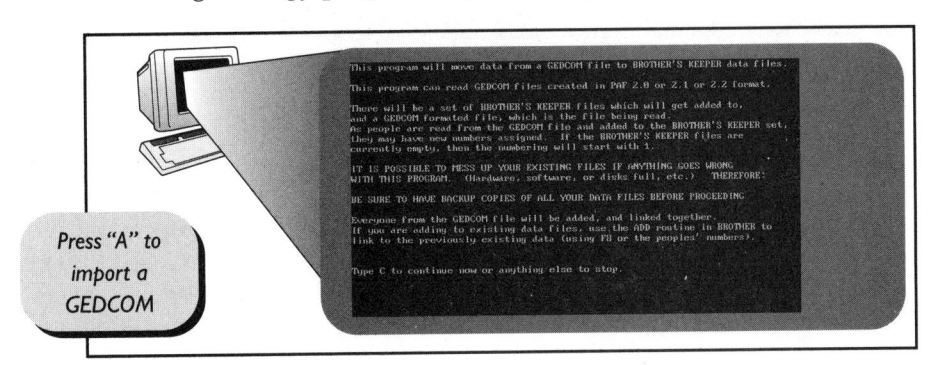

Press "A" to import a GEDCOM

131

6 Using Genealogy Programs

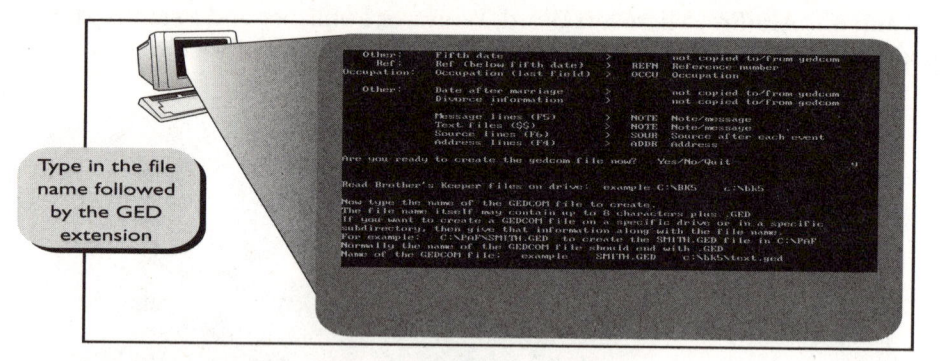

Type in the file name followed by the GED extension

You can also export GEDCOM files by selecting "X."

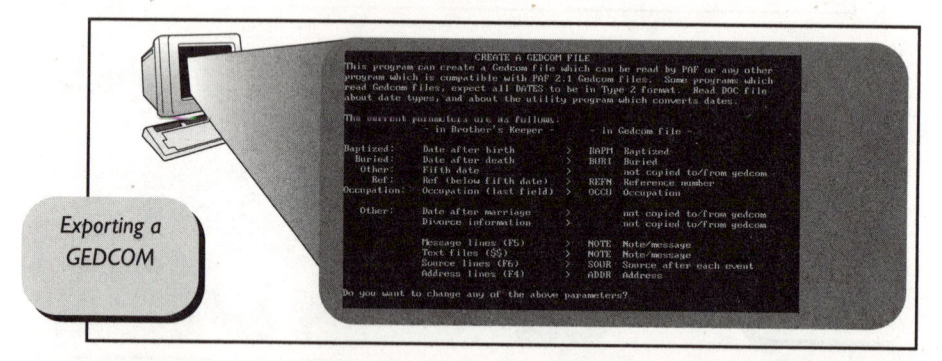

Exporting a GEDCOM

Brother's Keeper is a very good genealogy program that can handle just about all you'll need to put your family history in order. If you would prefer the new Windows version contact John Steed, 6907 Childsdale, Rockford, MI 49341. Please remember that you must either register the product after a specified time or uninstall it from your system.

Using Family Origins

Family Origins for Windows is an excellent genealogy program for a retail price of around $29. This low price helps make it one of the most popular genealogy programs available. It's simple to use, has flexible report and book printing capabilities and has the power to store a vast array of family history. You can put names, dates, places, stories, facts, descriptions, sources of information, relationships, graphics and photos into more than 50 fields, including

Using Genealogy Programs 6

birth, marriage, death, occupation and religion. You can also create your own labeled fields. Family Origins's new (for Ver. 5) multimedia scrapbook allows you to insert sound and video clips of your family in the database, too. Family Origins can store an unlimited number of people with an unlimited amount of personal information. The only constraint is the space available on your hard drive.

Another feature that is new to Version 5.0 is the ability to automatically create your own web pages. You can have your own virtual web site complete with associated pictures, notes, sources, index, surname list, GEDCOM file (for others to download) and your E-mail address. All from just a few clicks of your mouse directly from your Family Origins file. This completely eliminates the need to learn HTML code or any of the other website authoring tools on the market. For me, it was great. That feature alone was worth the upgrade price I paid. You will find two web sites on the companion CD-ROM that were created using just the Family Origins program.

Follow my examples to learn the basics of using Family Origins, from entering your family members' vital information to attaching the associated notes, sources and stories that make up your complete family history.

You'll also see how to import your digitized photos and integrate them into great-looking family reports. Family Tree (Pedigree) Reports or Ancestor's Reports (with or without graphics), a Family Group Sheet (again with or without notes and graphics) and a Modified Ancestor or Descendent report can all be printed by Family Origins. The "Book report" feature (in the **Reports** menu option) of Family Origins is an excellent tool for telling a more complete story, letting you print narrative books along with your charts. It places your notes and images together with family relationships to tell a more complete story of your family's history with your own words and pictures. And, Family Origins book reports are automatically indexed and include your bibliographies and sources where noted.

Finally, you'll learn how easy it is to import someone else's GEDCOM file (whether from another Family Origins database or another genealogy program) and how to create your own GEDCOM files to share with other family historians. It's an excellent program and easy to use.

6 Using Genealogy Programs

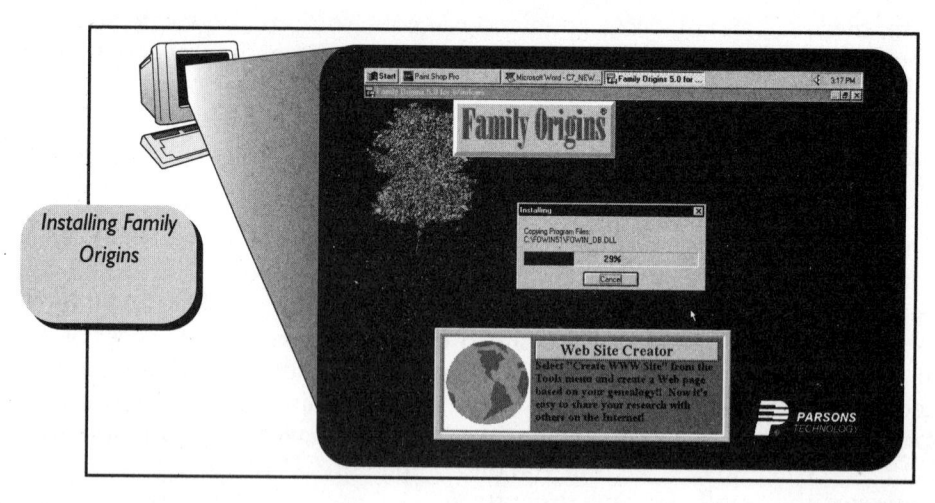

Installing Family Origins

You use Family Origins forms to enter your family members through the Pedigree chart (tree view) or the family group (card view) screens. You can choose the one that's easiest for you. One nice feature is that you can quickly flip between the screens by clicking the tabs just below the menu bar labeled Pedigree and Family Group. This is handy if you're in the tree view and need to see all the children of a marriage, which is shown in the family card page.

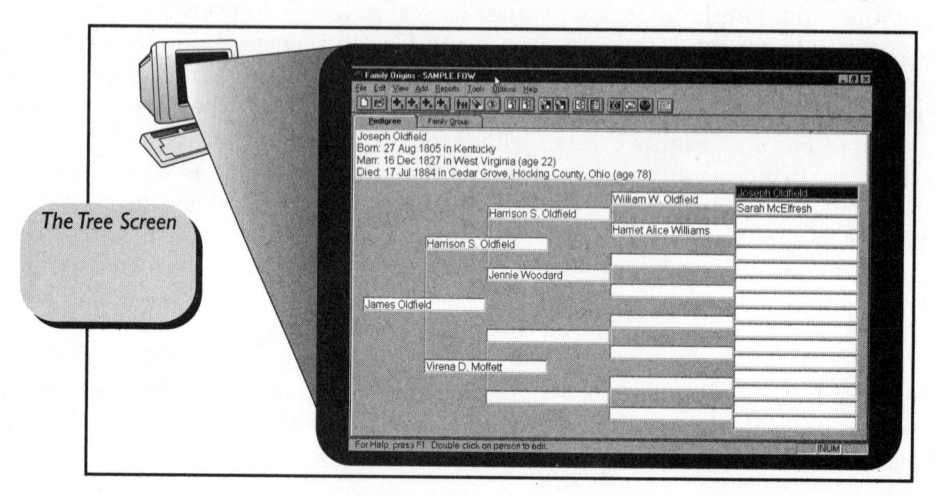

The Tree Screen

Using Genealogy Programs 6

The Family Group Screen

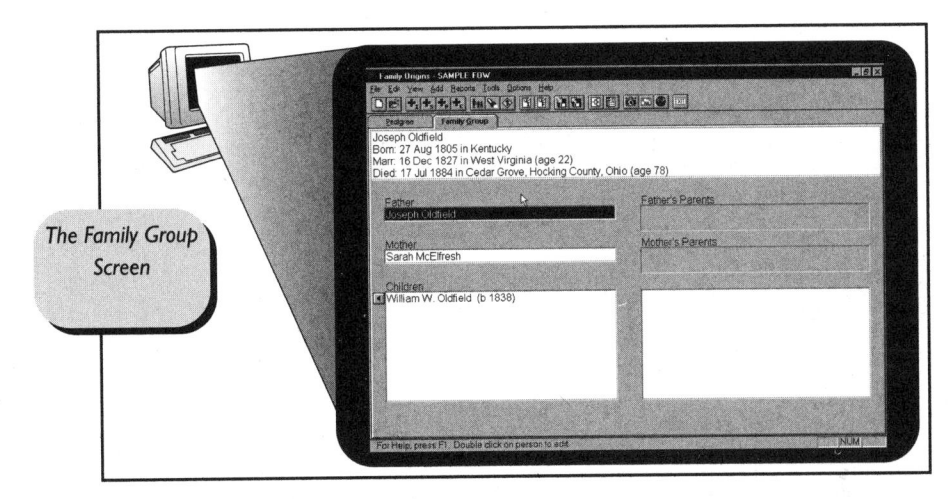

To begin entering your family members, select a box by highlighting it with your mouse pointer and select **Add** from the menu bar. When you enter your family, Family Origins will automatically ask you for more information about that individual and whether that person is linked (if necessary) with other family members you've entered.

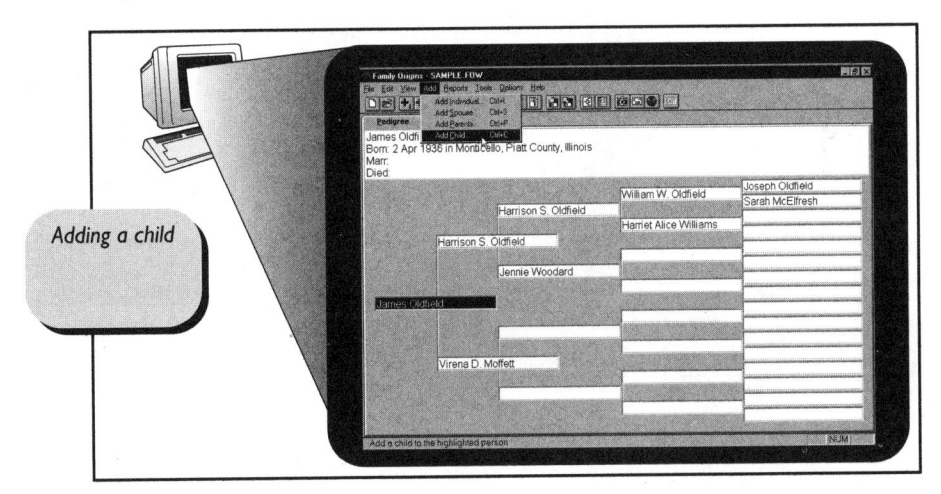

Adding a child

Family Origins will automatically open the Edit Individual box after selecting "Add Child..."

135

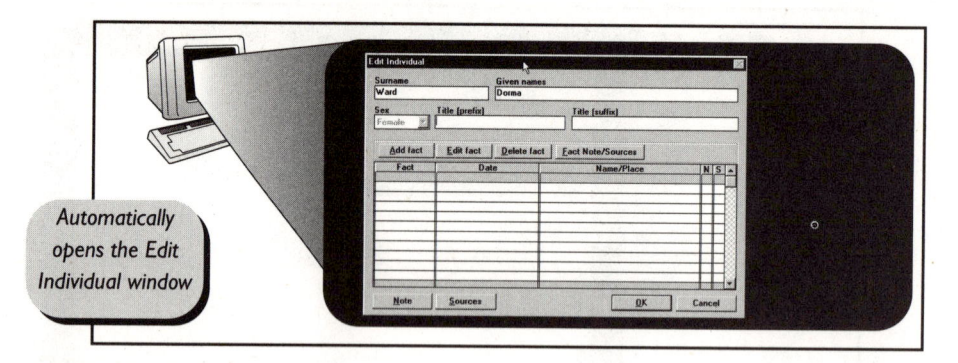

6 Using Genealogy Programs

Automatically opens the Edit Individual window

Adding information

In the Edit Individual window you can enter all your notes, sources and other information attached to this person. There are forms set up for this. This information will always be stored and printed (if specified) when this person is included in a report. Family Origins can handle as many sources and notes as you have for your family history.

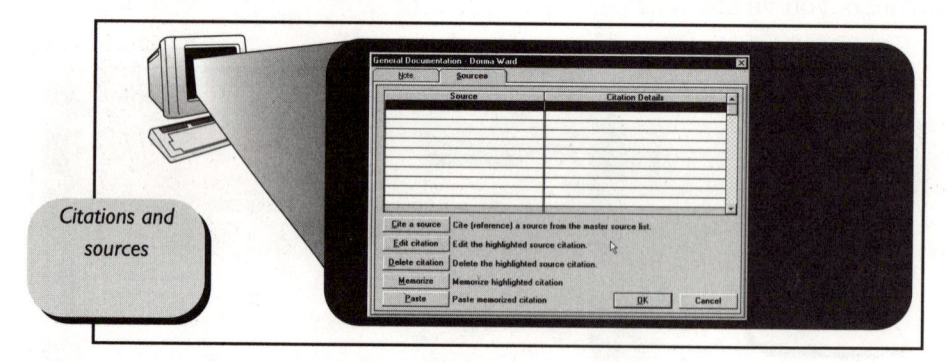

Citations and sources

Adding graphics and sound

To add a photo to someone's file, highlight that person by clicking on his or her name. Select **Edit/Multimedia Scrapbook** from the menu bar.

Using Genealogy Programs 6

Select Edit\Multimedia Scrapbook...

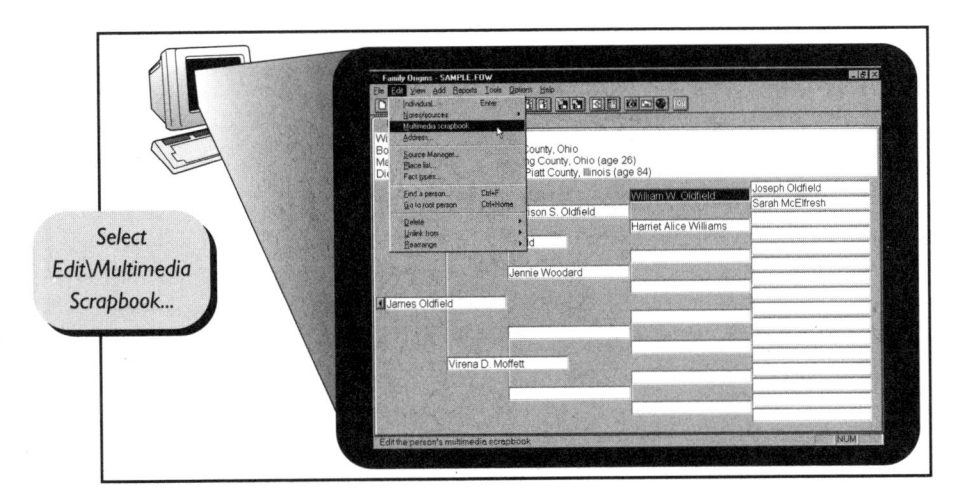

When the Multimedia Scrapbook window appears, click the empty box (a blue outline will appear) on the left and click [Add].

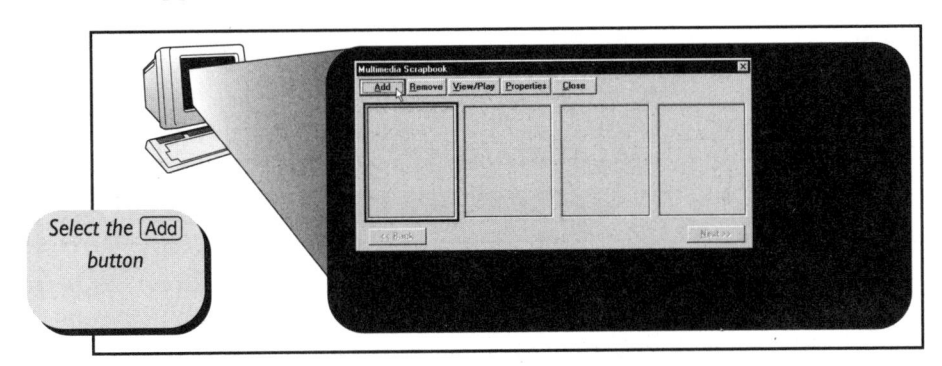

Select the [Add] button

Family Origins can load many of the popular graphic file formats, including PCX, JPG, BMP and PCD (Kodak Portfolio CD-ROM images). Click the [Browse...] button to locate your picture on your computer or CD-ROM, select it and click [OK] and [OK] again.

137

Using Genealogy Programs

An imported image

After it is loaded you can select the Properties button. Here you can type a caption and short description of the picture that will be printed with the image.

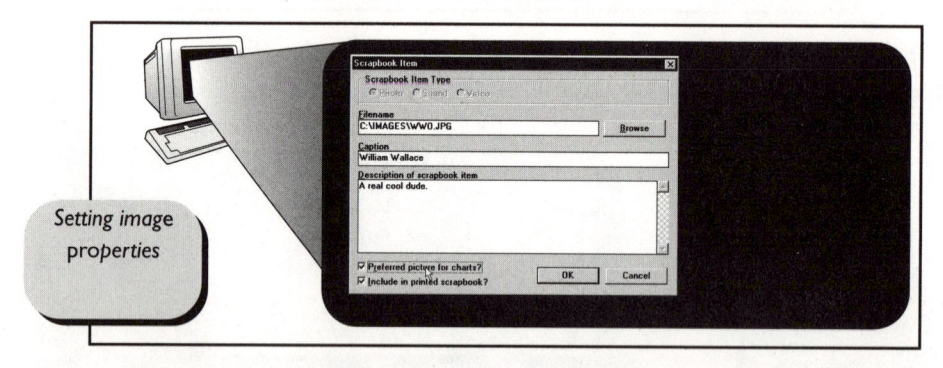

Setting image properties

Be sure to select the two options at the bottom left of the window: "Preferred picture for Charts?"—so if you have multiple images you can specify the one you want printed first, and "Include in printed Scrapbook?"—so it can be printed.

When you selected **Edit/Scrapbook** you may have noticed that Family Origins scrapbook can also add sounds (WAV file) and videos (AVI, MOV or MPG) to a person. These scrapbook options can make your family history into a multimedia event. To add a sound wave or video file to a family member, just repeat the process you followed to add a photo.

Using Genealogy Programs 6

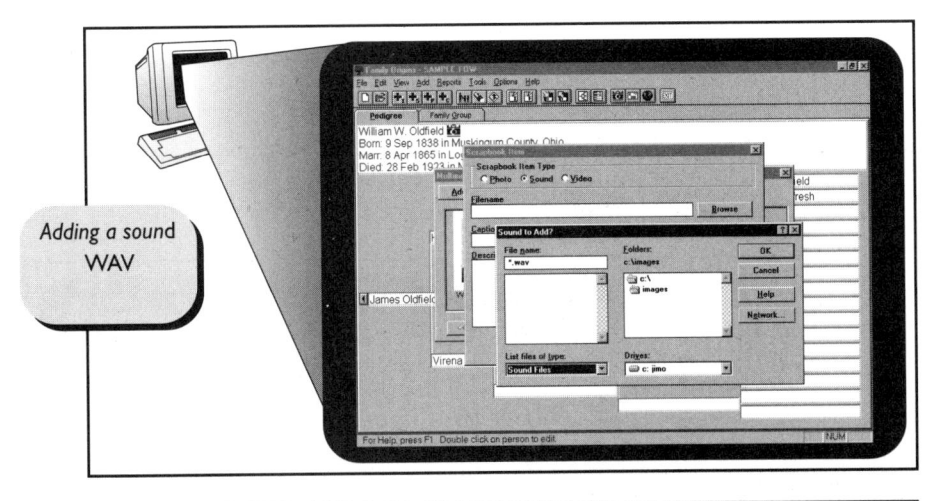

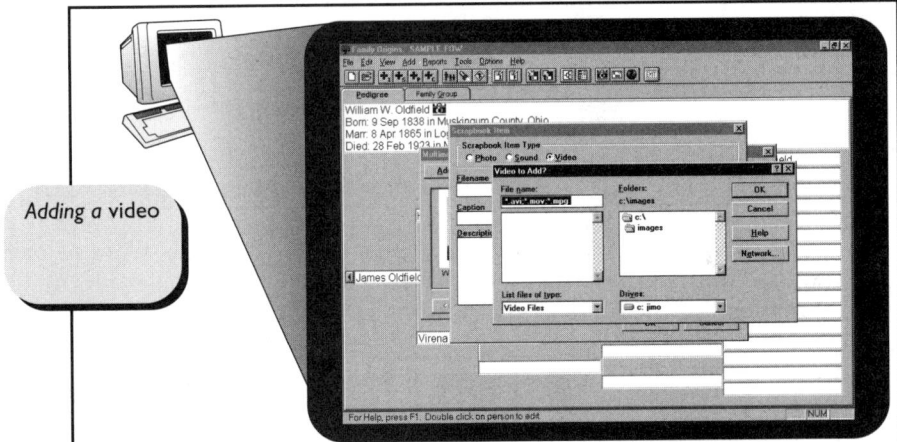

Adding a sound WAV

Adding a video

Reports

Several reports can be generated from the family information you've entered: Pedigree Chart, Family Group Chart, ancestor chart and modified reports (under the Book option). You also have the option of creating your own custom forms as well. The Pedigree and Family Group Charts and the print Book option can all incorporate photos.

6 Using Genealogy Programs

The **Reports/Book** option is an ancestor or descendant modified register report. This report is used to create your family history book. When you have entered your family members, their stories, pictures and maps, you'll have a professional-quality book of your family's history. To print the ancestors of a family member select that person. Select **Reports/Pedigree Charts..** and tell Family Origins the number of generations to display. Then click [OK].

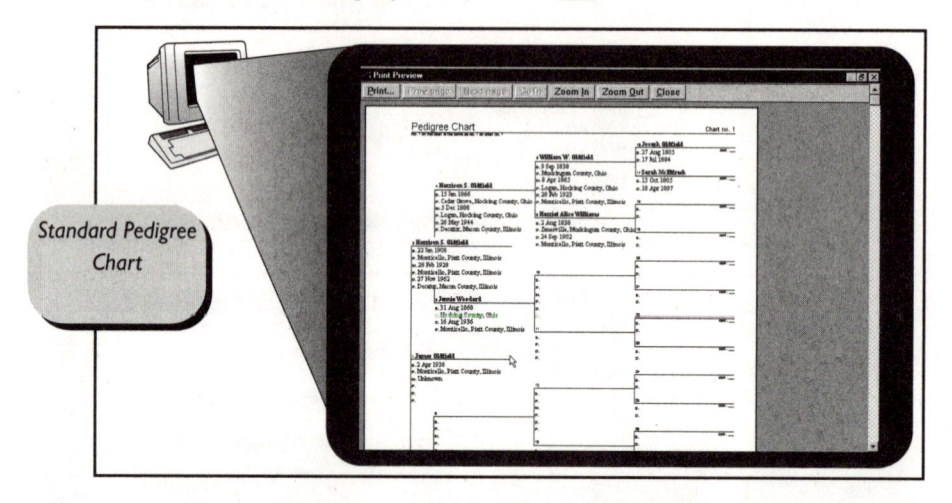

Standard Pedigree Chart

To print a family group sheet, select a person of the family you want to print. Select **Reports/Family Group Charts..** and tell Family Origins what information you want printed for the highlighted person or another family. Then click [OK].

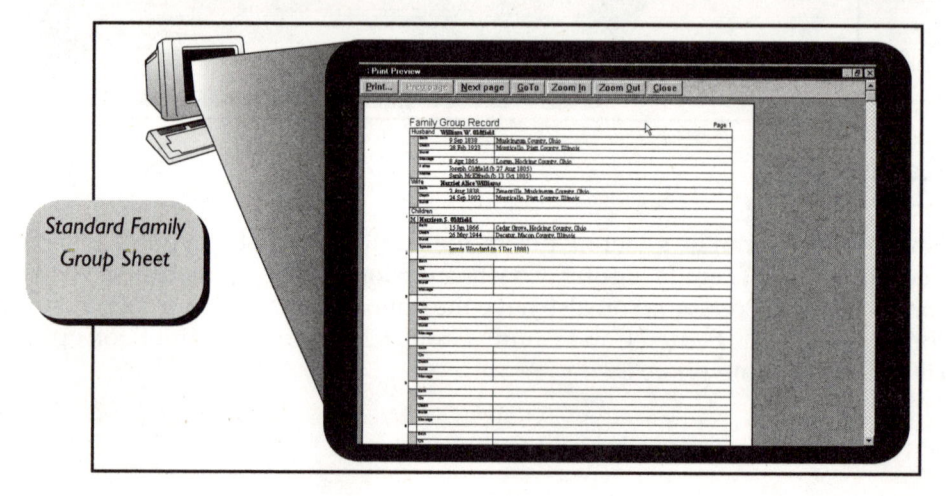

Standard Family Group Sheet

140

Using Genealogy Programs 6

To print photographs of the ancestors of a family member, select that person. Now choose **Reports/Photo Charts...** and select **Pedigree Chart**. Pick the number of generations and click OK.

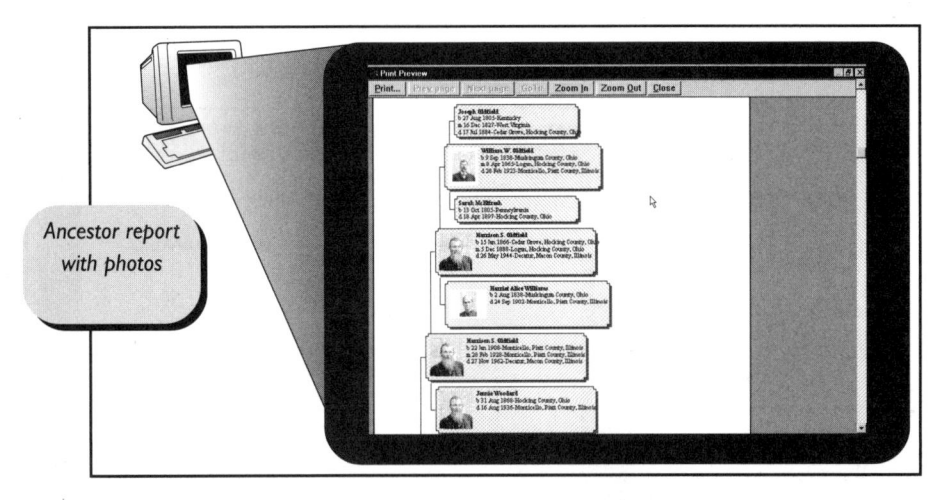

Ancestor report with photos

To print the descendants or ancestors of a family member, highlight that person. Select **Reports/Books....** You can print either this person's ancestors or descendants in a modified register. Tell Family Origins the information you want printed and click OK. Be sure that the "Include photos?" option has been selected.

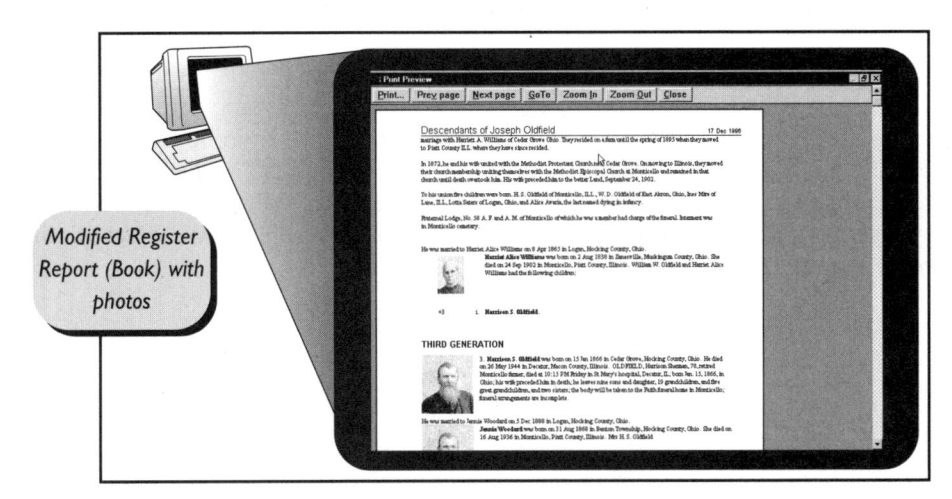

Modified Register Report (Book) with photos

141

6 Using Genealogy Programs

Family Origins has also added the ability to create your own customized reports. To create a custom report select **Reports/Custom Reports...**. You can include any number of fields in any order that you want them printed. You have complete control over the size, fonts and text that you want added. There are also four report templates already done which you can use as guides.

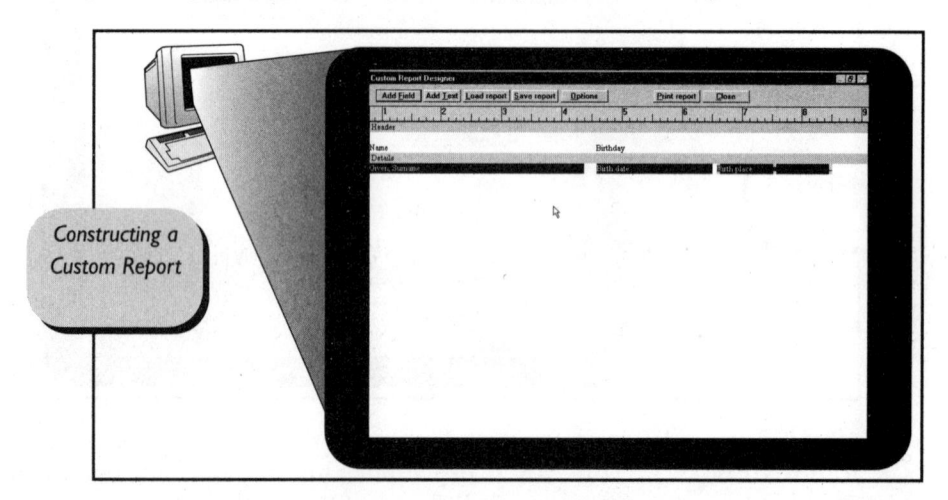

Constructing a Custom Report

BUILDING A FAMILY WEB SITE

After you have entered your family history you can publish it for the world wide web. This is a great way to share your family history with others (also see the chapter about getting online). You can have your own home page (with a service provider supplying the space) that others can visit and enjoy. You can add your E-mail address to it and anyone who visits your site can send you messages. Again, a great way to share your history. To begin, select **Tools/Create Web Page** from the menu bar.

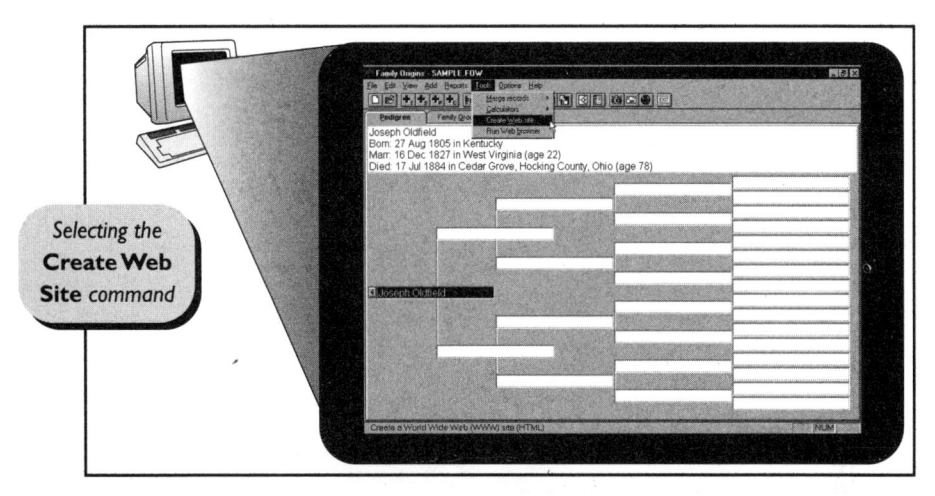

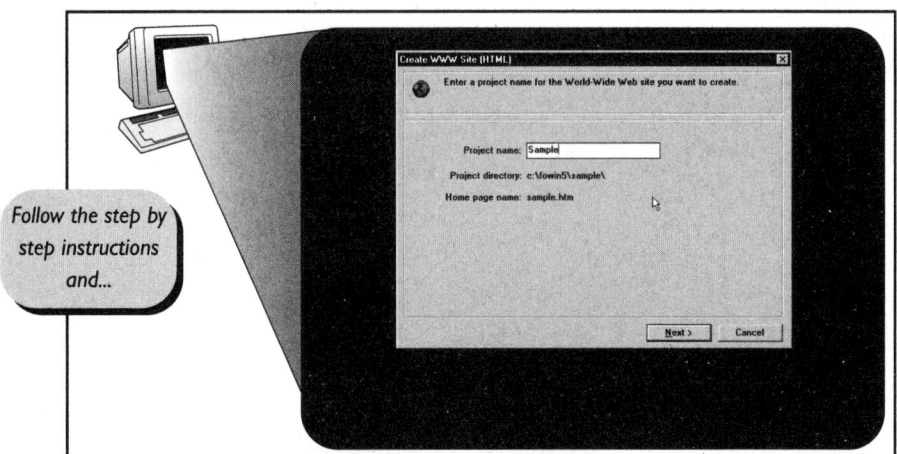

Using Genealogy Programs 6

*Selecting the **Create Web Site** command*

Follow the step by step instructions and...

6 Using Genealogy Programs

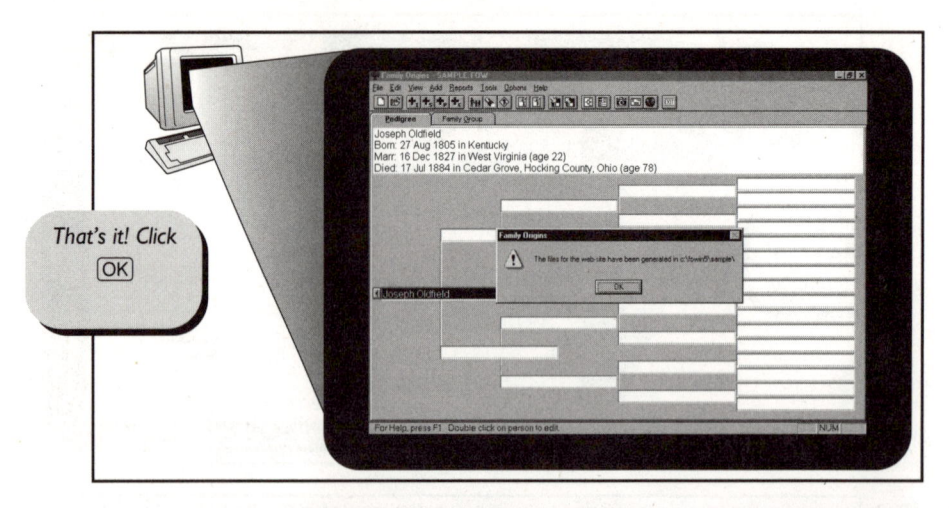

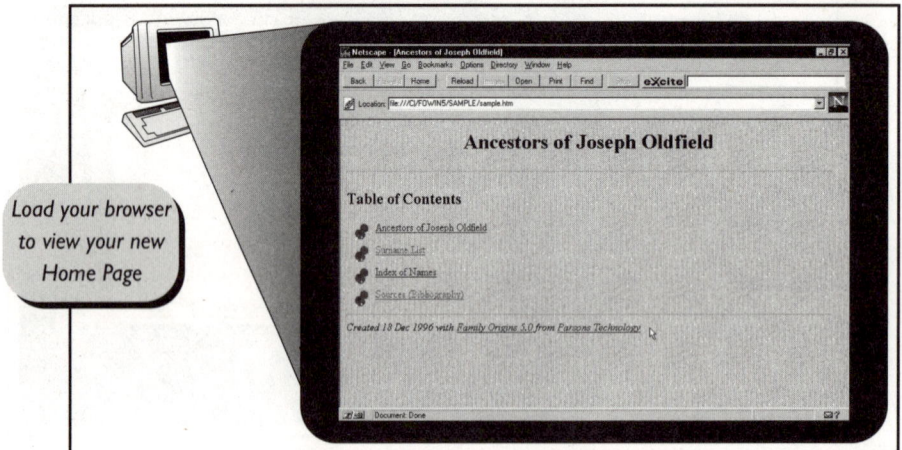

That's it! Click OK

Load your browser to view your new Home Page

Using Genealogy Programs 6

Importing and exporting GEDCOM files

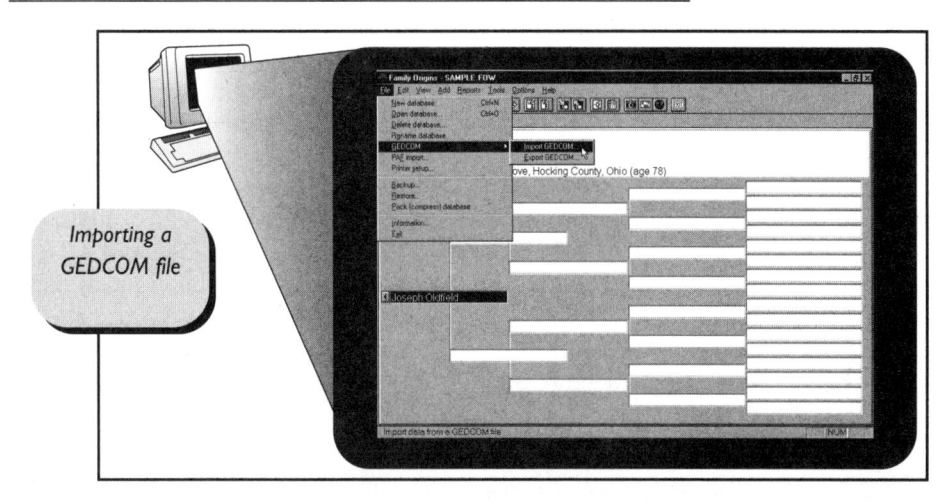

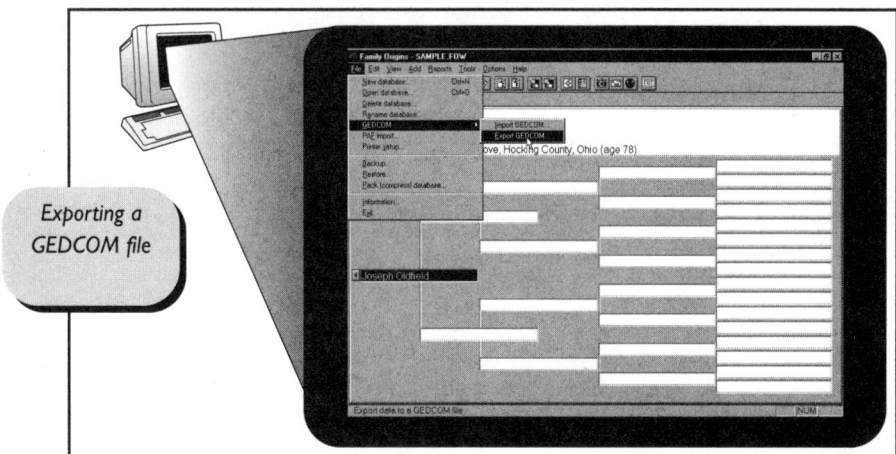

Importing a GEDCOM file

Exporting a GEDCOM file

You can import and export GEDCOM, as well as import PAF files directly into your database.

145

6 Using Genealogy Programs

Using Family Tree Maker for Windows

Family Tree Maker is advertised as the best selling family tree program. I don't doubt it. It is easy to use even without referring to the manual (a 450 plus page one at that), yet powerful enough to hold all your family history. It comes in three varieties: Family Tree Maker "Starter Edition," on floppy disk for $19.99, Family Tree Maker Standard Edition (CD) for $49.99 and the newer Deluxe Edition II for $89.99. The Deluxe Edition comes with five CDs—Family Tree Maker w/Family Archive CD, a 2 CD set of the World Family Tree and a 2 CD set of the Social Security Death Index. This edition has also just been updated to version 3.04, which includes 3 new reports added to an already large variety. These reports produce narrative family information that can be your published family history, combining all your notes, stories and photographs. If you buy Family Tree Maker, I recommend accepting the extra cost and buying the Deluxe Edition. The CDs that are included with it will save you a lot of time and travel.

Family Tree Maker Deluxe

The first CD contains the Family Tree Maker for Windows program and the Family Finder Index. The Family Finder Index (which can be loaded from within Family Tree Maker) is an index of over 115 million names. This database is compiled from the World Family Tree (from Banner Blue Div.), The US Census Index, The US Social Security Death Index (SSDI), Family Pedigrees (from Everton's Publishing), Marriage Archive Index, the 1784-1811 Military Records-US Volunteer Soldier Archive, State Index Archives, 1850-1880 US Mortality Index Archive and Land Records Archives.

Using Genealogy Programs 6

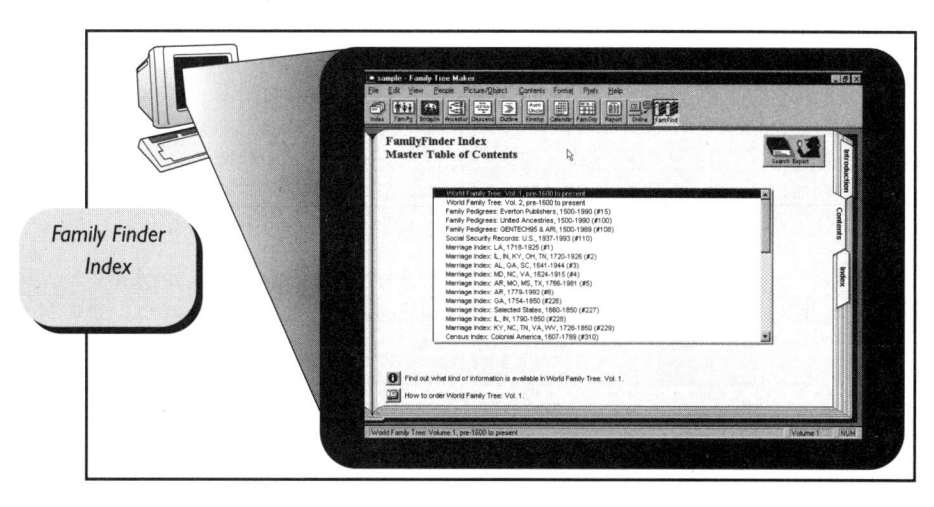

Family Finder Index

Beside the Family Finder Index, the CD also contains information from county courthouses, family associations, surname exchanges, surname registries, vital records offices, reunion committees, adoption registries, and national and state archives, historical societies, libraries, and genealogical societies. Plus, there is an over-1200-page genealogy "How-To" Guide. That's a lot of information on one CD. The Deluxe Edition also includes two 2-CD sets. One is the World Family Tree and the other is the SSDI. It's quite a package.

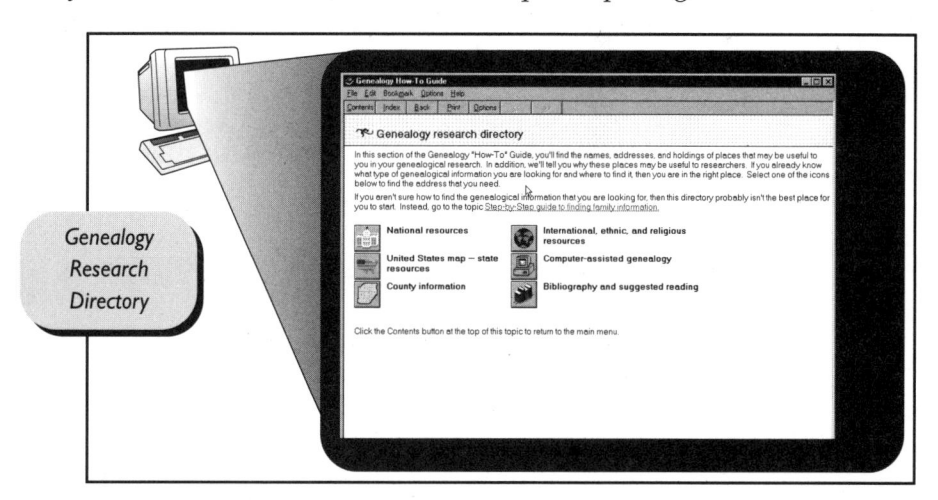

Genealogy Research Directory

147

6 Using Genealogy Programs

You may think with all this information packed into Family Tree Maker that it would be awkward or difficult to use. Nope. It is as easy to use as filling in the blanks can be. And, it keeps all your family information correctly organized, handling up to 2 million people. Each family member can be represented with names, dates, places, special events, medical information, notes, stories, and, with the Scrapbook feature, photographs, sounds and videos.

When you first run Family Tree Maker (FTM) you start with a blank family group sheet. Click your mouse in the husband or wife entry field and start putting your family members into the database. Always double-check your dates as you enter them. It's easy to reverse numbers. Also be sure to include your sources, notes and any medical information.

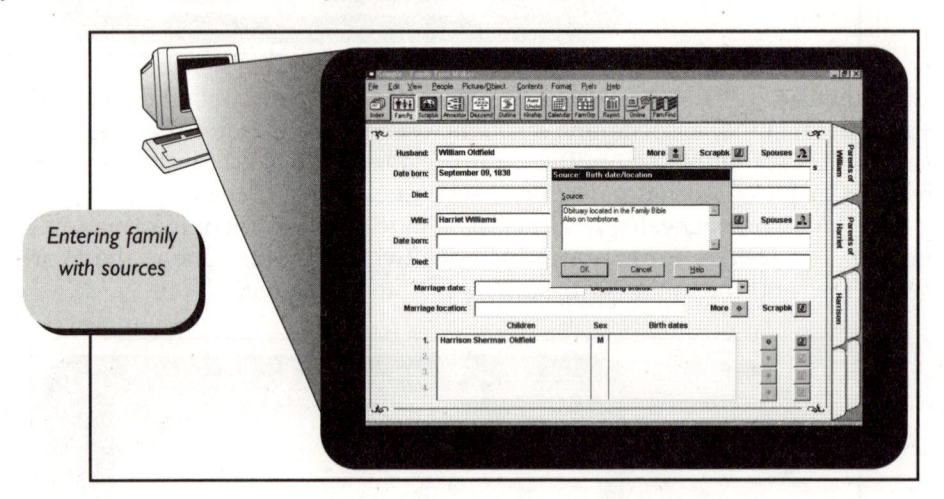

Entering family with sources

Using Genealogy Programs 6

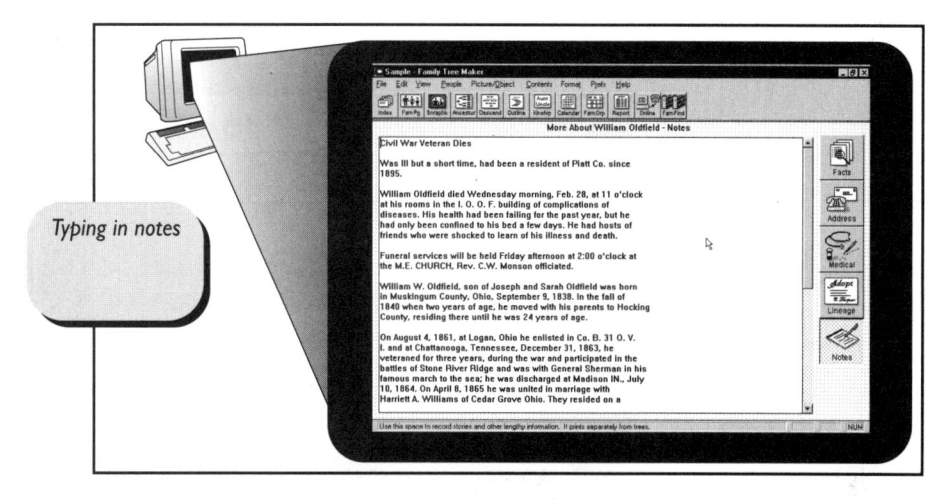

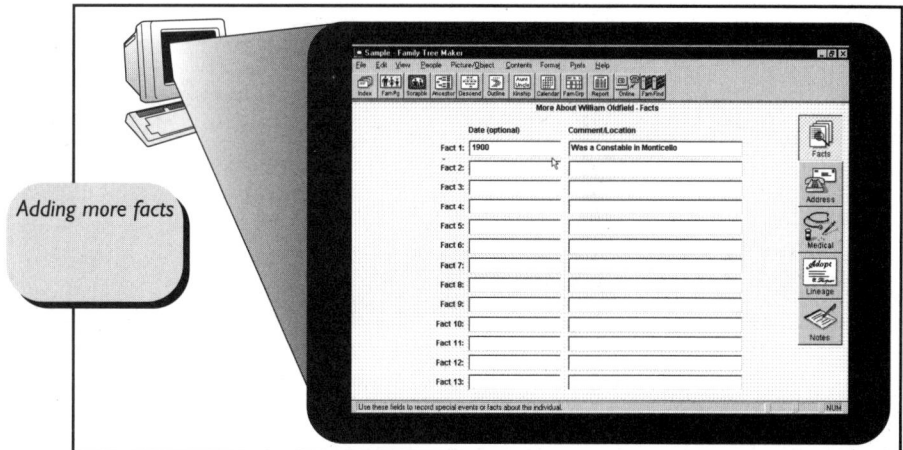

Typing in notes

Adding more facts

Adding graphics and sound

Family Tree Maker includes a great feature called "scrapbook." Using scrapbook you can add scanned or converted photographs, graphic files of all major programs, HTML pages, Acrobat PDF files, MIDI music, sound files and even video clips—just about any graphic, sound or video file you can think of can be included.

6 Using Genealogy Programs

Select Picture/Object to enter a picture

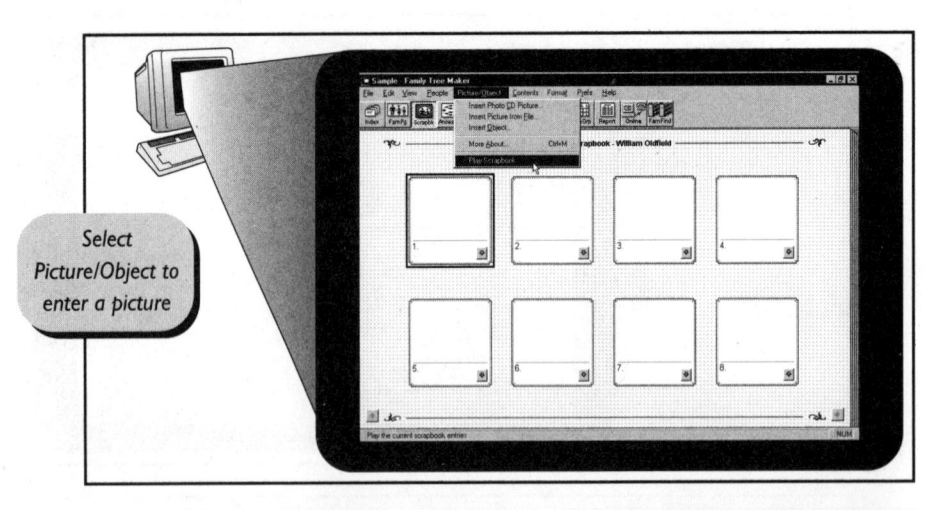

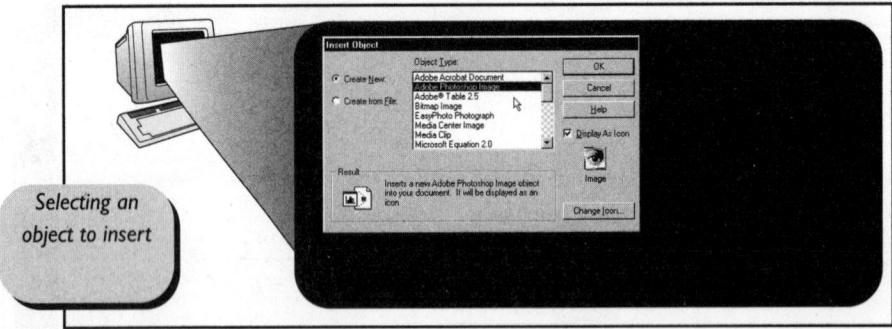

Selecting an object to insert

To insert a photograph on the family group sheet, click the Scrapbook icon to the right of the person's name. Select **Picture/Object** and then **Insert Picture from File...**. Locate the image and click [Open]. Your image will be loaded and the graphic editor will be displayed. Use the control buttons to "touch up," if necessary, and press the [OK] button when you are done. You will be back in the scrapbook again. If you do not have any other images or other objects, click the [FamPg] button on the menu bar to return to the family page of this person. You will now notice a small camera icon next to this person's name, which shows that there is an image linked to this person.

Using Genealogy Programs 6

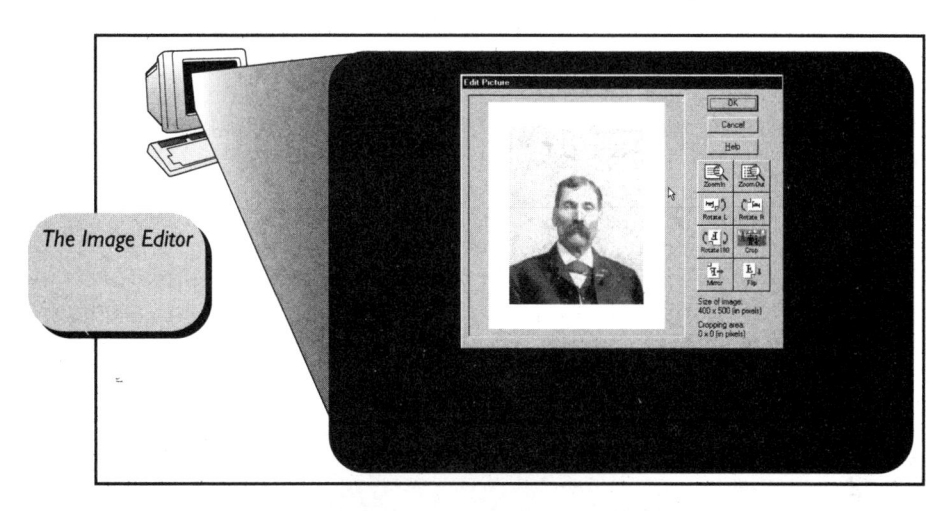

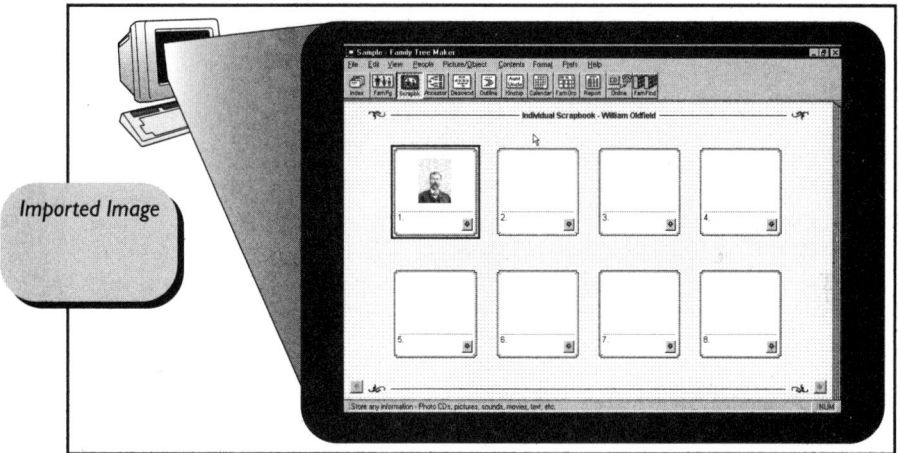

The Image Editor

Imported Image

Printing reports

When you are ready to print your family history, Family Tree Maker offers you several charts and reports. You can use the **View/Calendar...** command to print a year's worth of birthdays and anniversaries. Or you can print family group sheets for a family or the ancestors or descendants of a family. You can also print

6 Using Genealogy Programs

a Kinship report with labels and cards, ancestor, descendant and outline descendant trees, and LDS reports in standard formats. And you can create custom reports listing information you specify. There are even options to print name tags, stickers and other items!

Options are available for every report you choose to print under the **Contents** and **Format** menu commands. All reports are first printed to the screen for review. When you have the report on the screen, select the "Contents" command and choose what information to include (titles, footnotes and the number of generations to display) in the report. When you select the **Format** command you can choose what size boxes and fonts to use, the box styles and borders, and six different tree formats. Family Tree Maker creates great looking trees.

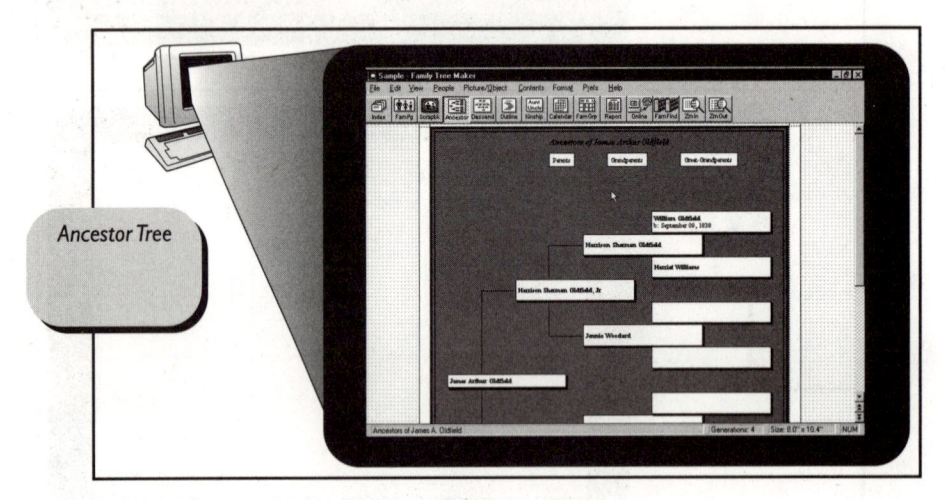

Ancestor Tree

152

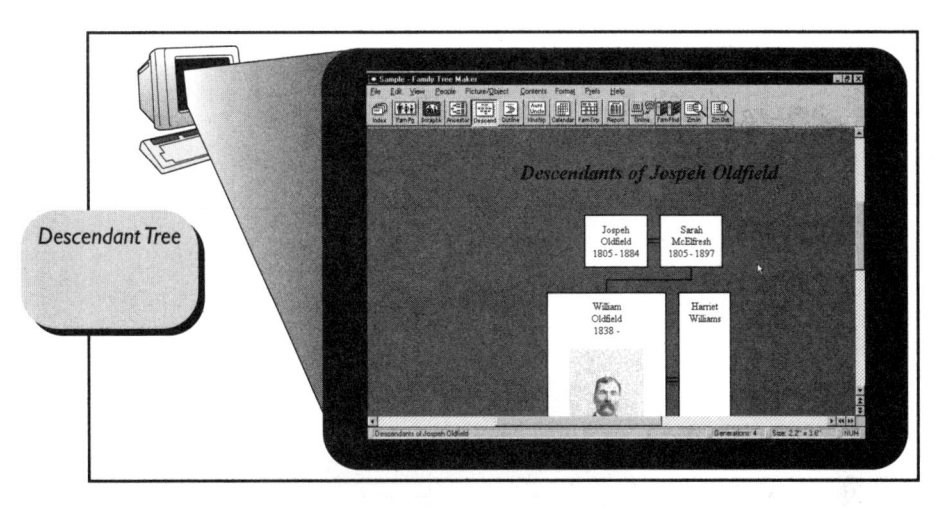

Using Genealogy Programs 6

Descendant Tree

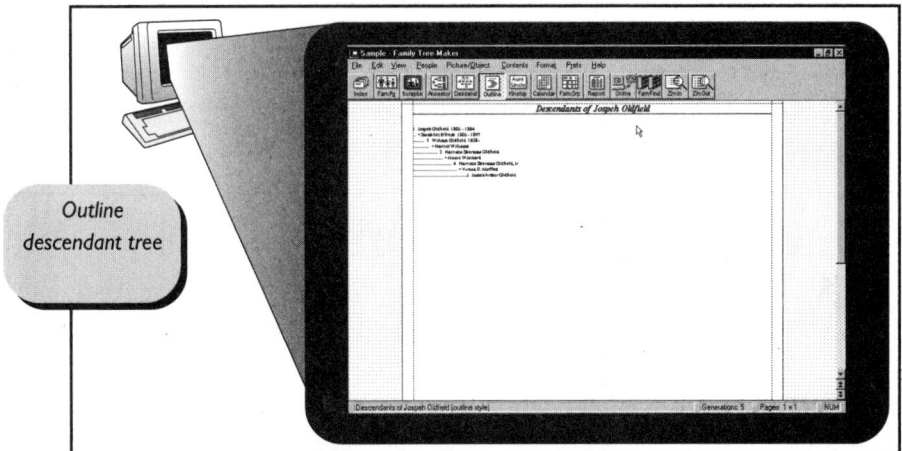

Outline descendant tree

153

6 Using Genealogy Programs

Descendant Tree

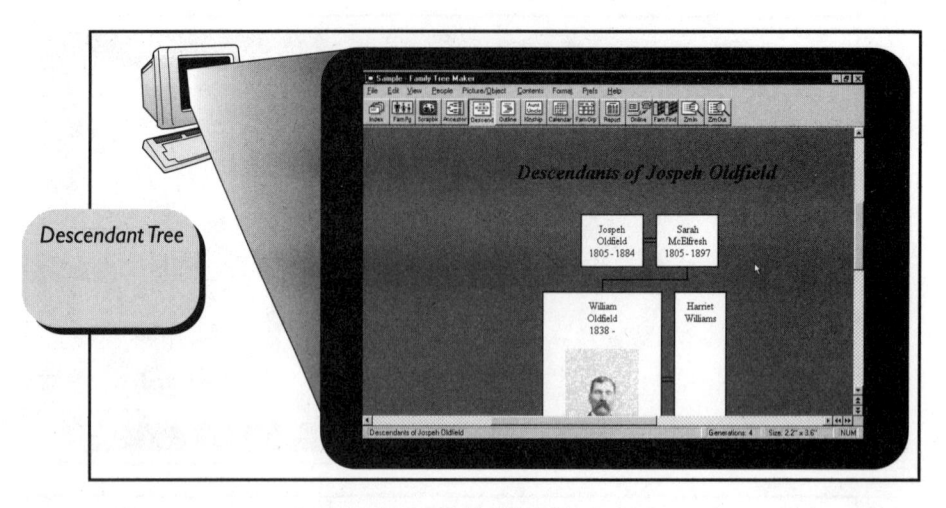

Importing and exporting GEDCOM files

Family Tree Maker also allows the loading and saving of GEDCOM files for transferring your family history between other programs.

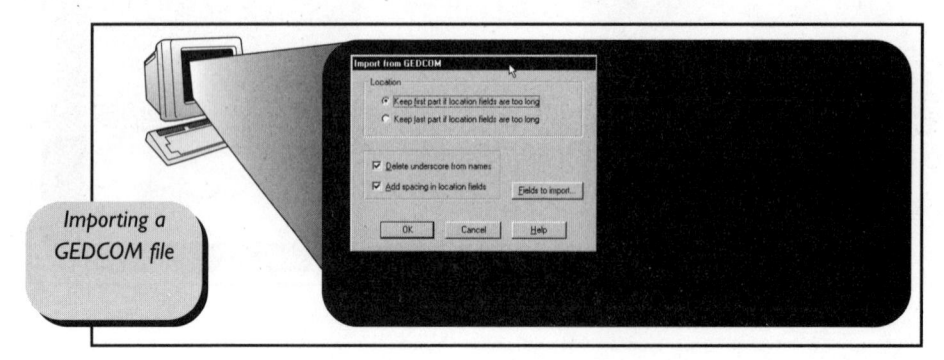

Importing a GEDCOM file

Using Genealogy Programs 6

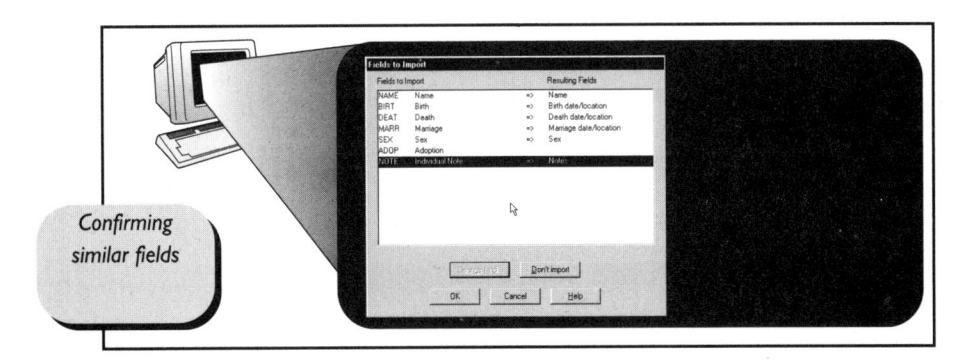

Confirming similar fields

To export a GEDCOM file of your family database, select **File/Copy/Export Family File**. In the "Save as type:" dialog box select the "*.GED" file type. Type a name (8 characters or less) in the "File name:" dialog box and click [Save].

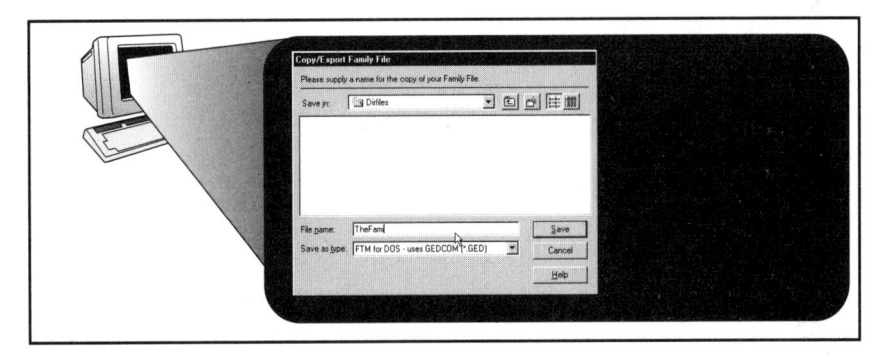

Saving a GEDCOM file

One final note: Broderbund sells a large variety of CD-ROMs for family research. If you purchased the Deluxe Edition of Family Tree Maker, you should buy their new CD "The Genealogist's All-in-One Address Book." To quote their advert: "This book is a one-stop resource needed by everyone engaged in family history research, from the beginner to the professional. With over 21,000 addresses and phone numbers, this CD contains three books compiled by Elizabeth Petty Bentley: County Courthouse Book, Directory of Family Associations, and The Genealogist's Address Book." I agree 100%. It is one of the few resources that you will keep using. Save some trees by buying the CD.

155

Using The Companion CD-ROM

Chapter 7

Using The Companion CD-ROM

The CD-ROM included with this guide will be an indispensable source of reference material as well as a sampler of selected software. I have included all the images, forms and family data examples you have seen in this guide on the CD-ROM for you to experiment with.

To run the CD-ROM in Windows 3.X, select "Run..." from the File pull-down menu located at the top left corner of your screen (this is the Windows' Program Manager screen). Type "D:\MENU.EXE" (where "D:" is the letter assigned to your CD-ROM drive) and click OK. Click OK again and the menu program will be loaded.

To run the CD-ROM in Windows 95, click the Start button, select **Run...**, type "D:\MENU.EXE" and click OK. This will load the CD's menu program.

The main menu of the companion CD-ROM

7 Using The Companion CD-ROM

If you DO NOT have Windows on your machine you can still install and evaluate **Brother's Keeper,** by John Steed, by running the INSTALL.EXE file located on the CD-ROM. Type "D:\BKINSTALL.EXE" at your DOS prompt and press ⌈Enter⌋.

WHAT'S ON THE CD-ROM

The following lists the directories and their contents as well as the instructions to access each one. With a little exploration on your part, you'll discover some great tools and techniques to help you write your own family history.

ADOBE	Adobe's Acrobat Reader program to read PDF files.
BK5STEED	This directory contains the latest (version 5.2b) of John Steed's Brother's Keeper genealogy program. Mr. Steed has continued to update and support his program for 10 plus years.
CATALOGS	This directory has 15 catalogs from some of the most respected names in genealogical publishing.
DATA	Contains various WAV, AVI, GED, DOC and TIF files.
DEMO	Contains EasyPhoto Demonstration, courtesy of Storm Technologies.
DISK1(2)	Contains the files to run Seattle FilmWorks's Photo Works demonstration.
FORMS	Contains many forms, including pedigree and family groups.
FOW5DEM	Family Origins Version 5 Demonstration. Limited features demonstration from one of the leaders in genealogy programs, Parsons Technology, Inc.
FT4WIN	Family Tree for Windows Demonstration, written by David Simmonds. An excellent family tree software program (shareware).
FTMDEMO	Family Tree Maker Demonstration, courtesy of Banner Blue Div. of Broderbund Software.
NR32	NavRoad Web Browser, by FAICO Information Solutions (Godfrey Ko).
PIX	This directory contains several of the images in the book.
R4DEMO	Roots IV Slide Show courtesy of the producer, CommSoft, Inc.
SFW	This directory contains sample images from Seattle FilmWorks.
UTES	Various shareware genealogy utilities.
VR_DEMO	Visual Roots Slide Show courtesy of the producer, CommSoft, Inc.
WEBSITE	This directory contains several sample web sites and HTML documents.

Using The Companion CD-ROM 7

ADOBE

From the pull-down menu (located in the top left corner of the Menu program and labeled "Abacus"), you can install Adobe's Acrobat Reader. This program allows you to read PDF (portable document file) files that are on the CD-ROM. The Abacus Catalog is in this format and can be located in this same directory. After installing Acrobat Reader, select **Load/File** and type "d:\adobe\catalog.pdf" and press Enter.

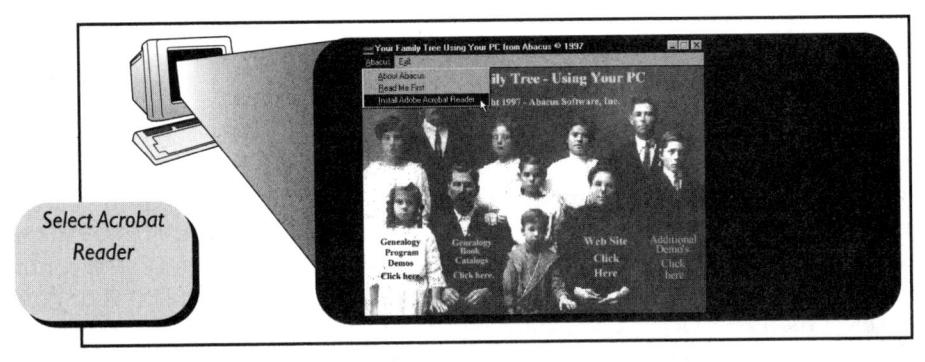

Select Acrobat Reader

You can also view the electronic edition of this guide by loading the Acrobat Reader, typing "d:\guide.pdf" and pressing *e*. The advantage to reading it with your PC is that you can quickly jump around the guide for specific information. You will also be able to go to the Appendix and see several "hot links" to commercial web sites.

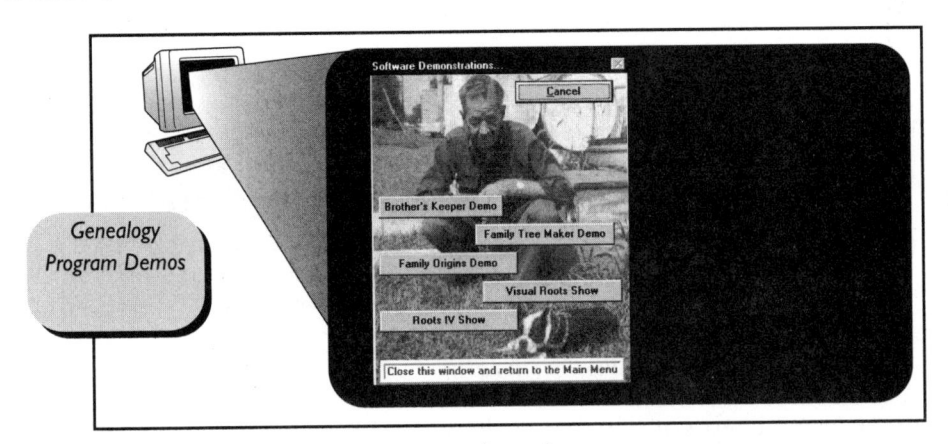

Genealogy Program Demos

161

7 Using The Companion CD-ROM

BK5STEED

Written and copyrighted (c) by John Steed. Brother's Keeper is one of the oldest and most reliable genealogy programs on the market today. This MS-DOS version may lack some of the fancy bells and whistles of Windows-based programs, however, it more than makes it up in speed and reliability. Be sure to refer to the chapter about Brother's Keeper to help you evaluate this outstanding shareware genealogy program.

FOW5DEMO

Family Origins, copyright (c) 1997 Parsons Technology. This is a demo version of Family Origins 5.0 for Windows genealogy software from Parsons Technology. This demo version is limited to 50 individuals, but the full working version supports unlimited family members. The full working version of Family Origins for Windows may be purchased from your local dealer, or directly from Parsons Technology by calling 1-800-223-6925 or 1-319-395-7300. You can also contact Parsons Technology at the addresses at the end of their readme.txt file. When you select the [Family Origins Demo] button from the menu program, the installation program will step you through installing it onto your hard drive.

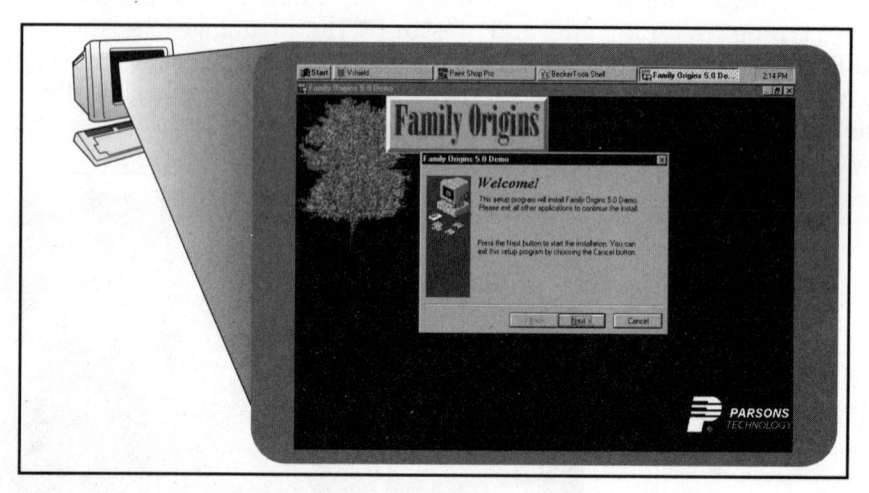

Some tips to running the Family Origins demo

A dialog box will appear which will allow you to:

Using The Companion CD-ROM 7

1. Create a new database

2. Open an existing database *or*

3. Exit from the program

If you would like to create a new database to enter some of your own information, then select the first option. The Family Origins demo also includes a sample database, which can be opened with the second option. This allows you to try the many features of Family Origins for Windows without having to type in a bunch of names first. To add people to your database, select **Add** from the main menu.

A submenu will appear to ask if you want to "Add an Individual, Parents, Spouse, or Child". Select "Individual" for the first person (you may also click the toolbar button with the Add symbol and the letter "I" for "individual"). Help files are not included with this demo. If you try to access **Help** from the **Help** menu, or by pressing F1 in any dialog, you will receive an error message that the help topic cannot be found.

FTMDEMO

Family Tree Maker copyright (c) Broderbund. This is a demonstration of Banner Blue Division of Broderbund Software's premiere genealogy program, Family Tree Maker Deluxe Edition. You can test the many features, including a variety of printable forms, to see if this is the right program for you. Be sure to read the chapter on this outstanding program package.

163

7 Using The Companion CD-ROM

FT4WIN

Copyrighted and written by David Simmonds of FT4WIN Software Enterprises, Family Tree for Windows Demonstration is an excellent family tree software program. It is shareware so you may try it out before purchasing. Please see the shareware notice in the back of the book for information. Its a very good program for your evaluation.

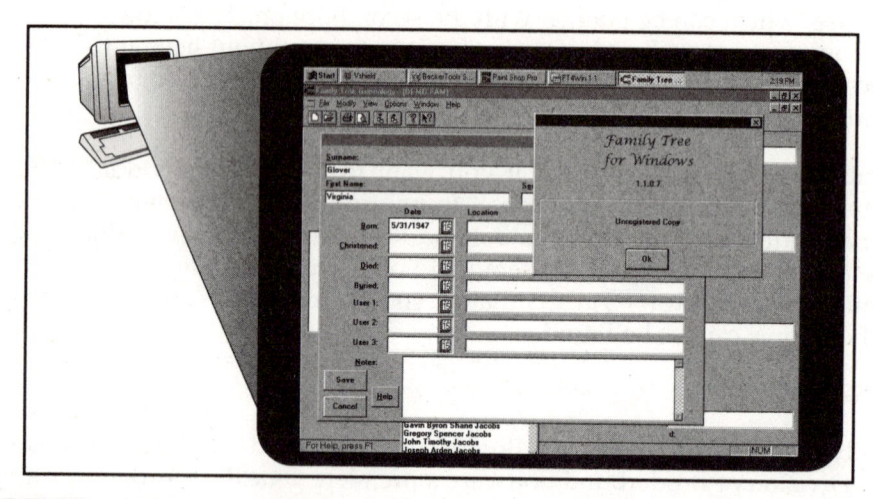

R4DEMO

This is Commsoft, Inc.'s ROOTS IV Slide Show. The Slide Show requires a VGA color system to show samples of printed reports. ROOTS IV, however, does not require a graphics card and monitor unless you wish to display images.

Using The Companion CD-ROM   7

Select Catalogs

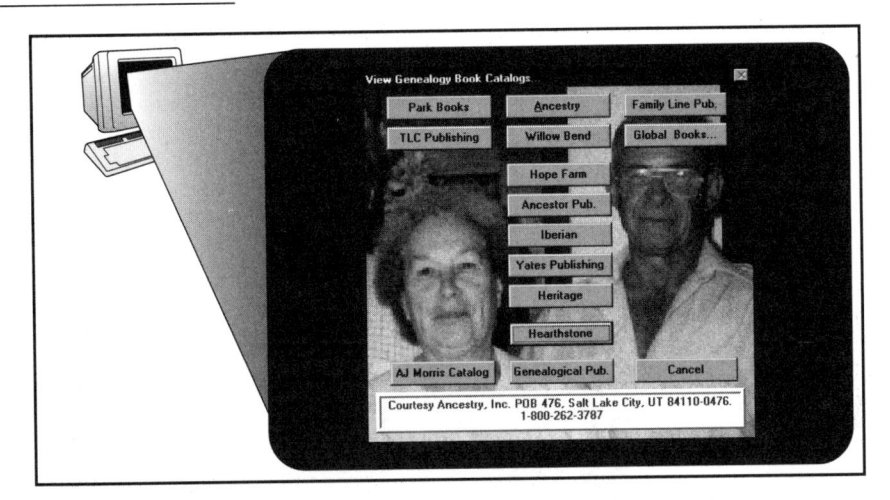

CATALOGS

Contains many catalogs from the best genealogical book publishers, service providers, booksellers and other companies serving the family historian. This is quite possibly one of the largest collections of genealogy books and supplies you will find in one place. If all of the catalogs were printed out at once, they would total over 1300 pages. The companies who were so generous to contribute include:

- ❖ A J Morris
- ❖ Ancestry
- ❖ Family Line
- ❖ Genealogical Publishing Company
- ❖ Hearthstone Books
- ❖ Hope Farm
- ❖ Parks Books
- ❖ Willow Brook
- ❖ Ancestor Publishing
- ❖ Everton's
- ❖ Global Heritage
- ❖ Heritage Books
- ❖ Iberian
- ❖ TLC
- ❖ Yates Publishing

165

7 Using The Companion CD-ROM

I highly recommend browsing these catalogs if you want to advance your family research.

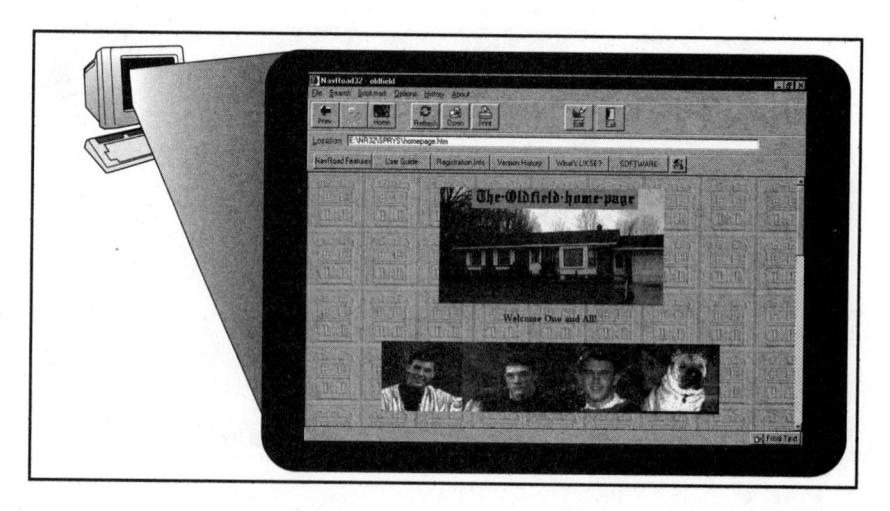

WEB SITE MENU

Directory - WEBSITE

NavRoad Web Browser

Copyright (c) 1997 by FAICO; GODFREY KO, PO BOX 710, MT GRAVATT 4122, QLD, AUSTRALIA. NavRoad Offline HTML Browser v1.40 - A small, powerful off-line HTML browser that runs off a floppy and requires no winsock.dll.

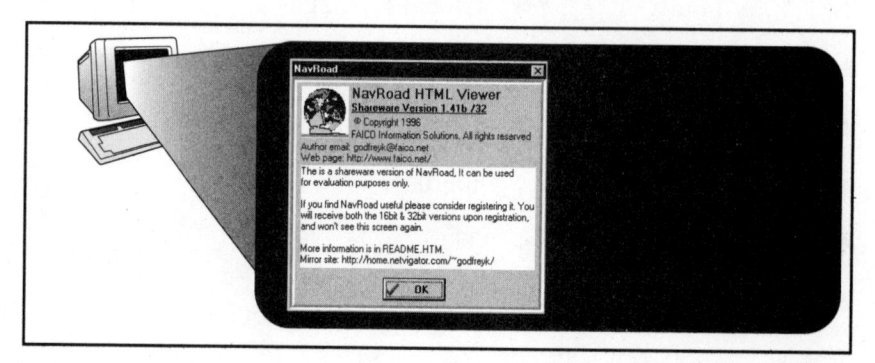

Using The Companion CD-ROM 7

This browser lets users view HTML files anytime, anywhere and supports all HTML 2 tags, and most HTML 3 tags. It also supports helper applications, image maps, bookmarks and directory buttons. You may export HTML files as plain text (without tags). With its customizable interface and Kiosk mode support this is a fast and easy solution for HTML files distribution. You may register NavRoad on-line with your credit cards (Visa, MasterCard, American Express, Novus brand cards) through REGNET by going to the following web sites:

- Single User Licensing
  http://www.xmission.com/~wintrnx/regnet/232p.htm

- Site Licensing
  http://www.xmission.com/~wintrnx/regnet/233p.htm

- Royalty Free Licensing
  http://www.xmission.com/~wintrnx/regnet/234p.htm

Sprynet homepage

This directory contains the complete Oldfield home page from sprynet's world wide web. This web site was created using Home Page Wizard, which is included with your subscription to SpryNet (a division of CompuServe). To view this website, click the [Home Page] button. Follow the links to view this basic family history web site.

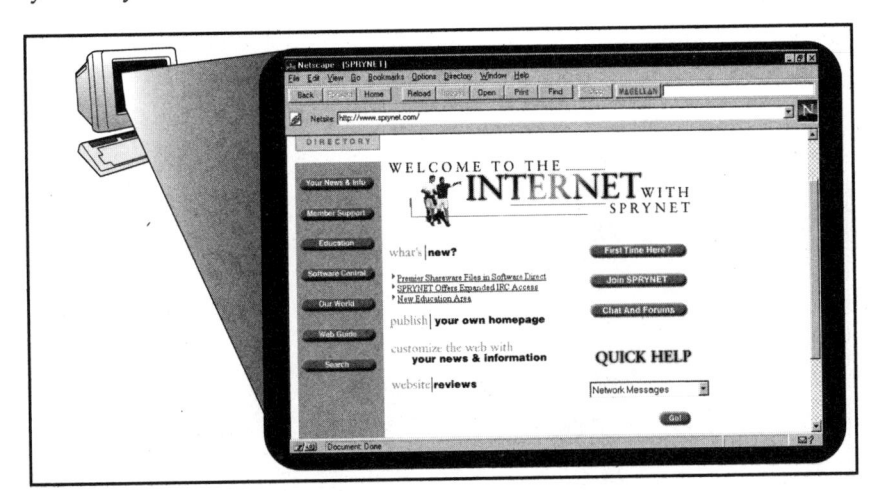

167

7 Using The Companion CD-ROM

Family Origins Demo web site

This is a web site created with Family Origins version 5.

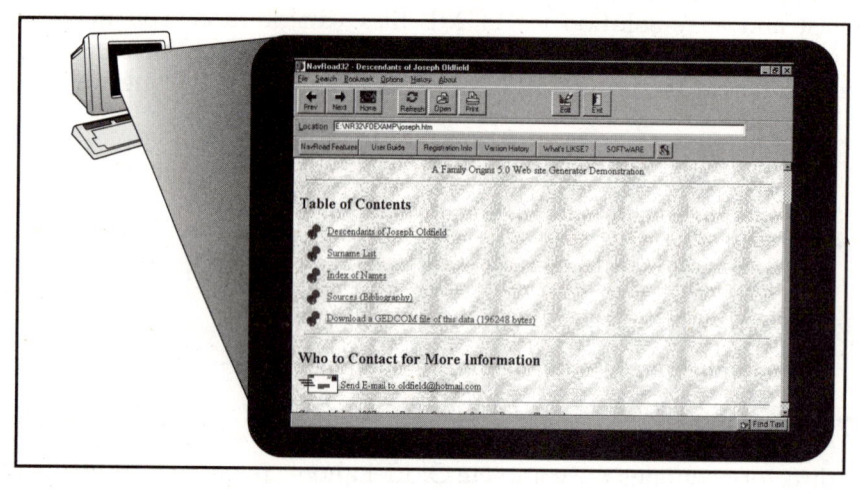

GED2HTML

GEDCOM to HTML Convertor copyright (c) 1995 Eugene W. Stark. This utility converts your GEDCOM files (created using your genealogy program) to HTML web pages. These pages can then be used to construct your own web site information to share with the world wide web. You can review this shareware program at: http://www.cs.sunysb.edu/~stark.

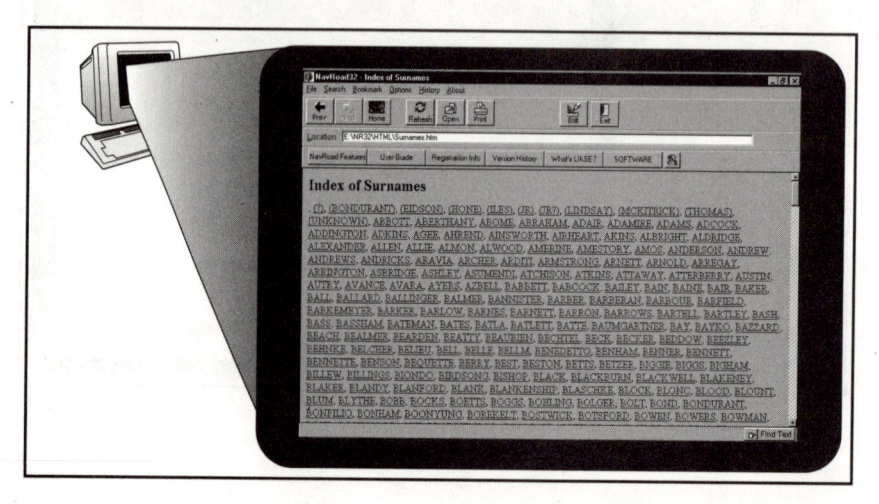

Using The Companion CD-ROM 7

Bookmark List

This 'virtual' web page contains one of the largest genealogy bookmark files anywhere. The more than 1400 bookmarks will lead you to over 10,000 more that you can explore. You can also see this bookmark file on the Abacus website at www.abacuspub.com.

In writing this book I've compiled a comprehensive collection of Internet web sites that I have visited and researched and that are of special interest to family history buffs. The enclosed file "famtree.htm" contains all these web site bookmarks (or favorites) that you too can use to research your own family tree. I have consolidated them into different folders so that they will be easier for you to use. I have also included an outline of the bookmarks and what each folder contains. Happy hunting!

Best Genealogy Sites Folder

This folder includes what I consider some of the best and informative genealogical web sites on the Internet.

Big List A through Z Folders

This is a large alphabetical list of web sites throughout the world. These include everything from family web sites to USGENWEB sites and many, many more.

Adoption Info and Sites Folder

I thought that many people would be interested in the genealogical issues of adoption. These are some of the most informative sites around.

Book Publishers & Sellers Folders

Alphabetically organized, these folders contains dozens of pointers to the very best genealogy book publishers, sellers and services.

Cemetery Information Folder

As you well know, cemeteries are a valuable aid to family historians. I have included several web sites that can help you with this research.

169

7 Using The Companion CD-ROM

Commercial Software Co. Folders

This folder contains a great assortment of genealogy software companies with web sites.

Finding People Folder

Lost someone? This is a very comprehensive list of web sites that can assist you in finding that lost one anywhere in the world. You will be surprised what (and who) you can find.

Genealogy Sites With Lists Folder

I chose to put several of the web sites which feature bookmark lists to other web sites pertaining to genealogy. Cyndi's list is both well organized and highly publicized.

Government and States Sites Folder

Your government at work. Many ".gov" web sites are listed to help you in your research.

Heraldry Folder

Many people are very fond of this area of genealogy. I would definitely check these out; they're very interesting.

International Folder

An alphabetical list by country of the most popular web sites in the world that can help you research your family history. From Australia to France, from Germany to Spain, to Ireland, Scotland and England, these bookmarks will help you travel the globe.

Magazines-Journals Folder

There are dozens of genealogy magazines, newsletters, journals and "e"-zines on the world wide web. All of these publications are good sources to help you research better.

Using The Companion CD-ROM

Mailing Lists - Genealogy Folder

This folder includes several web sites that you can subscribe to. There are also several web sites that can scan the usenet user groups for you. These include Deja News and Liszt. I have also included several web sites that will step you through subscribing to the variety of list servers on the internet.

Main Home Pages of Services Folder

I have included these bookmarks as a convenience to you. They include the world's most popular online services.

Maps Plus Folder

Maps help you with research and they're fun to read when included with your family history. These are some of the best sites to "map" out.

Photos Plus Folder

There are dozens of photography service companies, and this is a good list to start with.

ROOTS-L Folder

The very popular mail list service. If you subscribe to no other, try this one.

War, Conflicts & History Folder

And finally, there are literally thousands of web sites catering to war buffs. I have tried to include several web sites that can help you in your research. The most popular sites in this folder are the Civil War web pages. You will be surprised at the quantity and quality of information that these sites offer.

Add the famtree.htm file

You can easily add the famtree.htm file to either Netscape Navigator or Microsoft Internet Explorer. To install this bookmark file, exit this CD-ROM.

Follow these steps when installing the famtree.htm for Netscape Navigator:

171

7 Using The Companion CD-ROM

1. Start Netscape Navigator:

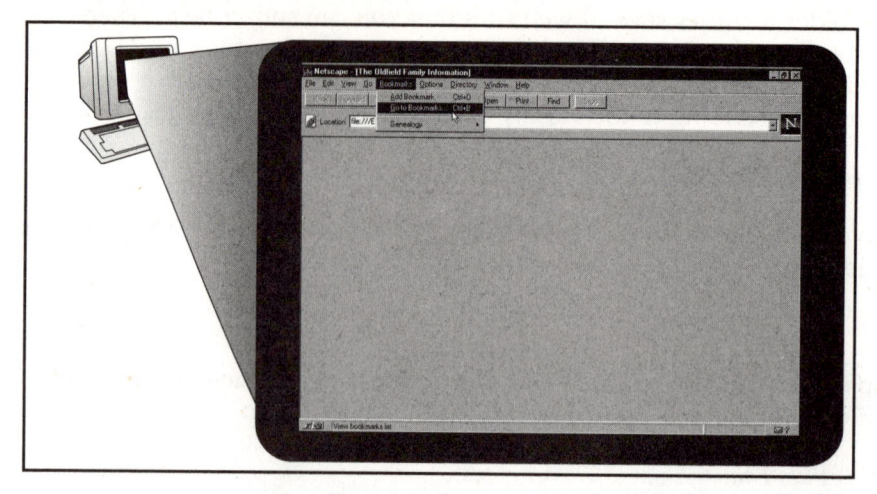

2. Click on menu item **Bookmarks / Go to Bookmarks...** to open the bookmark windows:

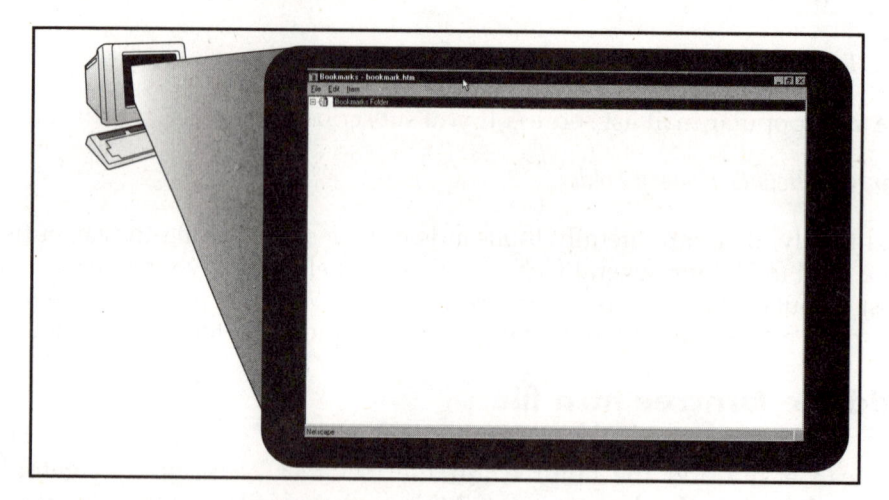

3. The Bookmarks window opens:

172

Using The Companion CD-ROM

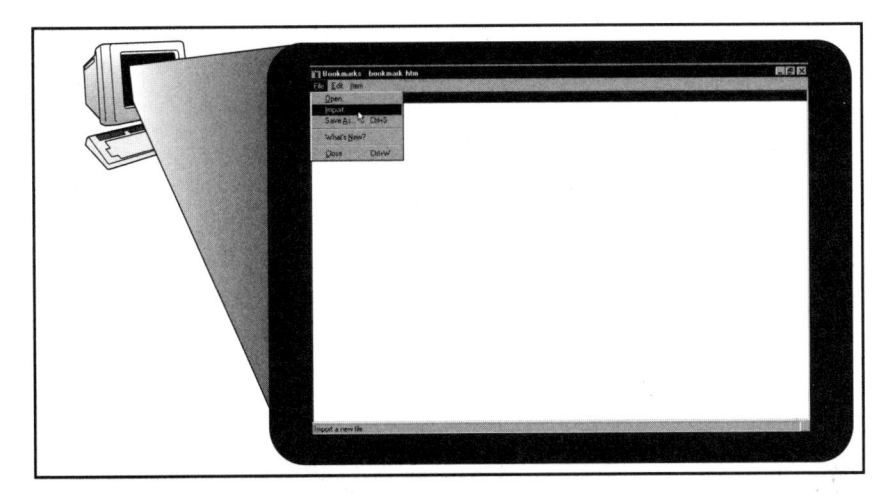

4. Click on menu item **File/Import** to open the Import bookmarks file window:

5. Select the file "famtree.htm.":

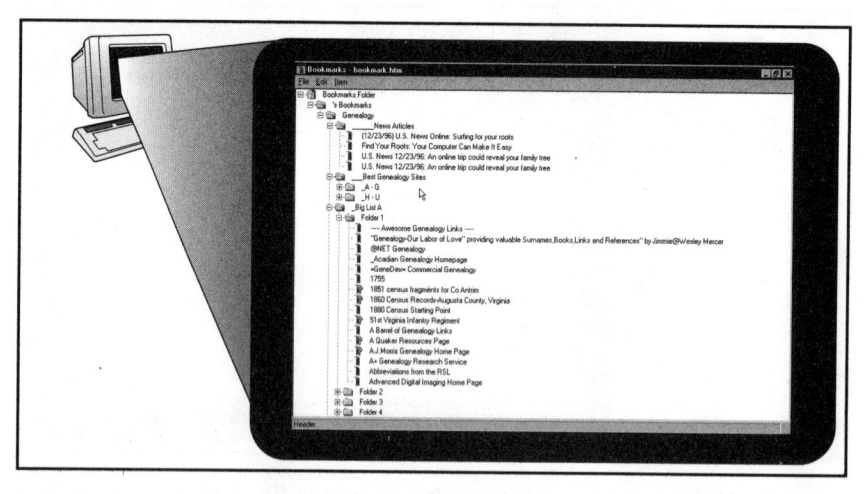

7 Using The Companion CD-ROM

6. The new family tree bookmarks are now available to you.

Installing the famtree.htm file for Microsoft Internet Explorer

1. Start Internet Explorer.

2. Click on menu item **File/Open**... and the Open dialog appears:

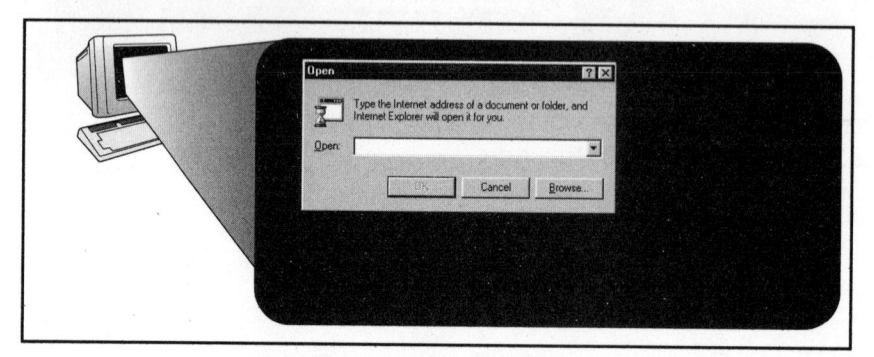

3. Click [Browse...] and select the file "famtree.htm":

174

Using The Companion CD-ROM 7

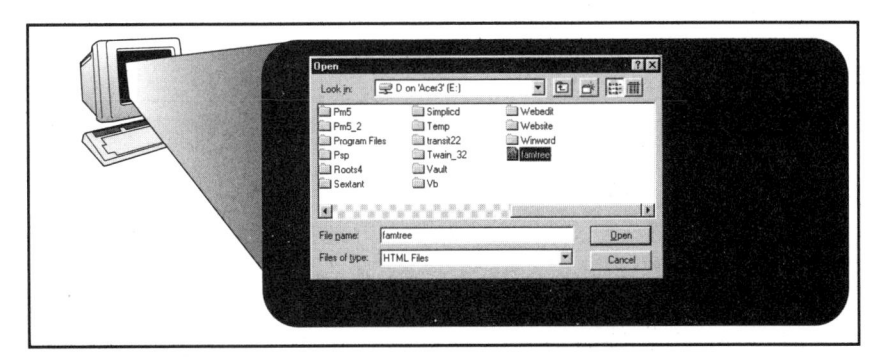

4. Click on menu item **Favorites / Add to Favorites** and the Add to Favorites dialog appears:

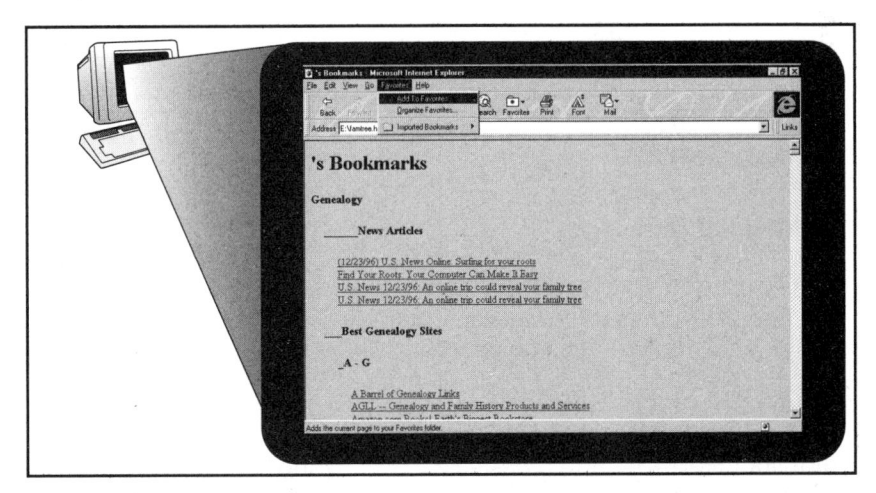

5. Click [OK].

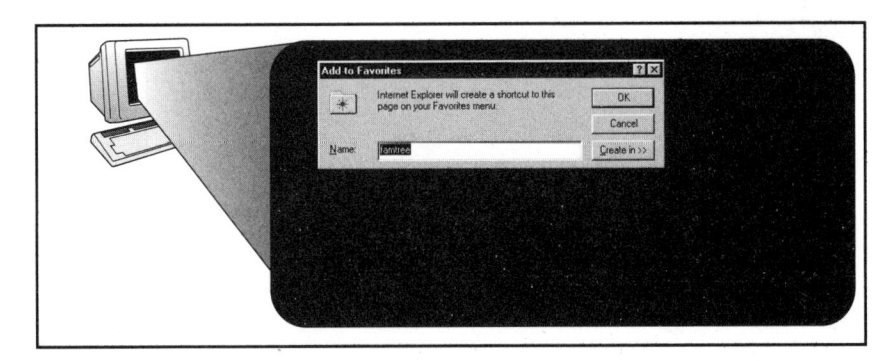

175

7 Using The Companion CD-ROM

6. The new family tree favorites are now available to you:

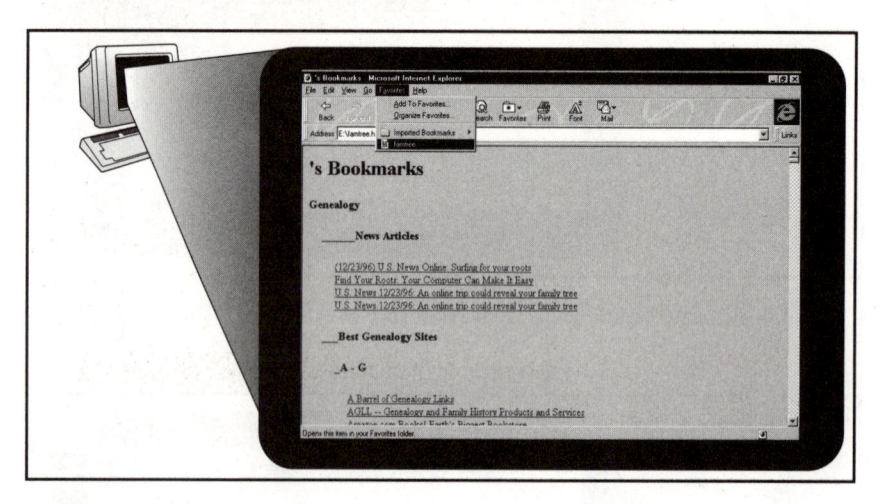

Additional demos

Select Additional Demos...

This menu contains a wide variety of genealogy utilities and demonstrations: a great selection of photography software, scanner software, calendars and much more.

EASY PHOTO DEMO

This will install Storm Technologies's Easy Photo slide show. It shows you the many functions and features of their software and hardware scanner. It is one of the easiest scanners to use to integrate your family photos into your genealogy software.

Using The Companion CD-ROM 7

SEATTLE FILMWORKS DEMO

Well known in the film industry, Seattle Film Works markets an excellent graphic package called Photo Works. Photo Works is a photography program that lets you catalog and modify your electronic photos. This demo is limited in some options that are available in the full commercial edition.

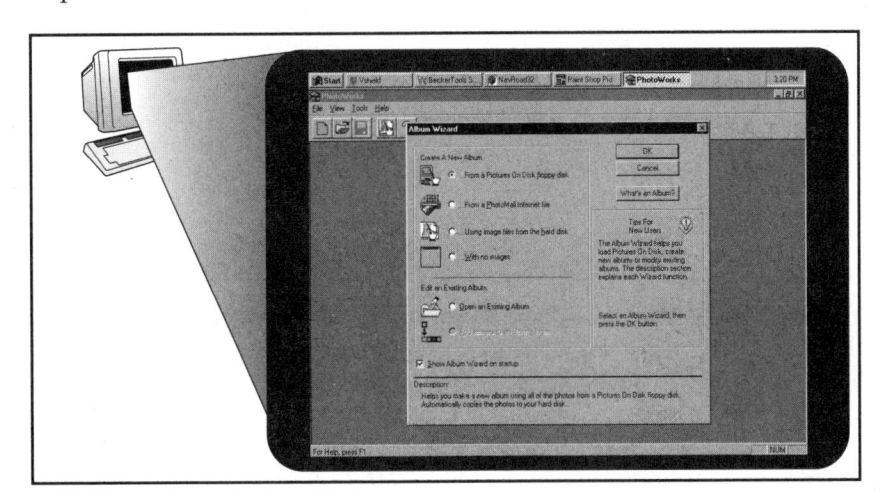

7 Using The Companion CD-ROM

Calendar Explorer

Copyright 1996 by Albert B. Collver, III, all rights reserved. Calendar Explorer is a 32-bit, Windows 95 and Windows NT program that allows you to explore the Western Church Year, including the Major and Minor Feasts, the date of both Eastern and Western Easter through the centuries, and the number of days between dates. The reports that you generate may be printed out or saved in text format. Other features include conversion between the Julian Calendar and the Gregorian Calendar dates as well as conversion to and from Julian Day Numbers. It offers a Year in Brief viewing mode that shows all 12 months of a given year in compact form. There is a Week Day finder that finds the week day for a given date—for example, Friday 13th or when your birthday will happen on a Monday. Calendar Explorer can also calculate the Lunar Quarters for any year between 4714 BC and 9999 AD.

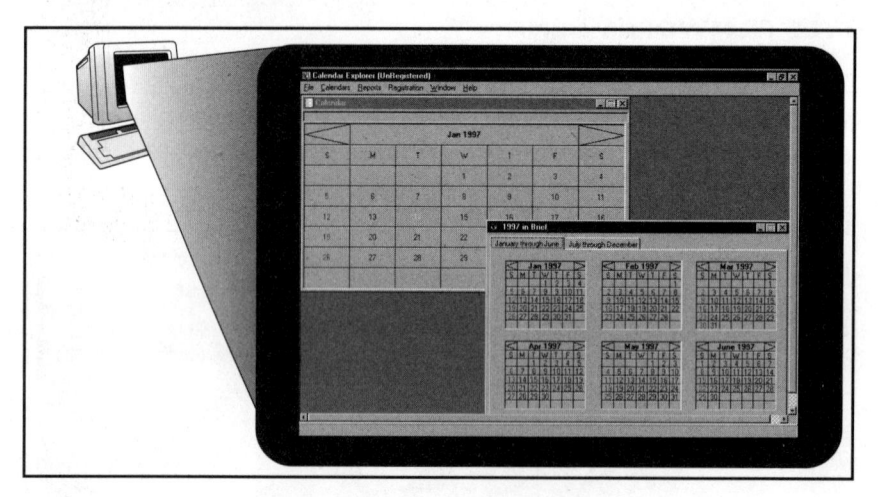

This program is being released as Shareware. You are free (and encouraged) to distribute this program via electronic networks or disks to friends, associates, neighbors, etc. This program may be registered electronically by logging onto CompuServe and typing SWREG. When asked for the program id number, please type "12019." Your CIS account will then be charged $17. When you download Calendar Explorer, there is a Registration program included that will allow you to register by e-mail, fax, or mail. Currencies from many countries as well as credit cards and checks are accepted. Kagi administers the registration of CE. You can also register by US Mail. Checks (drawn in US Funds) should be made to Albert Collver in the amount of $17. If you do not feel the program is

Using The Companion CD-ROM 7

worth registering, please tell the author why so it can be improved. The Registration information is included in Calendar Explorer's documentation. This new Version 1.71 also includes added printing and edit functions to Days Between Dates and Date Conversion Forms

Family Calendar for Windows

Copyright (c) Doug East, and located at: www.frii.com/~east.

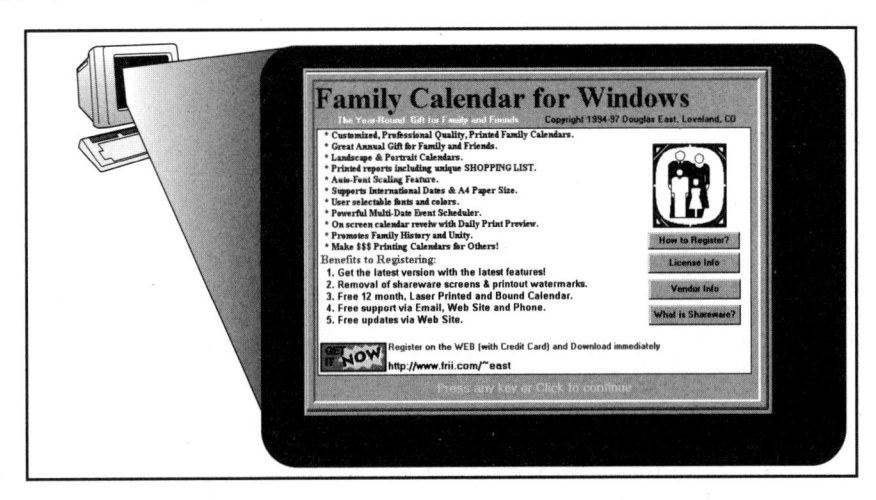

This is one of the best calendar programs with great features:

- ❖ Prints customized, professional quality, family oriented wall calendars.
- ❖ Prints unique (pocket/purse) sized Gift & Card Shopping List.
- ❖ Prints complete list of events.
- ❖ Prints blank data collection forms for friends and family.
- ❖ Auto-Font scaling feature.
- ❖ Supports International date formats and A4 paper size.
- ❖ Ships with three holiday files: US, Canada, Other
- ❖ Great annual gift for Family and Friends.

7 Using The Companion CD-ROM

- Promotes Family History and Unity.
- Make $$$$$ Printing Calendars for others!
- Version 2.0 Enhancements include:
- On-screen review of calendar w/daily print preview.
- User selectable fonts.
- Support for color printers.
- User selectable colors.
- Scheduling Tool for multi-date events.
- Landscape & Portrait printing modes.

WINMORET

v 1.01. Copyright (c) Sylvain Hogue. For Windows 3.1+. Converts calendar dates between Gregorian, Julian, Hebrew, Muslim, Christian and French Revolution calendars. It will show old style calendars for years before 1752 and spans 5000 years. This is a great tool with many features for genealogists.

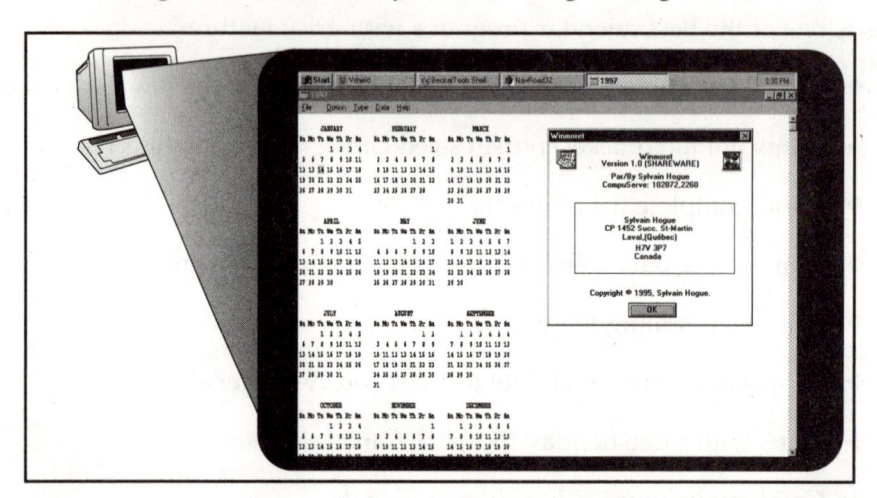

Using The Companion CD-ROM 7

ThumbsUp!

Copyright (c) 1997 Cerious Software, Inc. Thumbs+Plus v3.0-S. The most effective, elegant and inexpensive way to locate, view, edit, print and organize your graphic files in Windows 95, NT & 3.1. 30-day evaluation copy (shareware). ThumbsUp! can organize all your images into one convenient 'thumb nail' collection. This is an amazing utility — try it today!

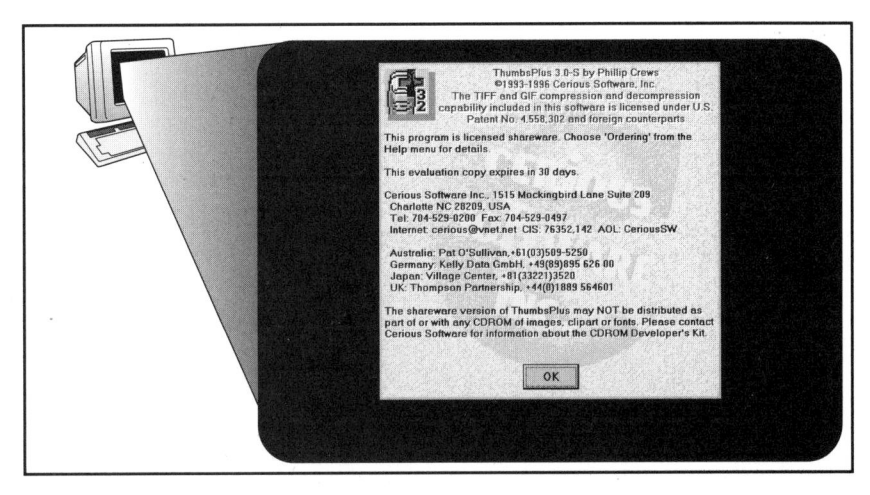

Graphic Work Shop

Copyright Steve Rimmer, Alchemy Mindworks. One of the very best graphic programs on the market today.

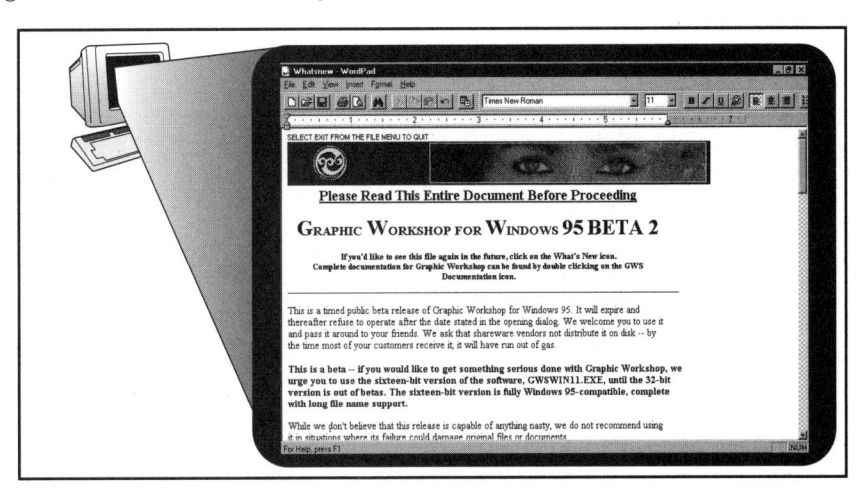

181

7 Using The Companion CD-ROM

FORMS

This directory includes sample request letters, family group forms and blank pedigree charts. These are provided to give you a head start with your research. Feel free to modify them to your own liking. They are in various text file formats including, Microsoft Works, Word 2.0, 6.0, Microsoft Write and standard ASCII text files.

Appendix

Appendix A
Glossary

During research, genealogists and family historians frequently encounter unfamiliar terms. A common example are diseases that afflicted ancestors and have since chae phrases are listed in the genealogy books catalogs on the CD-ROM. Listed below are common important terms you should be familiar with as you begin investigating your family's past.

Abstract

A summary of important information in a deed, will, or title.

Ahnentafel

A table of your ancestors, derived from the German words Ahnen (ancestor) and Tafel (table or list).

Ahnentafel numbering system

A numbering convention for keeping track of your ancestors. The numbers follow in succession that a person's father is twice that person's number, and that a person's mother is twice that person's number plus one, and so on.

Ancestor

Someone from whom you are descended.

Ancestor (or pedigree) chart

A report or chart that shows a person and all of their direct ancestors in a graphic format similar to a tree and its branches. Usually these charts are cascading, or they can be collapsed to fit more family members on a page.

Ancestral file

A database of someone's ancestors that is used to share with others.

Archives

A place where documents or records are stored.

185

Appendix A: Glossary

Bequeath

A term used to give personal property to someone else through a will.

Bibliography

A list of book sources used in research.

Birth certificate

A legal document stating when a person is born.

Canan

A particular branch or subset of a family tree.

Civil

Relations of the same generation, e.g. siblings and cousins.

Census

The counting of people. The Federal Government Census is taken every ten years since 1790 and includes information on the head of household, spouse, children, places of birth and ages at time of census. They are not available to the public until 70 years after the census is taken. The most recent available census is from 1920.

Citation

Reference of a source.

Collateral

your relatives from a different family line, including aunts, uncles and cousins.

Death certificate

A legal document of proof of someone's death.

Deed

A paper that verifies the transfer of ownership of property from one person or to another.

Descendancy chart

Report or chart that shows a person and all of his or her descendants in a graphical format, often represented as a tree and branches.

Descendant

A person who is descended from a particular ancestor, such as a child from the father and mother.

Direct line

How people are related through succeeding generations of children.

Emigrant

A person who emigrates from, or leaves, a country or region to settle in another.

Appendix A: Glossary

Estate

The assets and liabilities of a deceased person.

Family group sheet

The chart of names, dates and places used to record all members of a particular family, including husband, wife, and their children.

Family history

The history of a family as it relates to historical places and the times in which they lived.

Family History Centers

smaller branches of the Family History Library of the LDS church.

Family History Library

located in Salt Lake City, Utah, and maintained by the Church of Latter Day Saints (the Mormons), it holds the world's largest collection of microfilmed records, microfiche, and books and manuscripts, including family histories, local histories, indexes and periodicals. One of the best resources for help in genealogical research.

FamilySearch

A CD-ROM produced by the Mormon church and available in Family History Centers or the Family History Library. It contains the International Genealogical Index (IGI), Ancestral File, Social Security Death Index (SSDI), TempleReady and Military Death Indexes.

GEDCOM

Acronym for "GEnealogical Data COMmunication," a standard data format generated by genealogy programs to transfer information back and forth. It was created by the LDS Church.

Genealogy

The study of a family's origin and descent through generations.

Given name

one's first name, given at birth.

Grantee

The person who buys a property, found in land records.

Grantor

The person who sells a property, found in land records.

Appendix A: Glossary

Immigrant

A person who moves into a country or region.

Index

Alphabetical list of words.

International Genealogical Index (IGI)

a database of names (worldwide) maintained by the LDS Church.

LDS

Church of Jesus Christ of Latter-day Saints (The Mormons). They hold the world's largest repository of genealogical information.

Maiden name

A woman's surname prior to marriage (i.e., her name as a maiden).

Maternal

Referring to one's mother or her line of ancestors.

Microfiche

A sheet containing reduced copies of documents, records, books, etc.

Microfilm

A roll of film containing reduced copies of documents, records, books, etc.

Modified register

similar to a descendant report, but also includes notes and sources in a book form.

Naturalization

The process of becoming a citizen of the United States.

Note

information about a person, place or event. A cited source is more reliable.

Obituary

A written notice of a person's death (usually with pertinent family information) published in newspapers or other media.

Passenger list

list of the names of passengers who came to the United States in ships.

Paternal

Referring to one's father or his line of ancestors.

Appendix A: Glossary

Pedigree (or ancestor) chart

A report or chart that shows a person and all of their direct ancestors in a graphic format similar to a tree and its branches. Usually these charts are cascading, or they can be collapsed to fit more family members on a page.

Prefix title

The titles in front of names, such as Dr., Prof., Mr., Mrs., etc.

Primary record or evidence

The record created at or near the time of an event.

Probate

The settling of an estate when a person dies.

Secondary record

Records or evidence that was not created at or near the time of an event or were created or copied from original sources.

Social Security Death Index (SSDI)

index of Social Security Death Benefit records kept by the government.

Soundex

A letter and number coding system invented during the depression by the WPA. It is a way of giving sound codes to names in the federal census records. After converting a surname into its sound code you can search for all instances of a surname, even when it could be spelled in various ways.

Source

A book, document or person that provides primary information.

Suffix title

Titles after a name, such as Sr., Jr., or royal title.

Surname

Your last name

A common family name that is passed down directly through generations.

Vital records

People's records of births, marriages, and death.

Will

A legal document that expresses a person's wishes regarding the desolve of his or her property after death.

Appendix B
Resources

Appendix B contains a dated list of genealogy and historical groups across the country. These addresses came from several sources. I have not verified their accuracy and provide them *as is*. The following are arranged alphabetically by the two-letter postal state codes.

Alaska Historical Library and Museum, Juneau, AK 99801

Alaska Society S.A.R., 1925 N. Salem Dr., Anchorage, AK 99504

Fairbanks Genealogical Society, P.O. Box 60534, Fairbanks, AK 99709

Gastineau Genealogical Society, 3270 Nowell Ave., Juneau, AK 99801

Kenai Totem Tracers, 163 Main St. Loop, Kenai, AK 99611

Library (Genealogy), University of Alaska, College, AK 99701

State Library (Genealogy), Pouch G State Capitol, Juneau, AK 99801

Wrangell Genealogical Society, P.O. Box 928EP, Wrangell, AK 99929

Alabama Archives (Genealogy), World War Memorial Bldg., Montgomery, AL 36104

Alabama Genealogical Society Inc., P.O. Box 2296, Birmingham, AL 35229

Alabama Society S.A.R., 507 Bonnet Hill Cir., Mobile, AL 36609

American College of Heraldry, Drawer CG University of Alabama, Tuscaloosa, AL 35486

Baldwin County Genealogical Society, Box 501, Lillian, AL 36549

Birmingham Genealogical Society Inc., P.O. Box 2432, Birmingham, AL 35201

Bullock County Historical Society, P.O. Box 663, Union Springs, AL 36089

Butler County Historical Society, 309 Ft. Dale Rd., Greenville, AL 36037

Central Alabama Genealogical Society, P.O. Box 125, Selma, AL 36701

Civil War Descendants Society, P.O. Box 233, Athens, AL 35611

Genealogical Society of E. Alabama Inc., P.O. Drawer 1351, Auburn, AL 36830

Library (Genealogy), Wallace State Community College, Hanceville, AL 35077

Library (Genealogy), University of Alabama, University, AL 35486

Library (Genealogy), Auburn University, Auburn, AL 36830

Liles Memorial Library (Genealogy), 108 E. 10th St., Anniston, AL 36201

Mobile Genealogical Society Inc., P.O. Box 6224, Mobile, AL 36660

Natchez Trace Genealogical Society, P.O. Box 420, Florence, AL 35631

N.E. Alabama Genealogical Society Inc., P.O. Box 674, Gadsden, AL 35902

Appendix B: Resources

North Central Alabama Genealogical Society, P.O. Box 13, Cullman, AL 35056

Pea River Historical & Genealogical Society, P.O. Box 628, Enterprise, AL 36331

Piedmont Historical & Genealogical Society, P.O. Box 47, Spring Garden, AL 36275

Public Library (Genealogy), 212 S. Three Notch St., Andalusia, AL 36420

Public Library (Genealogy), 915 Monroe St., Huntsville, AL 35801

Public Library (Genealogy), 200 Clarke St., Cullman, AL 35055

Public Library (Genealogy), 218 N. Wood St., Florence, AL 35630

Public Library (Genealogy), 2020 7th Ave. N., Birmingham, AL 35203

Southeast Alabama Genealogical Society, P.O. Box 143, Dothan, AL 36302

Southern Society of Genealogical Inc., Box 295, Centre, AL 35960

Tennessee Valley Genealogical Society, P.O. Box 1568, Huntsville, AL 35807

Tuscaloosa Genealogical Society, 29 Dubois Terrace, Tuscaloosa, AL 35401

University Library (Genealogy), R.R. 5 Box 109, Piedmont, AL 36272

Arkansas Genealogical Society, P.O. Box 908, Hot Springs, AR 71902

Arkansas Society S.A.R., 1119 Scenic Way, Benton, AR 72015

Ashley County Genealogical Society, P.O. Box Drawer R, Crossett, AR 71635

Batesville Genealogical Society, P.O. Box 3883, Batesville, AR 72503

Baxter County Historical & Genealogical Society, 1505 Mistletoe, Mountain Home, AR 72653

Cal County Genealogical Club, 361 W. Main, Piggott, AR 72454

Crowley's Ridge Genealogical Society, Box 2091, State University, AR 72467

Dallas County Genealogical and Historical Society, C/o Dallas County Library, Fordyce, AR 71742

Desha County Historical Society, P.O. Box 432, Mcgehee, AR 71654

Faulkner County Historical Society, Conway, AR 72032

Frontier Researchers Genealogical Society, P.O. Box 2123, Fort Smith, AR 72902

Greene County Historical & Genealogical Society, 120 N. 12th St., Paragould, AR 72450

Hempstead County Genealogical Society, Box 1158, Hope, AR 71801

Historical & Genealogical Society of Marion Co., P.O. Box 554, Yellville, AR 72687

Jackson County Historical Society, 7 Pickens St., Newport, AR 72112

Jefferson County Genealogical Society, P.O. Box 2215, Pine Bluff, AR 71613

Madison County Genealogical & Historical Society, P.O. Box 427, Huntsville, AR 72740

Melting Pot Genealogical Society, P.O. Box 936, Hot Springs, AR 71902 0936

Montgomery County Historical Society, P.O. Box 520, Mount Ida, AR 71957

Northwest Arkansas Genealogical Society, P.O. Box K, Rogers, AR 72756

Ouachita-Calhoun Genealogical Society, P.O. Box 2092, Camden, AR 71701

Polk County Genealogical Society, P.O. Box 12, Hatfield, AR 71945

Professional Genealogists of Ark., 270 Midland Rd., Alexander, AR 72002

Public Library (Genealogy), 217 E. Dickson St., Fayetteville, AR 72701

Public Library (Genealogy), 200 Woodbine St., Hot Springs National Park, AR 71901

Public Library (Genealogy), 61 S. 8th St., Fort Smith, AR 72901

Public Library (Genealogy), 2801 Orange, North Little Rock, AR 72114

Public Library (Genealogy), 315 W. Oak, Jonesboro, AR 72401

Public Library (Genealogy), Clinton, AR 72031

Public Library (Genealogy), 116 E. 3rd St., Russellville, AR 72801

Public Library (Genealogy), 120 N. 12th St., Paragould, AR 72450

Public Library (Genealogy), 609 Caddo St., Arkadelphia, AR 71923

Public Library (Genealogy), 125 W. Central, Bentonville, AR 72712

Public Library (Genealogy), 700 Louisiana St., Little Rock, AR 72201

Appendix B: Resources

Public Library (Genealogy), 211 E. Lincoln, Hamburg, AR 71646

Public Library (Genealogy), 200 E. 8th Ave., Pine Bluff, AR 71601

Scott County Historical & Genealogical Society, P.O. Box 1560, Waldron, AR 72958

Southwest Arkansas Genealogical Society, 1022 Lawton Cir., Magnolia, AR 71753

Stone County Genealogical Society, P.O. Box 557, Mountain View, AR 72560

S.W. Arkansas Archives (Genealogy), Old Washington Historic State Park, Washington, AR 71862

Tri-County Genealogical Society, P.O. Box 580, Marvell, AR 72366

Union County Genealogical Society, E. 5th & N. Jefferson Sts., El Dorado, AR 71730

Union County Genealogical Society, Barton Library - 200 E. 5th, El Dorado, AR 71730

Yell County Historical & Genealogical Society, Box 622, Dardanelle, AR 72834

Apache Genealogical Society, P.O. Box 1084, Sierra Vista, AZ 85635

Arizona O.G.S., P.O. Box 6594, Mesa, AZ 85216

Arizona Society S.A.R., 1660 E. Greenway St., Mesa, AZ 85203

Arizona State Genealogical Society, Box 42075, Tucson, AZ 85733

Arizona State Geneal Library, 1700 W. Washington St. Basement, Phoenix, AZ 85007

Cochise Genealogical Society, P.O. Box 68, Pirtleville, AZ 85626

Genealogical Society of Arizona, P.O. Box 27237, Tempe, AZ 85282

Genealogical Society of Yuma, P.O. Box 2905, Yuma, AZ 85366 2905

Genealogical Workshop of Mesa, P.O. Box 6052, Mesa, AZ 85208

Green Valley Genealogical Society, P.O. Box 1009, Green Valley, AZ 85614

Lake Havasu Genealogical Society, P.O. Box 953, Lake Havasu City, AZ 86403

Library (Genealogy), 318 University of Arizona, Phoenix, AZ 85007

The Heritage Library, R.R. 1 Box 60H, McNeal, AZ 85617

Mohave County Genealogical Society, 400 W. Beale St., Kingman, AZ 86401

Northern Arizona Genealogical Society, P.O. Box 695, Prescott, AZ 86302

Northern Gila County Genealogical Society, P.O. Box 952, Payson, AZ 85547

Phoenix Genealogical Society, 4607 W. Rovey Ave., Glendale, AZ 85301

Public Library (Genealogy), P.O. Box 27470, Tucson, AZ 85726

Sun Cities Genealogical Society, P.O. Box 1448, Sun City, AZ 85372

Amador County Genealogical Society, 322 Via Verde Sutter Terr, Sutter Creek, CA 95685

Antelope Valley Genealogical Society, P.O. Box 1049, Lancaster, CA 93534

Augustan Society Library, 1510 Cravens Ave., Torrance, CA 90501

Cal State Genealogical Alliance, P.O. Box 401, Wildomar, CA 92595 0401

Calaveras Genealogical Society, 753 S. Main St., Angels Camp, CA 95222 0184

California Society S.A.R., P.O. Box 1776, San Diego, CA 92112 1776

California Genealogical Society, P.O. Box 77105, San Francisco, CA 94107 0105

Colusa County Genealogical Society, P.O. Box 973, Williams, CA 95987

Conejo Valley Genealogical Society Inc., P.O. Box 1228, Thousand Oaks, CA 91358

Contra Costa County Genealogical Society, P.O. Box 910, Concord, CA 94522

East Bay Genealogical Society, P.O. Box 20417, Oakland, CA 94620

Escondido Genealogical Society, P.O. Box 2190, Escondido, CA 92025

Family History Center, 4780 Lincoln Ave., Oakland, CA 94602 2535

Family History Center, 875 Quince Ave., Santa Clara, CA 95051 5292

Family History Center, 10741 Santa Monica Blvd., Los Angeles, CA 90025

Family History Center, 55 Casa St., San Luis Obispo, CA 93405 1801

Family History Center, 2175 Santiago Ave., San Jose, CA 95100

Genealogical Assn.. of Sacramento, P.O. Box 28297, Sacramento, CA 95828

Appendix B: Resources

Genealogical Society Morongo Basin, P.O. Box 234, Yucca Valley, CA 92286

Genealogical Society of Riverside, P.O. Box 2557, Riverside, CA 92516

Genealogical Society of Siskiyou Co., P.O. Box 225, Yreka, CA 96097

German Genealogical Society America, 1420 N. Claremont Blvd #106A, Claremont, CA 91711

Glendora Genealogical Group, P.O. Box 1141, Glendora, CA 91740

Hemet-San Jacinto Genealogical Society, P.O. Box 2516, Hemet, CA 92543

Huntington Library (Genealogy), San Marino, CA 91108

Immigrant Genealogical Society, P.O. Box 7369, Burbank, CA 91510 7369

India Wells Valley Genealogical Society, Box 842, Ridgecrest, CA 93556

Jewish Genealogical Society of L.A., P.O. Box 55443, Sherman Oaks, CA 91413

Kern County Genealogical Society, P.O. Box 2214, Bakersfield, CA 93303

Lake County Museum/ Genealogical, 255 N. Forbes, Lakeport, CA 95453

Library (Genealogy), University of California, Berkeley, CA 94720

Library (Genealogy), University of California, Davis, CA 95616

Livermore/amador Genealogical Society, P.O. Box 901, Livermore, CA 94551

Los Angeles Public Library - Genealogical Periodicals, 630 W. 5th St., Los Angeles, CA 90071

Marin County Genealogical Society, P.O. Box 1511, Novato, CA 94947

Mendocino Coast Genealogical Society, P.O. Box 762, Fort Bragg, CA 95437

Mira Loma Genealogical Library, P.O. Box 527, Mira Loma, CA 91752

Napa Valley Genealogical & Biographical Society, P.O. Box 385, Napa, CA 94559 0385

Native Daughters of the Golden West, 555 Baker St., San Francisco, CA 94117 1405

North California O.G.S., P.O. Box 60191, Sacramento, CA 95860 0101

NSDAR San Francisco Chap, 121 Edgehill Way, San Francisco, CA 94127 1003

NSDAR Sequoia Chap, 152 Yosemite Rd., San Rafael, CA 94903

Orange County Genealogical Society, C/o Huntington Beach Library, Huntington Beach, CA 92648

Pocahontas Genealogical Society, 3628 Cherokee Ln, Modesto, CA 95356

Public Library (Genealogy), 2635 Homestead Rd., Santa Clara, CA 95051

Public Library (Genealogy), 2450 Stevenson Blvd., Fremont, CA 94538

Public Library (Genealogy), Ocean at Pacific Ave., Long Beach, CA 90802

Public Library (Genealogy), 2450 Stevenson Blvd., Fremont, CA 94538

Public Library (Genealogy), 420 S. Broadway, Santa Maria, CA 93454

Public Library (Genealogy), 113 N. F St., Tulare, CA 93274

Public Library (Genealogy), 3rd and E. Sts., Santa Rosa, CA 95404

Public Library (Genealogy), 285 E. Walnut St., Pasadena, CA 91101

Public Library (Genealogy), 1095 N. 7th St., San Jose, CA 95112

Public Library (Genealogy), 625 S. Garey Ave., Pomona, CA 91766

Public Library (Genealogy), 820 E St., San Diego, CA 92101

Public Library (Genealogy), 3581 7th St., Riverside, CA 92502

Public Library (Genealogy), 719 4th St., Yreka, CA 96097

Public Library (Genealogy), 1500 I St., Modesto, CA 95354

Public Library (Genealogy), 480 Winston Dr., San Francisco, CA 94132

Public Library (Genealogy), 14th and Oak St., Oakland, CA 94612

Public Library (Genealogy), P.O. Box 442, Terra Bella, CA 93270

Questing Heirs Genealogical Society Inc., P.O. Box 15102, Long Beach, CA 90815

S. California Chapter O.G.S., P.O. Box 5057, Los Alamitos, CA 90721 5057

S. California Genealogical Society, P.O. Box 4377, Burbank, CA 91503

194

Appendix B: Resources

S. F. Bay Area Jewish Genealogical Society, 3916 Louis Rd., Palo Alto, CA 94303 4541

Sacramento German Genealogical Society, P.O. Box 660061, Sacramento, CA 95866

San Bernardino Valley Genealogical Society, P.O. Box 26020, San Bernardino, CA 92406

San Diego Genealogical Society, 2925 Kalmia St., San Diego, CA 92104

San Fernando Valley Genealogical Society, 21904 Kingsbury St., Chatsworth, CA 91311

San Joaquin Genealogical Society, P.O. Box 4817, Stockton, CA 95204

San Luis Obispo County Genealogical Society Inc., P.O. Box 4, Atascadero, CA 93423

San Mateo Genealogical Society, P.O. Box 5083, San Mateo, CA 94402

San Ramon Valley Genealogical Society, P.O. Box 305, Diablo, CA 94528

Santa Barbara Genealogical Society, P.O. Box 1303, Goleta, CA 93116

Santa Clara County Historical & Genealogical Society, 2635 Homestead Rd., Santa Clara, CA 95051

Santa Cruz Genealogical Society, P.O. Box 72, Santa Cruz, CA 95063

Santa Maria Valley Genealogical Society, P.O. Box 1215, Santa Maria, CA 93456

Sar San Franscisco Chap, 898 Cordilleras Ave., San Carlos, CA 94070

Sequoia Genealogical Society Inc., P.O. Box 3473, Visalia, CA 93278

Southern California O.G.S., P.O. Box 5057, Los Alamitos, CA 90721 5057

Soc of California Pioneers, 456 Mcallister St., San Francisco, CA 94102

Soc of Mayflower Desc of Calif, 405 14th St. Terr Level, Oakland, CA 94612

Solano County Genealogical Society Inc., P.O. Box 2494, Fairfield, CA 94533

Sonoma County Genealogical Society, P.O. Box 2273, Santa Rosa, CA 95405

Sons of the Rev Library, 600 S. Central Ave., Glendale, CA 91204

South Bay Cities Genealogical Society, P.O. Box 11069, Torrance, CA 90510 9998

Stanislaus County Genealogical Society, P.O. Box 4735, Modesto, CA 95352

State Archives (Genealogy), 1020 O St. Rm 200, Sacramento, CA 95814

State Library (Genealogy), P.O. Box 942837, Sacramento, CA 94237 0001

Sutro Library, 480 Winston, San Francisco, CA 94132

Sutter-Yuba Genealogical Society, P.O. Box 1274, Yuba City, CA 95991

Taft Genealogical Society, P.O. Box 7411, Taft, CA 93268

Tehama Genealogical & Historical Society, P.O. Box 415, Red Bluff, CA 96080

Trw Genealogical Society, One Space Park S1435, Redondo Beach, CA 90278

Tuolumne County Genealogical Society, P.O. Box 3956, Sonora, CA 95370

Vandenberg Genealogical Society, P.O. Box 814, Lompoc, CA 93438

Ventura County Genealogical Library, 651 E. Main St., Ventura, CA 93003

Ventura County Genealogical Society, P.O. Box 24608, Ventura, CA 93002

Whittier Area Genealogical Society, 5821« Greenleaf Ave., Whittier, CA 90601

Yorba Linda Genealogical Society, 44751 Liibra Place, Yorba Linda, CA 92686

Yucaipa Valley Genealogical Society, P.O. Box 32, Yucaipa, CA 92399

Ancestor Seekers Genealogical Society, P.O. Box 693, Castle Rock, CO 80104

Archuleta County Genealogical Society, P.O. Box 1611, Pagosa Springs, CO 81147

Aurora Genealogical Society of Colorado, P.O. Box 31439, Aurora, CO 80041

Boulder Colorado Genealogical Group, 856 Applewood Dr., Lafayette, CO 80026

Boulder Genealogical Society, P.O. Box 3246, Boulder, CO 80307

Brighton Genealogical Society, P.O. Box 1005, Brighton, CO 80601

Colorado Council of Genealogical Societies, P.O. Box 24379, Denver, CO 80224

Colorado Genealogical Society, P.O. Box 9218, Denver, CO 80209

Colorado O.G.S., P.O. Box 1106, Longmont, CO 80502 1106

Appendix B: Resources

Colorado Society S.A.R., P.O. Box 9671, Denver, CO 80209

Columbine Genealogical & Historical Society Inc., P.O. Box 2074, Littleton, CO 80161

Estes Park Genealogical Society, 2517 Longview Dr., Estes Park, CO 80517

Foothills Genealogical Society of Colorado, P.O. Box 15382, Lakewood, CO 80215

Fore-Kin Trails Genealogical Society, P.O. Box 1024, Montrose, CO 81402

Friend Genealogical Library, 1448 Que St., Penrose, CO 81240

Genealogical Society of Hispanic America, P.O. Box K, Denver, CO 80209

High Country Genealogical Society, P.O. Box 576, Gunnison, CO 81230

Larimer County Genealogical Society, P.O. Box 9502, Ft. Collins, CO 80525 9502

Library (Genealogy), Colorado College, Colorado Springs, CO 80903

Library (Genealogy), University of Colorado, Boulder, CO 80304

Logan County Genealogical Society, P.O. Box 294, Sterling, CO 80751

Longmont Genealogical Society, P.O. Box 6081, Longmont, CO 80501

Mesa County Genealogical Society, Box 1506, Grand Junction, CO 81502

Morgan County Genealogical Society, 3 Princeton Ct, Brush, CO 80723

Ouray Genealogical Society, Box 494, Ouray, CO 81427

Pikes Peak Genealogical Society, P.O. Box 1262, Colorado Springs, CO 80901

Prowers County Genealogical Society, P.O. Box 175, Lamar, CO 81052

Public Library (Genealogy), 1000 Canyon Blvd., Boulder, CO 80302

Public Library (Genealogy), 1357 Broadway, Denver, CO 80203

Public Library (Genealogy), 20 N. Cascade, Colorado Springs, CO 80902

Public Library (Genealogy), 2227 23rd Ave., Greeley, CO 80631

Public Library (Genealogy), 919 7th St., Greeley, CO 80631

Public Library (Genealogy), 1125 Pine St., Boulder, CO 80306

Public Library (Genealogy), 100 Abriendo Ave., Pueblo, CO 81005

Public Library (Genealogy), City Hall, Montrose, CO 81401

Public Library (Genealogy), 21 W. Kiowa St., Colorado Springs, CO 80903

San Luis Valley Genealogical Society, P.O. Box 911, Alamosa, CO 81101 0911

Sisson Memorial Library (Genealogy), P.O. Box 849, Pagosa Springs, CO 81147

Southeastern Colorado Genealogical Society Inc., P.O. Box 4086, Pueblo, CO 81003

Stagecoach Library (Genealogy), 1840 S. Wolcott Ct, Denver, CO 80219

Weld County Genealogical Society, P.O. Box 278, Greeley, CO 80631

White River Trace Genealogical Society, 425 12th St., Meeker, CO 81641

Yuma Area Genealogical Society, P.O. Box 24, Yuma, CO 80759

College Library (Genealogy), 300 Summit St., Hartford, CT 06106

College Library (Genealogy), Mohegan Ave., New London, CT 06320

Connecticut Historical Society, 1 Elizabeth St., Hartford, CT 06105

Ct Society of Genealogical Inc., P.O. Box 435, Glastonbury, CT 06033

Farmington Museum (Genealogy), 37 High St., Farmington, CT 06032

Ferguson Library (Genealogy), 96 Broad St., Stamford, CT 06901

Fr-Can Genealogical Society of Ct, P.O. Box G45, Tolland, CT 06084

Indian/Colonial Research Ctr (Genealogy), Old Mystic, CT 06372

Jewish Genealogical Society of Ct, 17 Salem Walk, Milford, CT 06460

Middlesex Genealogical Society, 45 Old Kings Hwy, Darien, CT 06820

New Haven Colony Historical Society, 114 Whitney Ave., New Haven, CT 06510

Polish Genealogical Society of Ct, 8 Lyle Rd., New Britain, CT 06053

Public Library (Genealogy), 1080 Old Post Rd., Fairfield, CT 06430

Public Library (Genealogy), 840 Main St., East Hartford, CT 06108

Appendix B: Resources

Public Library (Genealogy), 46 Church St., Seymour, CT 06483

Public Library (Genealogy), 925 Broad St., Bridgeport, CT 06603

Public Library (Genealogy), 50 North St., Suffield, CT 06078

Public Library (Genealogy), Lyme St., Old Lyme, CT 06371

Public Library (Genealogy), 20 S. Main St., West Hartford, CT 06107

Public Library (Genealogy), 20 High St., New Britain, CT 06050

Public Library (Genealogy), 133 Elm St., New Haven, CT 06510

Public Library (Genealogy), 5 High St., Bristol, CT 06010

Public Library (Genealogy), 205 Main St., West Hartford, CT 06107

Public Library (Genealogy), 134 Newfield St., Middletown, CT 06457

Public Library (Genealogy), 63 Huntington St., New London, CT 06320

Public Library (Genealogy), 720 Pequot Ave., Southport, CT 06490

Public Library (Genealogy), 170 Main St., Danbury, CT 06810

Public Library (Genealogy), 261 Main St., Norwich, CT 06360

Public Library (Genealogy), 25 Main St., Newtown, CT 06470

Public Library (Genealogy), 267 Grand St., Waterbury, CT 06702

Public Library (Genealogy), 255 Main St., Southington, CT 06489

Public Library (Genealogy), 500 Main St., Hartford, CT 06103

Public Library (Genealogy), Hill Rd., Groton, CT 06340

Public Library (Genealogy), 50 N. Main St., Hartford, CT 06103

Soc of Mayflower Desc In Conn, 36 Arundel Ave., Hartford, CT 06107

Southington Genealogical Society, 239 Main St., Southington, CT 06489

Stamford Genealogical Society Inc., Box 249, Stamford, CT 06904

State Library (Genealogy), 231 Capitol Ave., Hartford, CT 06115

University Library (Genealogy), Box 1603A Yale Station, New Haven, CT 06520

Anderson House Library (Genealogy), 2118 Massachusetts Ave. N.W., Washington, DC 20008

Libr of Congress Genealogical Rm, Thomas Jefferson Annex, Washington, DC 20540

National Institute on Genealogical Research, P.O. Box 14274, Washington, DC 20044 4274

National Society Daughters of American Colonists, 2205 Massachusetts Ave. N.W., Washington, DC 20008

NSDAR Library, 1776 D St. N.W., Washington, DC 20006

Public Library (Genealogy), 901 G St. N.W., Washington, DC 20001

Delaware Genealogical Society, 505 Market St. Mall, Wilmington, DE 19801

Delaware Society S.A.R., P.O. Box 2169, Wilmington, DE 19899

Free Library (Genealogy), 10th & Market Sts., Wilmington, DE 19801

Library (Genealogy), University of Delaware, Newark, DE 19711

State Archives (Genealogy), Hall of Records, Dover, DE 19901

Alachua County Genealogical Society, P.O. Box 12078 University Station, Gainesville, FL 32604

Bay County Genealogical Society, P.O. Box 662, Panama City, FL 32401

Bonita Springs Genealogical Club, 27312 Shriver Ave. S.E., Bonita Springs, FL 33923

Brevard Genealogical Society, P.O. Box 1123, Cocoa, FL 32922

Central Florida Genealogical & Historical Society, P.O. Box 177, Orlando, FL 32802

Charlotte County Genealogical Society, P.O. Box 2682, Port Charlotte, FL 33952

Citrus County Genealogical Society, Rm 102 Old Courthouse, Inverness, FL 32650

Desoto Corr Institute Library (Genealogy), P.O. Box 1072, Arcadia, FL 33821

Florida Chapter O.G.S., 3809 Esplanade Ct, Tampa, FL 33624 4756

Florida Genealogical Society, P.O. Box 18624, Tampa, FL 33679

Florida Society of Genealogical Research, 8461 54th St., Pinellas Park, FL 33565

Florida State Genealogical Society, P.O. Box 10249, Tallahassee, FL 32302

Appendix B

197

Appendix B: Resources

Genealogical Group of Seminole Co., P.O. Box 2148, Casselberry, FL 32707

Genealogical Society of Broward County Inc., P.O. Box 485, Fort Lauderdale, FL 33302

Genealogical Society of Collier Co., P.O. Box 7933, Naples, FL 33941

Genealogical Society of Greater Miami, P.O. Box 162905, Miami, FL 33116 2905

Genealogical Society of Hernando Co., P.O. Box 1793, Brooksville, FL 34605 1793

Genealogical Society of North Brevard, P.O. Box 897, Titusville, FL 32780

Genealogical Society of Okaloosa Co., P.O. Box 1175, Fort Walton Beach, FL 32549

Genealogical Society of Okeechobee, P.O. Box 731, Okeechobee, FL 34973

Genealogical Society of Santa Rosa Co., 805 Alabama St., Milton, FL 32570

Genealogical Society of Sarasota Inc., P.O. Box 1917, Sarasota, FL 34230

Genealogical Society of Southern Brevard, P.O. Box 786, Melbourne, FL 32902

Geneva Historical & Genealogical Society, P.O. Box 145, Geneva, FL 32732

Highlands County Genealogical Society, 116 E. Main St., Avon Park, FL 33825

Historical & Genealogical Library, 100 E. Main St., Bartow, FL 33830

Historic Ocala/marion County Genealogical Society, P.O. Box 1206, Ocala, FL 32678 1206

Historical & Genealogical Library, County Courthouse, Tampa, FL 33602

Imperial Polk Genealogical Society, P.O. Box 10, Kathleen, FL 33849 0045

Jewish Genealogical Society of Broward Co., 1859 N. Pine Island Rd. #128, Ft. Lauderdale, FL 33322

Jewish Genealogical Society of Greater Miami, 9370 S.W. 88th Terr, Miami, FL 33176

Jewish Genealogical Society of Miami, 6310 S.W. 33 St., Miami, FL 33155

Keystone Genealogical Society, P.O. Box 50, Monticello, FL 32344

Lake County Kinseekers Genealogical Society, P.O. Box 2711, Leesburg, FL 34729 2711

Lee County Genealogical Society, 921 S.W. 39th Terr, Cape Coral, FL 33914

Lehigh Acres Genealogical Society, P.O. Box 965, Lehigh Acres, FL 33936

Manasota Genealogical Society, 1405 4th Ave. N., Bradenton, FL 34206

Osceola County Dept. Genealogical Research, 326 Eastern Ave., Saint Cloud, FL 34769

Osceola County Historical Society, 1750 Palmetto Dr., Kissimmee, FL 34743

Palm Beach County Genealogical Society Inc., P.O. Box 1746, W. Palm Beach, FL 33402

Public Library (Genealogy), 10 N. Rosalind Ave., Orlando, FL 32801

Public Library (Genealogy), 1001 Blvd of the Arts, Sarasota, FL 34277

Public Library (Genealogy), 1301 Barcarrota Blvd W., Bradenton, FL 34205

Public Library (Genealogy), 1 Biscayne Blvd N., Miami, FL 33132

Public Library (Genealogy), 222 E. University Ave., Gainesville, FL 32601

Public Library (Genealogy), 2050 Lee St., Fort Myers, FL 33901

Public Library (Genealogy), 130 E. Howry Ave., Deland, FL 32724

Public Library (Genealogy), 122 N. Ocean Ct, Jacksonville, FL 32202

Public Library (Genealogy), 216 Reid St., Palatka, FL 32177

Public Library (Genealogy), 430 Delannoy Ave., Cocoa, FL 32922

Public Library (Genealogy), 26876 Pine Ave., Bonita Springs, FL 33923

Public Library (Genealogy), 1600 21St St., Vero Beach, FL 32960

Public Library (Genealogy), 900 N. Ashley St., Tampa, FL 33602

Public Library (Genealogy), 540 E. Fee St., Melbourne, FL 32901

Public Library (Genealogy), Central Ave., Naples, FL 33940

Public Library (Genealogy), City Island, Daytona Beach, FL 32114

Putnam County Genealogical Society, P.O. Box 418, Palatka, FL 32178

Ridge Genealogical Society, P.O. Box 477, Babson Park, FL 33827

Southern Hillsborough Genealogists, Rt. 1 Box 400, Palmetto, FL 34221

Appendix B: Resources

Southern Genealogical Exchange, 1580 Blanding Blvd., Jacksonville, FL 32203

St. Augustine Genealogical Society, 1960 N. Ponce De Leon Blvd., Saint Augustine, FL 32084

State Library (Genealogy), R A Gray Bldg., Tallahassee, FL 32301

Suncoast Genealogical Society, P.O. Box 977, Crystal Beach, FL 34681

Tallahassee Genealogical Society, P.O. Box 4371, Tallahassee, FL 32315

Treasure Coast Genealogical Society, P.O. Box 3401, Fort Pierce, FL 34948

Volusia Genealogical & Historical Society, P.O. Box 2039, Daytona Beach, FL 32115

West Florida Genealogical Society, P.O. Box 947, Pensacola, FL 32594 0947

West Pasco Genealogical Society, 2225 23rd Ct, New Port Richey, FL 34655

Yonge Library (Genealogy), University of Florida, Gainesville, FL 32601

Augusta Genealogical Society, P.O. Box 3743, Augusta, GA 30904

Bulloch County Historical Society, P.O. Box 42, Statesboro, GA 30458

Carroll County Genealogical Society, P.O. Box 576, Carrollton, GA 30117

Central Georgia Genealogical Society, P.O. Box 2024, Warner Robins, GA 31093

Clark-Oconee Genealogical Society, P.O. Box 6403, Athens, GA 30604

Cobb County Genealogical Society, P.O. Box 1413, Marietta, GA 30061

Coweta Chatter Genealogical & Historical Society, Hwy 54 Rt. 1, Sharpsburg, GA 30277

Coweta County Genealogical Society Inc., P.O. Box 1014, Newnan, GA 30264

Delta Genealogical Society, 504 Mcfarland Ave., Rossville, GA 30741

Delta Genealogical Society, 504 Mcfarland Ave., Rossville, GA 30741

Genealogical Society of Original Muscogee Co., 120 Bradley Dr., Columbus, GA 31906

Georgia Genealogical Society, P.O. Box 38066, Atlanta, GA 30334

Georgia Society S.A.R., 2869 Reese Rd., Columbus, GA 31907

Gs/of Henry & Clayton Cos, P.O. Box 1296, Mcdonough, GA 30253

Huxford Genealogical Society, P.O. Box 595, Homerville, GA 31634

Muscogee Genealogical Society, P.O. Box 761, Columbus, GA 31902

Northeast Ga Historical & Genealogical Society, P.O. Box 907643, Gainesville, GA 30501 0911

N.W. Georgia Historical & Genealogical Society, P.O. Box 5063, Rome, GA 30161

Odom Genealogical Library, 204 5th St. S.E., Moultrie, GA 31768

Public Library (Genealogy), 1180 Washington Ave., Macon, GA 31201

Public Library (Genealogy), Margaret Mitchell Sq, Atlanta, GA 30303

Public Library (Genealogy), 120 W. Dougherty St., Athens, GA 30601

Public Library (Genealogy), Shotwell & Monroe, Bainbridge, GA 31717

Public Library (Genealogy), 208 Gloucester St., Brunswick, GA 31521

Public Library (Genealogy), Watkinsville, GA 30677

Public Library (Genealogy), 902 Greene St., Augusta, GA 30901

Public Library (Genealogy), Pike St., Lawrenceville, GA 30245

Public Library (Genealogy), 127 N. Main, Gainesville, GA 30501

Public Library (Genealogy), 617 E. Ward St., Douglas, GA 31533

Public Library (Genealogy), Winder, GA 30680

Public Library (Genealogy), 207 5th Ave. N.E., Eastman, GA 31023

Public Library (Genealogy), 215 Sycamore St., Decatur, GA 30030

Public Library (Genealogy), 124 S. Main St., Statesboro, GA 30458

Public Library (Genealogy), 401 Lee Ave., Waycross, GA 31501

Public Library (Genealogy), 2002 Bull St., Savannah, GA 31401

Public Library (Genealogy), 218 Perry St., Rome, GA 30161

Public Library (Genealogy), 30 Atlanta St., Marietta, GA 30060

Appendix B: Resources

Public Library (Genealogy), Bradley Dr., Columbus, GA 31906

Richard Ratcliff Genealogical Society, Rt. 5 Box 454, Tocca, GA 30577

Savannah Area Genealogical Society, P.O. Box 15385, Savannah, GA 31416

Savannah Historical Society, 501 Whittaker St., Savannah, GA 31401

Savannah Valley River Genealogical Society, County Library - Benson St., Hartwell, GA 30643

Southern Georgia Genealogical Society, P.O. Box 246, Ochlocknee, GA 31773

State Archives (Genealogy), 330 Capitol Ave., Atlanta, GA 30334

State Library (Genealogy), 301 State Judicial Bldg., Atlanta, GA 30334

S.W. Georgia Genealogical Society, P.O. Box 4672, Albany, GA 31706

West Georgia Genealogical Society, P.O. Box 1051, La Grange, GA 30241

D.A.R. Memorial Library, 1914 Makiki Hts Dr., Honolulu, HI 96822

Hawaii Society S.A.R., 1564 Piikea St., Honolulu, HI 96818

Hawaiian Historical Society, 560 Kawaiahao St., Honolulu, HI 96813

Libr of Hawaii (Genealogy), King & Punchbowl Sts., Honolulu, HI 96813

Adair County Anquestors Genealogical Society, Rt. 1 Box 23, Menlo, IA 50164

Adams County Genealogical Society, P.O. Box 117, Prescott, IA 50859

Appanoose County Genealogical Society, 1009 Shamrock #402, Centerville, IA 52544

Boone County Genealogical Society, Box 453, Boone, IA 50036

Botna Valley Genealogical Society, P.O. Box 633, Oakland, IA 51560

Bremer County Genealogical Society, Rt. 1 Box 132, Plainfield, IA 50666

Buena Vista Genealogical Society, P.O. Box 811, Storm Lake, IA 50588

Carroll County Genealogical Society, P.O. Box 21, Carroll, IA 51401

Cass County Genealogical Society, 706 Hazel St., Atlantic, IA 50022

Central Iowa Genealogical Society, Box 945, Marshalltown, IA 50158

Cherokee County Tree Stumpers, P.O. Box 247, Cleghorn, IA 51014

Chickasaw County Genealogical Society, P.O. Box 434, New Hampton, IA 50659

Clarke County Genealogical Society, R.R. 2 Box 5, Murray, IA 50174

Clayton County Genealogical Society, P.O. Box 846, Elkader, IA 52043

Crawford County Genealogical Society, P.O. Box 26, Vail, IA 51465

Davis County Genealogical Society, 701 E. Main St., Bloomfield, IA 52537

Delaware County Genealogical Society, 200 E. Main St., Manchester, IA 52057

Des Moines County Genealogical Society, P.O. Box 493, Burlington, IA 52601

Dubuque County Genealogical Society, P.O. Box 13, Dubuque, IA 52004

Franklin Genealogical Society of Hampton, Rt. 1 Box 119, Geneva, IA 50633

Gateway Genealogical Society, 618 14th Ave., Camanche, IA 52730

Gateway Society, 380 23rd Place, Clinton, IA 52732

Greater Sioux County Genealogical Society, 327 First Ave. N.E., Sioux Center, IA 51250

Greene County Genealogical Society, P.O. Box 133, Jefferson, IA 50129 0133

Guthrie County Genealogical Society, P.O. Box 96, Jamaica, IA 50128

Hancock County Genealogical Society, Box 81, Klemme, IA 50449

Hardin County Genealogical Society, P.O. Box 252, Eldora, IA 50627

Harrison County Genealogical Society, 222 N. 6th, Missouri Valley, IA 51555

Henry County Genealogical Society, P.O. Box 81, Mount Pleasant, IA 52641

Historical Museum (Genealogy), 210 W. Main St., Ottumwa, IA 52501

ILL-IA-MO Searcher, R.R. 1 Box 182, Keokuk, IA 52632

Iowa City Genealogical Society, Box 822, Iowa City, IA 52244

Iowa Genealogical Society, P.O. Box 7735, Des Moines, IA 50322 7735

Appendix B: Resources

Iowa Historical & Genealogical Library, E. 12th St. & Grand Ave., Des Moines, IA 50319

Iowa Lakes Genealogical Society, Box 91, Everly, IA 51338

Iowa Society S.A.R., 227 Clinton St., Boone, IA 50036

Jackson County Genealogical Society, Box 1065, Maquoketa, IA 52060

Jasper County Genealogical Society, P.O. Box 163, Newton, IA 50208

Jefferson County Genealogical Society, Rt. 1 Box 50, Fairfield, IA 52556

Jones County Genealogical Society, P.O. Box 174, Anamosa, IA 52205

Keo-Mah Genealogical Society, P.O. Box 616, Oskaloosa, IA 52577 0616

Key City Genealogical Society, P.O. Box 13, Dubuque, IA 52801

Lee County Genealogical Society of Ia, P.O. Box 303, Keokuk, IA 52632 0303

Lime Creek Genealogical Society, 115 E. L St., Forest City, IA 50436

Linn County Heritage Society, P.O. Box 175, Cedar Rapids, IA 52406

Madison County Genealogical Society, P.O. Box 26, Winterset, IA 50273 0026

Marion County Genealogical Society, P.O. Box 385, Knoxville, IA 50138

Mid-America Genealogical Society, P.O. Box 316, Davenport, IA 52801

Mills County Genealogical Society, 109 N. Vine St., Glenwood, IA 51534

Monroe County Genealogical Society, 203 Benton Ave., Albia, IA 52531

Museum (Genealogy), Park Ave. & South St., Waterloo, IA 50701

Museum Library (Genealogy), Box 84, Toledo, IA 52342

Nishnabotna Genealogical Society, Rt. 2 Box 129, Harlan, IA 51537

North Central Iowa Genealogical Society, P.O. Box 237, Mason City, IA 50401 0237

Northeast Iowa Genealogical Society, 503 South St., Waterloo, IA 50701

Northwest Iowa Genealogical Society, 46 First St. S.W., Le Mars, IA 51031

Old Fort Genealogical Society, P.O. Box 1, Fort Madison, IA 52627

Page County Genealogical Society, Rt. 2 Box 236, Shenandoah, IA 51610

Palo Alto County Genealogical Society, 207 N. Wallace St., Emmetsburg, IA 50536

Pioneer Sons & Daughters Genealogical Society, P.O. Box 2103, Des Moines, IA 50310

Poweshiek County Historical & Genealogical Society, P.O. Box 280, Montezuma, IA 50171

Public Library (Genealogy), S. Market & 2nd St., Oskaloosa, IA 52577

Public Library (Genealogy), 6th & Jackson Sts., Sioux City, IA 51101

Public Library (Genealogy), Donnellson, IA 52625

Public Library (Genealogy), Glenwood, IA 51534

Public Library (Genealogy), 702 Greene St., Boone, IA 50036

Public Library (Genealogy), 501 N. 4th St., Burlington, IA 52601

Public Library (Genealogy), 46 1St St. S.W., Le Mars, IA 51031

Public Library (Genealogy), 7305 Aurora Ave., Urbandale, IA 50322

Public Library (Genealogy), 36 N. Center St., Marshalltown, IA 50158

Public Library (Genealogy), 21 E. 3rd St., Spencer, IA 51301

Public Library (Genealogy), 21 E. 3rd St., Spencer, IA 51301

Public Library (Genealogy), 310 N. Maple, Creston, IA 50801

Public Library (Genealogy), Mason City, IA 50401

Ringgold County Genealogical Society, 608 S. Elm St., Creston, IA 50801 3613

Sac County Genealogical Society, P.O. Box 234, Lytton, IA 50561

Scott County Genealogical Society, P.O. Box 3132, Davenport, IA 52808

Story County Genealogical Society, 125 S. 3rd St., Ames, IA 50010

Tama County Tracers Genealogical Society, P.O. Box 84 200 North Broadway, Toledo, IA 52342

Taylor County Genealogical Society, P.O. Box 8, Gravity, IA 50848

Union County Genealogical Society, 310 N. Maple St., Creston, IA 50801

Appendix B: Resources

Wapello County Genealogical Society, P.O. Box 163, Ottumwa, IA 52501

Warren County Genealogical Society, Rt. 2 802 Kennedy St., Indianola, IA 50125

Washington Genealogical Society, Box 446, Washington, IA 52353

Wayne County Genealogical Society, 304 N. Franklin, Corydon, IA 50060

Webster County Genealogical Society, P.O. Box 1584, Fort Dodge, IA 50501

West Liberty Historical Society, 600 E. 4th, West Liberty, IA 52776

Woodbury County Genealogical Society, P.O. Box 624, Sioux City, IA 51102

Wright County Genealogical Searchers, P.O. Box 225, Clarion, IA 50525

Bonner County Genealogical Society, P.O. Box 27, Dover, ID 83825

Caldwell Genealogical Group, 3504 S. Illinois, Caldwell, ID 83605

Family Scanner Chapter Igs, P.O. Box 581, Caldwell, ID 83605

Idaho County Chapter Igs, 215 W. North, Grangeville, ID 83530

Idaho Genealogical Society, P.O. Box 326, Grangeville, ID 83530

Idaho Genealogical Society Inc., 4620 Overland Rd. Rm 204, Boise, ID 83705 2867

Idaho Genealogical Library, 325 W. State, Boise, ID 83702

Kamiak Genealogical Society, Box 322, Kamiah, ID 83536

Kootenai County Genealogical Society, 8385 N. Government Way, Hayden Lake, ID 83854

Latah County Genealogical Society, 327 E. 2Nd, Moscow, ID 83843

Library (Genealogy), Lewis-Clark State College, Lewiston, ID 83501

Library (Genealogy), College of Southern Idaho, Twin Falls, ID 83301

Library (Genealogy), N.W. Nazerene College, Nampa, ID 83651

Library (Genealogy), Ricks College, Rexburg, ID 83440

Library (Genealogy), N. Idaho College, Coeur D'alene, ID 83814

Library (Genealogy), Idaho State University, Pocatello, ID 83209

Library (Genealogy), Boise State University, Boise, ID 83725

Library (Genealogy), College of Idaho, Caldwell, ID 83605

Library (Genealogy), Iniv of Idaho, Moscow, ID 83843

Magic Valley Chapter Igs, Rt. 2 770 S. River Dr., Heyburn, ID 83336

North Idaho Genealogical Society, C/o 1623 Birch Ave., Coeur D'alene, ID 83814

Pocatello Branch Genealogical Society, 156 1/2 S. 6th Ave., Pocatello, ID 83201

Public Library (Genealogy), Mccall, ID 83638

Public Library (Genealogy), 533 Thain Rd., Lewiston, ID 83501

Shoshone County Genealogical Society, P.O. Box 183, Kellogg, ID 83837

Treasure Valley Chapter Igs, 325 W. State St., Boise, ID 83702

Twin Rivers Genealogical Society, P.O. Box 386, Lewiston, ID 83501

Upper Snake River Valley Historical Society, P.O. Box 244, Rexburg, ID 83440

Valley County Genealogical Society, P.O. Box 697, Cascade, ID 83611

Blackhawk County Genealogical Society, P.O. Box 3913, Rock Island, IL 61204 3913

Bond County Genealogical Society, P.O. Box 172, Greenville, IL 62246

Carnegie Public Library (Genealogy), 6th and Van Buren Sts., Charleston, IL 61920

Carroll County Genealogical Society, P.O. Box 347, Savanna, IL 61074

Champaign County Genealogical Society, 201 S. Race, Urbana, IL 61801

Chicago Genealogical Society, P.O. Box 1160, Chicago, IL 60690

Christian County Genealogical Society, P.O. Box 174, Taylorville, IL 62568

Clay County Genealogical Society, Box 94, Louisville, IL 62858

Coles County Genealogical Society, P.O. Box 225, Charleston, IL 61920

Cumberland County Historical & Genealogical Society, Greenup, IL 62428

Decatur Genealogical Society, P.O. Box 1548, Decatur, IL 62526

Appendix B: Resources

Decatur Genealogical Library, 356 N. Main St., Decatur, IL 62523

Douglas County Genealogical Society, P.O. Box 113, Tuscola, IL 61953

Dunton Genealogical Society, 500 N. Dunton, Arlington Heights, IL 60004

Dupage County Genealogical Society, P.O. Box 133, Lombard, IL 60148

Edgar County Genealogical Society, P.O. Box 304, Paris, IL 61944

Edwards County Genealogical Society, P.O. Box 205, Albion, IL 62257

Effingham County Genealogical Society, P.O. Box 1166, Effingham, IL 62401

Elgin Genealogical Society, P.O. Box 1418, Elgin, IL 60121

Fayette County Genealogical Society, Box 177, Vandalia, IL 62471

Federation of Genealogical Societies, P.O. Box 271, Western Springs, IL 60558 0271

Fellowship of Bethren Genealogists, 1451 Dundee Ave., Elgin, IL 60120

Fox Valley Genealogical Society, 705 N. Brainard St., Naperville, IL 60563

Frankfort Area Genealogical Society, P.O. Box 427, West Frankfort, IL 62896

Freeburg Historical & Genealogical Society, Box 69, Freeburg, IL 62243

Freeport Public Library Genealogical Rm, 314 W. Stephenson St., Freeport, IL 61032

Ft. Lamotte Genealogical & Historical Society, Lamotte Township Library, Palestine, IL 62451

Fulton County Historical & Genealogical Society, 45 N. Park Dr., Canton, IL 61520

Genealogical & Historical Research Ctr, 320 E. 161St Place, South Holland, IL 60473

Genealogical Committee/ Stephenson County Historical Society, 110 Coates Place, Freeport, IL 61032

Genealogical Forum of Elmhurst, 120 E. Park, Elmhurst, IL 60126

Genealogical Guild of Lasalle Co., P.O. Box 278, Utica, IL 61373

Genealogical Society of Dekalb Co., P.O. Box 295, Sycamore, IL 60178

Genealogical Society of Southern Il, Lohn A Logan College Rt. 2, Carterville, IL 62918

Great River Genealogical Society, Quincy Public Library, Quincy, IL 62302

Greene County Historical & Genealogical Society, P.O. Box 137, Carrollton, IL 62016

Hancock County Historical Society, Box 68, Carthage, IL 62321 0068

Henry County Genealogical Society, P.O. Box 346, Kewanee, IL 61443

Henry Historical & Genealogical Society, 610 North St., Henry, IL 61537

Ill Chapter Palatines to America, 5753 Washington St., Downers Grove, IL 60516 1310

Ill Mennonite Historical & Genealogical Society, P.O. Box 819, Metamora, IL 61548

Illiana Genealogical & Historical Society, P.O. Box 207, Danville, IL 61834

Illiana Jewish Genealogical Society, 3033 Bob-o-Link Rd., Flossmoor, IL 60422

Illinois State Genealogical Society, P.O. Box 10195, Springfield, IL 62791

Iroquois County Genealogical Society, 103 W. Chery St., Watseka, IL 60970

Jacksonville Area Genealogical & Historical Society, P.O. Box 21, Jacksonville, IL 62651

Jasper County Genealogical & Historical Society, Newton Public Library, Newton, IL 62448

Jewish Genealogical Society of Illinoia, 818 Mansfield Ct, Schaumburg, IL 60194

Kane County Genealogical Society, P.O. Box 504, Geneva, IL 60134

Kankakee Valley Genealogical Society, P.O. Box 442, Bourbonnais, IL 60914

Kendall County Genealogical Society, P.O. Box 1086, Oswego, IL 60543

Kishwaukee Genealogists, P.O. Box 5503, Rockford, IL 61125 0503

Knox County Genealogical Society, P.O. Box 13, Galesburg, IL 61401

Laharpe Historical & Genealogical Society, P.O. Box 289, Laharpe, IL 61450

Lake County Genealogical Society, P.O. Box 721, Libertyville, IL 60048 0721

Lasalle County Genealogical Guild, Box 534, Ottawa, IL 61350

Appendix B: Resources

Lawrence County Genealogical Society, Rt. 1 Box 44, Bridgeport, IL 62417

Lewis & Clark Genealogical Society, P.O. Box 485, Godfrey, IL 62035

Lexington Genealogical & Historical Society, 318 W. Main St., Lexington, IL 61753

Library (Genealogy), University of Illinois, Urbana, IL 61801

Logan County Genealogical Genealogical Society, P.O. Box 283, Lincoln, IL 62656

Macoupin County Genealogical Society, P.O. Box 95, Staunton, IL 62088

Madsion County Genealogical Society, P.O. Box 631, Edwardsville, IL 62025 0631

Marion County Genealogical & Historical Society, P.O. Box 342, Salem, IL 62881

Marissa Historical & Genealogical Society, P.O. Box 27, Marissa, IL 62257

Mason County Genealogical Society, P.O. Box 246, Havana, IL 62644

Mason County Lds Genealogical Project, Rt. 1 Box 193, Havana, IL 62644

Mcdonough County Genealogical Society, P.O. Box 202, Macomb, IL 61455

Mchenry County Genealogical Society, P.O. Box 184, Crystal Lake, IL 60039 0184

Mclean County Genealogical Society, P.O. Box 488, Normal, IL 61761

Mclean County Genealogical Society, Old County Courthouse, Bloomington, IL 61701

Montgomery County Genealogical Society, P.O. Box 212, Litchfield, IL 62056

Moultrie County Historical & Genealogical Society, P.O. Box Mm, Sullivan, IL 61951

Mt. Vernon Genealogical Society, 101 S. Seventh St., Mt. Vernon, IL 62864

Newberry Library - Genealogical, 60 W. Walton St., Chicago, IL 60610

North Suburban Genealogical Society, 768 Oak St., Winnetka, IL 60093

Northwest Sub Council of Genealogy, P.O. Box AC, Mt. Prospect, IL 60056

Odell Historical & Genealogical Society, P.O. Box 82, Odell, IL 60460

Ogle County Genealogical Society, P.O. Box 251, Oregon, IL 61061

Palatines to America Il Chap, P.O. Box 3884, Quincy, IL 62305

Peoria Genealogical Society, Box 1489, Peoria, IL 61655

Piatt County Historical & Genealogical Society, P.O. Box 123, Monticello, IL 61856

Pike & Calhoun Cos Genealogical Society, P.O. Box 104, Pleasant Hill, IL 62366

Polish Genealogical Society, 984 N. Milwaukee Ave., Chicago, IL 60622

Public Library (Gencalogy), 131 N. Chestnut, Assumption, IL 62510 0227

Public Library (Genealogy), 314 W. Stephenson St., Freeport, IL 61032

Public Library (Genealogy), 307 N. Vermillion St., Danville, IL 61832

Public Library (Genealogy), Charleston Ave. & 17th St., Mattoon, IL 61938

Public Library (Genealogy), 768 Oak St., Winnetka, IL 60093

Public Library (Genealogy), 1930 Glenview Rd., Glenview, IL 60025

Public Library (Genealogy), 106 W. Meek St., Abingdon, IL 61410

Public Library (Genealogy), 215 N. Wyman St., Rockford, IL 61101

Public Library (Genealogy), 202 E. Washington, Bloomington, IL 61701

Public Library (Genealogy), 2400 Gabriel Ave., Zion, IL 60099

Public Library (Genealogy), 215 S. 5th St., Vandalia, IL 62471

Public Library (Genealogy), P.O. Box 300, Channahon, IL 60410

Public Library (Genealogy), 107 N.E. Monroe St., Peoria, IL 61602

Public Library (Genealogy), N. Center St., Plano, IL 60545

Public Library (Genealogy), Galesburg, IL 61401

Public Library (Genealogy), Galena, IL 61036

Public Library (Genealogy), 60 West Side Sq, Monmouth, IL 61462

Public Library (Genealogy), 10 W. Cossitt, La Grange, IL 60525

Public Library (Genealogy), 200 N. Grove Ave., Elgin, IL 60120

Public Library (Genealogy), 4209 Joliet Ave., Lyons, IL 60534

Appendix B: Resources

Public Library (Genealogy), 306 W. Main, Staunton, IL 62088

Randolph County Genealogical Society, 600 State St. Rm 306, Chester, IL 62233

Richfield County Genealogical & Historical Society, Box 174, Olney, IL 62450

Rock Island County Genealogical Society, P.O. Box 632, Moline, IL 61265

Rockford Public Library Genealogical Rm, 215 N. Wyman St., Rockford, IL 61101

Saline County Genealogical Society, P.O. Box 4, Harrisburg, IL 62946

Sangamon County Genealogical Society, P.O. Box 1829, Springfield, IL 62705

Schuyler County Geneal Ctr, Madison & Congress, Rushville, IL 62681

Schuyler County Historical & Genealogical Society, 200 S. Congress St., Rushville, IL 62681

Schuyler-Brown Historical & Genealogical Society, P.O. Box 96, Rushville, IL 62681

Shelby County Historical & Genealogical Society, 151 S. Washington, Shelbyville, IL 62565

South Suburban Genealogical & Historical Society, P.O. Box 96, South Holland, IL 60473

St. Clair Genealogical Society, P.O. Box 431, Belleville, IL 62220

State Archives (Genealogy), Archives Bldg., Springfield, IL 62706

State Library (Genealogy), Old State Capitol, Springfield, IL 62706

Stephenson County Genealogical Society, P.O. Box 514, Freeport, IL 61032

Tazewell County Genealogical Society, P.O. Box 312, Pekin, IL 61555

Tinley Moraine Genealogists, P.O. Box 521, Tinley Park, IL 60477

Tri-Co Genealogical Society, P.O. Box 355, Augusta, IL 62311

Union County Genealogical & Historical Research Comm, 101 E. Spring St., Anna, IL 62906

Veteren's Home Library (Genealogy), 1707 N. 12th, Quincy, IL 62301

Vogel Genealogical Research Library, 305 1St St., Holcomb, IL 61043

Warren County Genealogical Society, P.O. Box 761, Monmouth, IL 61462 0761

Waverly Genealogical & Historical Society, P.O. Box 15, Waverly, IL 62692

Whiteside County Genealogists, Box 145, Sterling, IL 61081

Will/grundy County Genealogical Society, P.O. Box 24, Wilmington, IL 60481

Winnebago & Boone Cos Genealogical Society, P.O. Box 10166, Rockford, IL 61131 0166

Zion Genealogical Society, 2400 Gabriel Ave., Zion, IL 60099

Allen County Genealogical Society, P.O. Box 12003, Fort Wayne, IN 46862

Allen County Public Library, P.O. Box 2270, Ft. Wayne, IN 46801 2270

American Legn Nat Hq Library (Genealogy), 700 N. Pennsylvania St., Indianapolis, IN 46204

Bartholomew County Genealogical Society, P.O. Box 2455, Columbus, IN 47202

Brown County Genealogical Society, P.O. Box 1202, Nashville, IN 47448

Cass County Genealogical Society, P.O. Box 373, Logansport, IN 46947

Delaware County Historical Alliance, P.O. Box 1266, Muncie, IN 47308

Elkhart County Genealogical Society, 1812 Jeanwood Dr., Elkhart, IN 46514

Genealogical Sec Kosciusko County Historical Society, P.O. Box 1071, Warsaw, IN 46580

Hendricks County Genealogical Society, 101 S. Indiana St., Danville, IN 46122

Historical Ctr (Genealogy), 317 W. Monroe St., Plymouth, IN 46563

Howard County Genealogical Society, 220 N. Union, Kokomo, IN 46901

Indiana Society S.A.R., 5401 Central Ave., Indianapolis, IN 46220

Jackson County Genealogical Society, 415 S. Walnut St., Seymour, IN 47274

Laporte County Genealogical Society, 904 Indiana Ave., La Porte, IN 46350

Library (Genealogy), Goshen College, Goshen, IN 46526

Marion-Adams Genealogical Society, 308 Main St., Sheridan, IN 46069

Marshall County Genealogical Society, 317 W. Monroe, Plymouth, IN 46563

Appendix B: Resources

Miami County Genealogical Society, P.O. Box 542, Peru, IN 46970

Monroe County Genealogical Society, E. 6th St. & Washington, Bloomington, IN 47401

Montgomery County Historical Society Genealogical Sec, 222 S. Washington St., Crawfordsville, IN 47933

North Central Indiana Genealogical Society, 2300 Canterbury Dr., Kokomo, IN 46901

Noble County Genealogical Society, 109 N. York St., Albion, IN 46701

Northwest Territory Genealogical Society, Vincennes University, Vincennes, IN 47591

N.W. Indiana Genealogical Society, 103 Jefferson St., Valparaiso, IN 46383

Orange County Genealogical Society, P.O. Box 344, Paoli, IN 47454

Public Library (Genealogy), 600 S. Washington St., Marion, IN 46952

Public Library (Genealogy), 1 Library Sq, Terre Haute, IN 47807

Public Library (Genealogy), New Albany, IN 47150

Public Library (Genealogy), 106 N. Market St., Rockville, IN 47872

Public Library (Genealogy), 122 W. Wayne, South Bend, IN 46601

Public Library (Genealogy), 121 S. Riverside, Winamac, IN 46996

Public Library (Genealogy), 554 Locust St., Middletown, IN 47356

Public Library (Genealogy), E. North St., Winchester, IN 47394

Public Library (Genealogy), 21 1St Ave., Evansville, IN 47710

Public Library (Genealogy), 603 S. Jackson St., Auburn, IN 46706

Public Library (Genealogy), Worthington, IN 47471

Public Library (Genealogy), 101 S. Indiana St., Danville, IN 46122

Public Library (Genealogy), N.E. Court, Paoli, IN 47454

Public Library (Genealogy), N. Main St., Lynn, IN 47355

Public Library (Genealogy), 44 E. Park Dr., Huntington, IN 46750

Public Library (Genealogy), 208 W. Clinton St., Frankfort, IN 46041

Public Library (Genealogy), 315 E. Center St., Warsaw, IN 46580

Public Library (Genealogy), 100 E. 4th St., Michigan City, IN 46360

Public Library (Genealogy), 188 W. Hill St., Wabash, IN 46992

Public Library (Genealogy), 220 N. Main, Kokomo, IN 46901

Public Library (Genealogy), 16 S. 10th St., Noblesville, IN 46060

Public Library (Genealogy), 111 E. 12th St., Anderson, IN 46016

Public Library (Genealogy), 103 Jefferson St., Valparaiso, IN 46383

Public Library (Genealogy), 103 Jefferson St., Valparaiso, IN 46383

Public Library (Genealogy), 616 E. Broadway, Logansport, IN 46947

Public Library (Genealogy), S. Franklin St., Bloomfield, IN 47424

Public Library (Genealogy), 904 Indiana Ave., La Porte, IN 46350

Public Library (Genealogy), 1120 Stafford Rd., Plainfield, IN 46168

Public Library (Genealogy), N. Columbia St., Union City, IN 47390

Public Library (Genealogy), 420 W. Main St., Madison, IN 47250

Public Library (Genealogy), 127 E. Madison St., Tipton, IN 46072

Pulaski County Genealogical Society, Rt. 4 Box 121, Winamac, IN 46996

Randolph County Genealogical Society, Rt. 3, Winchester, IN 47394

South Bend Area Genealogical Society, P.O. Box 1222, South Bend, IN 46624

Southern In Genealogical Society, P.O. Box 665, New Albany, IN 47150

Speedway Genealogical Club, 5633 W. 25 St., Speedway, IN 46224

State Library (Genealogy), 140 N. Senate Ave., Indianapolis, IN 46204

State Library (Genealogy), 315 W. Ohio St., Indianapolis, IN 46202

Tippecanoe County Area Genealogical Society, 909 South St., Lafayette, IN 47901

Tri-State Genealogical Society, 21 First Ave., Evansville, IN 47741

Appendix B: Resources

Wabash Valley Genealogical Society Inc., P.O. Box 85, Terre Haute, IN 47808

Washington County Historical Society, 307 E. Market St., Salem, IN 47167

Wayne County Genealogical Society, 1150 N. A St., Richmond, IN 47374

Atchison County Genealogical Society, Public Library 4th & Kansas, Atchison, KS 66002

Barton County Genealogical Society Inc., P.O. Box 425, Great Bend, KS 67530

Bethel College Library (Genealogy), 300 E. 27th St., North Newton, KS 67117

Blue Valley Genealogical Society, P.O. Box 53, Marysville, KS 66508

Bluestem Genealogical Society, P.O. Box 582, Eureka, KS 67045

Branches & Twigs Genealogical Society, Rt. 1, Kingman, KS 67068

Canute Genealogical Society, 1000 S. Allen St., Chanute, KS 66720

Cherokee County Genealogical Society, P.O. Box 33, Columbus, KS 66725 0033

Cloud County Genealogical Society, Rt. 3, Concordia, KS 66901

Cowley County Genealogical Society, P.O. Box 102, Arkansas City, KS 67005

Crawford County Genealogical Society, 211 W. 4th St., Pittsburg, KS 66762

D.A.R. Kansas State Library, 303 University, Dodge City, KS 67801

Decatur County Genealogical Society, 307 N. Rodehaver, Oberlin, KS 67749

Douglas County Genealogical Society, P.O. Box 3664, Lawrence, KS 66046 0664

East Central Kansas Genealogical Society, P.O. Box 101, Garnett, KS 66032

Finney County Genealogical Society, P.O. Box 592, Garden City, KS 67846

Flint Hills Genealogical Society, P.O. Box 555, Emporia, KS 66801

Ft. Hays Genealogical Society, Forsyth Library F.H.S. University, Hays, KS 67601

Harper County Genealogical Society, Public Library - 10th & Oak, Harper, KS 67058

Historical Museum (Genealogy), 118 E. 6th St., Emporia, KS 66801

Hodgeman County Genealogical Society, P.O. Box 441, Jetmore, KS 67854

Jefferson County Genealogical Society, P.O. Box 174, Oskaloosa, KS 66066

Johnson County Genealogical Society Inc., P.O. Box 8057, Shawnee Mission, KS 66208

Kansas Genealogical Society, P.O. Box 103, Dodge City, KS 67801

Kansas Council Genealogical Society, P.O. Box 3858, Topeka, KS 66604 6858

Labette Genealogical Society, Box 826, Parsons, KS 67357

Leavenworth County Genealogical Society Inc., P.O. Box 362, Leavenworth, KS 66048

Liberal Area Genealogical Society, P.O. Box 1094, Liberal, KS 67905

Miami County Genealogical Society, P.O. Box 123, Paola, KS 66071

Midwest Historical & Genealogical Society Inc., P.O. Box 1121, Wichita, KS 67201

Montgomery County Genealogical Society, Box 444, Coffeyville, KS 67337

Morris County Genealogical Society, Box 42A Rt. 2, White City, KS 66872

North Central Kansas Genealogical Society, Box 251, Cawker City, KS 67430

Norton County Genealogical Society, P.O. Box 446, Norton, KS 67654

Old Fort Genealogical Society, 502 S. National, Fort Scott, KS 66701

Osage County Genealogical Society, P.O. Box 563, Lyndon, KS 66451

Osborne County Genealogical & Historical Society Inc., 307 West Main, Osborne, KS 67473

Phillips County Genealogical Society, Box 114, Phillipsburg, KS 67661

Public Library (Genealogy), 8400 Shawnee Mission Pky, Merriam, KS 66203

Public Library (Genealogy), 6th & Minnesota Sts., Kansas City, KS 66101

Public Library (Genealogy), 720 North Oak, Newton, KS 67114

Public Library (Genealogy), 210 N. 7th, Garden City, KS 67846

Public Library (Genealogy), Iola, KS 66749

Public Library (Genealogy), 213 W. 5th Ave., Arkansas City, KS 67005

Public Library (Genealogy), 211 W. 4th St., Pittsburg, KS 66762

Appendix B: Resources

Public Library (Genealogy), 220 S. Main St., Wichita, KS 67202

Public Library (Genealogy), Independence, KS 67301

Public Library (Genealogy), 1515 W. 10th, Topeka, KS 66604

Rawlins County Genealogical Society, P.O. Box 203, Atwood, KS 67730

Reno County Genealogical Society, P.O. Box 5, Hutchinson, KS 67504

Republic County Genealogical Society, Rt. 1, Belleville, KS 66935

Riley County Genealogical Society, 2005 Claflin Rd., Manhattan, KS 66502

Santa Fe Trail Genealogical Society, P.O. Box 387, Syracuse, KS 67878

S.E. Kansas Genealogical Society, P.O. Box 393, Iola, KS 66749

Sherman County Historical & Genealogical Society, P.O. Box 684, Goodland, KS 67735

Smoky Valley Genealogical Society & Library Inc., 211 West Iron Ste 205, Salina, KS 67501

Stafford County Historical & Genealogical Society, 100 South Main, Stafford, KS 67578

Stevens County Genealogical Society, H.C. 01 Box 12, Hugoton, KS 67951

Topeka Kansas Genealogical Society, P.O. Box 4048, Topeka, KS 66604 0048

West Kansas Archives (Genealogy), Forsyth Library, Hays, KS 67601

Washington County Genealogical Society, P.O. Box 31, Washington, KS 66968

Wichita Genealogical Society, P.O. Box 3705, Wichita, KS 67201 3705

Woodson County Genealogical Society, 608 N. Prairie, Yates Center, KS 66783

Adair County Genealogical Society, P.O. Box 613, Columbia, KY 42728

Ancestral Trails Historical Society, P.O. Box 613, Columbia, KY 42728

Bicentennial Heritage Corp, R.F.D. 2 Box 574, Liberty, KY 42539

Breathitt County Genealogical Society, 1024 College Ave., Jackson, KY 41339

Bullitt County Genealogical Society, P.O. Box 960, Shepherdsville, KY 40165

Butler County Historical & Genealogical Society, P.O. Box 435, Morgantown, KY 42261

Christian County Genealogical Society, 1101 Bethel St., Hopkinsville, KY 42240

Clay County Genealogical & Historical Society Inc., P.O. Box 394, Manchester, KY 40962

Corbin Genealogical Society, P.O. Box 353, Corbin, KY 40701

Eastern Ky Genealogical Society, Box 1544, Ashland, KY 41101

Fayette County Genealogical Society, P.O. Box 8113, Lexington, KY 40533

Fulton County Genealogical Society, P.O. Box 31, Fulton, KY 42041

Genealogical Society of Hancock Co., Old Courthouse, Hawesville, KY 42348

Graves County Genealogical Society, P.O. Box 245, Mayfield, KY 42066

Green County Historical Society, P.O. Box 276, Greensburg, KY 42743

Harlan County Genealogical Society, P.O. Box 1498, Harlan, KY 40831

Harodsburg County Historical Society Genealogical Committee, Box 316, Harrodsburg, KY 40330

Hart County Historical Society, P.O. Box 606, Munfordville, KY 42765

Hopkins County Genealogical Society, P.O. Box 51, Madisonville, KY 42431

Jefferson County Genealogical & Historical Society, 1211 Brookley Dr., Louisville, KY 40229

Jewish Genealogical Society of Louisville, 3600 Dutchman Ln, Louisville, KY 40205

Johnson County Historical / Genealogical Society, P.O. Box 788, Paintsville, KY 41240

Kentucky Genealogical Society, P.O. Box 153, Frankfort, KY 40601

Kentucky Historical Society Library, 300 W. Broadway, Frankfort, KY 40621

Kin Hunters, P.O. Box 151, Russellville, KY 42276

Letcher County Genealogical & Historical Society, P.O. Box 312, Whitesburg, KY 41858

Library (Genealogy), Western Kentucky University, Bowling Green, KY 42101

Library (Genealogy), Murray State University, Murray, KY 42071

Appendix B: Resources

Library (Genealogy), University of Kentucky, Lexington, KY 40506

Louisville Genealogical Society, P.O. Box 5164, Louisville, KY 40205

Marshall County Genealogical Society, P.O. Box 373, Benton, KY 42025

Mason County Genealogical Society, P.O. Box 266, Maysville, KY 41056

Mccracken County Genealogical Society, 4640 Buckner Ln, Paducah, KY 42001

Metcalfe County Historical Society, P.O. Box 359, Edmonton, KY 42129

Muhlenberg County Genealogical Society, Public Library - Broad St., Paducah, KY 42001

National Society of the S.A.R. Inc., 1000 S. Fourth St., Louisville, KY 40203

Nelson County Genealogical Roundtable Inc., P.O. Box 409, Bardstown, KY 40004

Perry County Genealogical & Historical Society Inc., H.C. 32 Box 550, Vicco, KY 41773

Public Library (Genealogy), 307 Greensburg St., Columbia, KY 42728

Public Library (Genealogy), 114 S. Harrison St., Princeton, KY 42445

Public Library (Genealogy), High St., Hazard, KY 41701

Public Library (Genealogy), 101 S. Main St., Henderson, KY 42420

Public Library (Genealogy), Box 258, Warsaw, KY 41095

Public Library (Genealogy), 5 & Scott, Covington, KY 41011

Public Library (Genealogy), 312 Main St., Fulton, KY 42041

Public Library (Genealogy), 1740 Central Ave., Ashland, KY 41101

Public Library (Genealogy), 109 S. Main St., Winchester, KY 40391

Public Library (Genealogy), 116 E. 4th St., London, KY 40741

Public Library (Genealogy), 203 Harrison St., Greenup, KY 41144

Public Library (Genealogy), 159 S. Main St., Monticello, KY 42633

Public Library (Genealogy), Hardinsburg, KY 40143

Public Library (Genealogy), P.O. Box 498, Hyden, KY 41749

Public Library (Genealogy), 210 Pike Ave., Pikeville, KY 41501

Public Library (Genealogy), 4 & York Sts., Louisville, KY 40203

Public Library (Genealogy), 110 N. Main St., Cynthiana, KY 41031

Public Library (Genealogy), 450 Griffith Ave., Owensboro, KY 42301

Public Library (Genealogy), 2nd & Market Sts., Lexington, KY 40507

Scott County Genealogical Society, Public Library - E. Main, Georgetown, KY 40324

South Central Ky Historical / Genealogical Society, P.O. Box 157, Glasgow, KY 42142 0157

Southern Ky Genealogical Society, P.O. Box 1905, Bowling Green, KY 42101

State Library (Genealogy), 300 Coffee Tree Rd., Frankfort, KY 40602 0537

Taylor County Historical Society, P.O. Box 14, Campbellsville, KY 42718

The Filson Club, 1310 S. Third St., Louisville, KY 40208

West Central Ky Family Research Assn., P.O. Box 1932, Owensboro, KY 42302

Alexandria Historical & Genealogical Library, 503 Washington, Alexandria, LA 71301

Allen Genealogical & Historical Society, P.O. Box 789, Kinder, LA 70648

Ark-La-Tex Genealogical Assn.. Inc., P.O. Box 4462, Shreveport, LA 71104

Baton Rouge Genealogical & Historical Society, P.O. Box 80565 S.E. Station, Baton Rouge, LA 70898

Central Louisiana Genealogical Society, P.O. Box 12206, Alexandria, LA 71315 2006

Centroplex Library (Genealogy), 120 St. Louis St., Baton Rouge, LA 70821

Diocecse Archives (Genealogy), P.O. Box 2028, Baton Rouge, LA 70821

East Ascension Genealogical & Historical Society, P.O. Box 1006, Gonzales, LA 70707

Evangeline Genealogical & Historical Society, P.O. Box 664, Ville Platte, LA 70586

Genealogical Research Society of New Orleans, P.O. Box 51791, New Orleans, LA 70151

German-Acadian Coast Historical/Genealogical Society, P.O. Box 417, Destrehan, LA 70047

Appendix B: Resources

Jefferson Genealogical Society, P.O. Box 961, Metairie, LA 70004

Jennings Genealogical Society, 136 Greenwood Dr., Jennings, LA 70546

Lafourche Heritage Society, 412 Menard St., Thibodaux, LA 70301

Library (Genealogy), Louisiana State University, Baton Rouge, LA 70803

Library (Genealogy), Tulane University, New Orleans, LA 70118

Louisiana D.A.R., 2564 Donald Dr., Baton Rouge, LA 70809

Louisiana Genealogical and Historical Society, P.O. Box 3454, Baton Rouge, LA 70821

Memorial Library (Genealogy), 424 Texas St., Shreveport, LA 71120

Natchitoches Genealogical & Historical Assn., P.O. Box 1349, Natchitoches, LA 71458 1349

North Louisiana Genealogical Society, P.O. Box 324, Ruston, LA 71270

Plaquemines Parish Genealogical Society, 203 Hwy 11 S, Buras, LA 70041

Public Library (Genealogy), 411 Washington St., Alexandria, LA 71301

Public Library (Genealogy), 509 W. Alabama, Ruston, LA 71270

Public Library (Genealogy), 1800 Stubbs Ave., Monroe, LA 71201

Public Library (Genealogy), 219 Loyola Ave., New Orleans, LA 70112

Public Library (Genealogy), P.O. Box 1471, Baton Rouge, LA 70821

Public Library (Genealogy), P.O. Box 578, Amite, LA 70422

Shreve Memorial Library Genealogical Dept, 424 Texas St. P.O. Box 21523, Shreveport, LA 71120

Southwest Louisiana Genealogical Society, P.O. Box 5652, Lake Charles, LA 70606

St. Bernard Genealogical Society, P.O. Box 271, Chalmette, LA 70044

State Archives (Genealogy), 3851 Essen Ln, Baton Rouge, LA 70804

State Library (Genealogy), State Capitol Ground, Baton Rouge, LA 70804

Terrebonne Genealogical Society, P.O. Box 295 Station 2, Houma, LA 70360

American Antiquarian Society, 185 Salisbury St., Worcester, MA 01609

American-Portugese Genealogical Society, P.O. Box 644, Taunton, MA 02780

Berkshire Family Historical Assn., P.O. Box 1437, Pittsfield, MA 01202

Bristol County Chapter Mass Society / Genealogy, 459 Madison St., Fall River, MA 02720

Connecticut Valley Historical Museum, 194 State St., Springfield, MA 01130

Essex Institute (Genealogy), 132 Essex St., Salem, MA 01970

Essex Society of Genealogy, P.O. Box 313, Lynnfield, MA 01940 0313

Genealogical Roundtable, 20 Lobloily Ln, Wayland, MA 01778 1429

General Society of Mayflower Desc, Box 3297, Plymouth, MA 02361

Hampden Chapter Mass Society / Genealogy, 25 Edison Dr., Ludlow, MA 01056

Irish Ancestral Research Assn., Box 619, Sudbury, MA 01776

Jewish Genealogical Society of Boston, P.O. Box 366, Newton, MA 02161 0004

Jones Library (Genealogy), 43 Amity St., Amherst, MA 01002

Mass Society Mayflower Desc, 101 Newbury St., Boston, MA 02116

Massachusetts Genealogical Council, P.O. Box 5393, Cochituate, MA 01778

Massachusetts Society of Genealogical Inc., Box 215, Ashland, MA 01721

Memorial Library (Genealogy), P.O. Box 2571, Holyoke, MA 01041

Middlesex Chapter Mass Society / Genealogy, 244 Flanders Rd., Westborough, MA 01581

Nehgs, 99-101 Newbury, Boston, MA 02116

Old Colony Historical Society, 66 Church St., Taunton, MA 02780

Plymouth Colony Genealogy, 60 Sheridan St., Brockton, MA 02402

Public Library (Genealogy), 99 Main St., Haverhill, MA 01830

Public Library (Genealogy), P.O. Box 286, Boston, MA 02117

Public Library (Genealogy), 74 N. Main St., Attleboro, MA 02703

Appendix B: Resources

Public Library (Genealogy), 18 Summer St., Lynnfield, MA 01940

Public Library (Genealogy), Box 338, Eastham, MA 02642

Public Library (Genealogy), 304 Main St., Brockton, MA 02401

Public Library (Genealogy), 220 State St., Springfield, MA 01103

Public Library (Genealogy), 69 Main St., Swansea, MA 02777

Public Library (Genealogy), 402 Main St., Greenfield, MA 01301

Public Library (Genealogy), Pleasant St., New Bedford, MA 02740

State Library (Genealogy), Beacon Hill, Boston, MA 02155

Sturgis Library (Genealogy), Main St., Barnstable, MA 02630

The Essex Genealogist, 18 Summer St., Lynnfield, MA 01940

Western Mass Genealogical Society, P.O. Box 206, Springfield, MA 01108

Yarmouth Library (Genealogy), 297 Main St., Yarmouth Port, MA 02675

Anne Arundel Genealogical Society, P.O. Box 221, Pasadena, MD 21122

Baltimore County Genealogical Society, P.O. Box 10085, Towson, MD 21204

Calvert County Genealogical Comm, P.O. Box 358, Prince Frederick, MD 20678

Carroll County Genealogical Society, 50 E. Main St., Westminster, MD 21157

Catonville Historical Society & Genealogical Sec, P.O. Box 9311, Baltimore, MD 21228

Genealogical Club / Montgomery County Historical Society, 103 W. Montgomery Ane, Rockville, MD 20850

Genealogical Society of Allegany Co., P.O. Box 3103, Cumberland, MD 21502

Genealogical Society of Cecil Co., Box 11, Charlestown, MD 21914

Genealogical Library, 1000 Stoneybrook Dr., Kensington, MD 20895

Howard County Genealogical Society, P.O. Box 274, Columbia, MD 21045

Lower Del-Mar-Va Genealogical Society, P.O. Box 3602, Salisbury, MD 21802 3602

Maryland Genealogical Society, 201 W. Monument St., Baltimore, MD 21201

Maryland Society S.A.R., 7977 Timmons Rd., Union Bridge, MD 21791

National Capital Buckeye, P.O. Box 105, Bladensburg, MD 20710

Peabody Library (Genealogy), 17 E. Mt. Vernon Place, Baltimore, MD 21202

Prince George's County Genealogical Society, P.O. Box 819, Bowie, MD 20718

Public Library (Genealogy), 307 N. Washington St., Snow Hill, MD 21863

Public Library (Genealogy), 305 Gay St., Cambridge, MD 21613

Public Library (Genealogy), 400 Cathedral St., Baltimore, MD 21201

St. Mary's County Genealogical Society, General Delivery, Callaway, MD 20620

State Library (Genealogy), 361 Rose Blvd., Annapolis, MD 21401

Upper Shore Genealogical Society of Md, P.O. Box 275, Easton, MD 21601

Washington Dc Temple Br Genealogical Library, P.O. Box 49, Kensington, MD 20895

Bath/patten Free Library Genealogical Rm, 33 Summer St., Bath, ME 04530

Cherryfield - Narraguagus Historical Society, P.O. Box 96, Cherryfield, ME 04622

Maine Genealogical Society, P.O. Box 221, Farmington, ME 04938

Memorial Library (Genealogy), 800 Main St., Westbrook, ME 04092

Old York Historical Society, P.O. Box 312, York, ME 03909

Public Library (Genealogy), Court & Spring Sts., Auburn, ME 04210

Public Library (Genealogy), 145 Harlow St., Bangor, ME 04401

Public Library (Genealogy), 33 Summer St., Bath, ME 04530

Public Library (Genealogy), 112 Main St., Kennebunk, ME 04043

State Library (Genealogy), 800 Main St., Westbrook, ME 04092

Sunrise Research Institute, P.O. Box 158, Whitneyville, ME 04692

A.c.e. Genealogical Society, 315 Jackson, Petosky, MI 49770

Appendix B

211

Appendix B: Resources

Albion Historical Society, 509 S. Superior St., Albion, MI 49224

Bay County Genealogical Society, P.O. Box 27, Essexville, MI 48732

Branch County Genealogical Society, P.O. Box 443, Coldwater, MI 49036

Calhoun County Genealogical Society, 501 S. Superior St., Albion, MI 49224

Cheboygan County Genealogical Society, P.O. Box 51, Cheboygan, MI 49721

Cmu Library Genealogical Rm, Mount Pleasant, MI 48858

Dearborn Genealogical Society, 915 Brady, Dearborn, MI 48124

Delta County Genealogical Society, 1900 - 3rd Ave., Escanaba, MI 49829

Detroit Society for Genealogical Research, 5201 Woodward Ave., Detroit, MI 48202

Dickinson County Genealogical Society, 401 Iron Mountain St., Iron Mountain, MI 49801

Downriver Genealogical Society, P.O. Box 476, Lincoln Park, MI 48146

Eaton County Genealogical Society, 100 Lawrence Ave., Charlotte, MI 48813

Farmington Genealogical Society, 23500 Liberty, Farmington, MI 48334

Flint Genealogical Society, P.O. Box 1217, Flint, MI 48501

Four Flags Area Genealogical Society, P.O. Box 414, Niles, MI 49120

French-Can Heritage Society Mich, P.O. Box 10028, Lansing, MI 48901 0028

Gaylord Fact-Finders Genealogical Society, Rt. 2 Box 2033A, Grayling, MI 49738

Genealogical Assn.. of S.W. Mich, Box 573, Saint Joseph, MI 49085

Genealogical Historical Research Ctr, 305 E. Filer St., Ludington, MI 49431

Genealogical of Clinton County Historical Society, P.O. Box 23, St. Johns, MI 48879 0023

Genealogical Society of Flemish Americans, 18740 Thirteen Mile Rd., Roseville, MI 48066

Genealogical Society of Monroe Co., P.O. Box 1428, Monroe, MI 48161

Genealogical Society of Washtenaw County Mi Inc., P.O. Box 7155, Ann Arbor, MI 48107

Grand Haven Genealogical Society, 407 Columbus, Grand Haven, MI 49417

Grand Traverse Genealogical Society, 430 S. Airport Rd. E., Traverse City, MI 49684

Gratiot County Historical Society, 228 W. Center St., Ithaca, MI 48847

Holland Genealogical Society, 300 River Ave., Holland, MI 49423

Huron Shores Genealogical Society, 110 S. State St., Oscoda, MI 48750 1633

Huron Valley Genealogical Society, 1100 Atlantic, Milford, MI 48381

Jackson County Genealogical Society, 108 E. Meadow Heights, Jackson, MI 49203

Jewish Genealogical Society of Mich, 4987 Bantry Dr., West Bloomfield, MI 48322

Kalamazoo Valley Genealogical Society, P.O. Box 405, Comstock, MI 49041

Kalkaska Genealogical Society, P.O. Box 353, Kalkaska, MI 49646

Kinseekers, 5697 Old Maple Tr, Grawn, MI 49637

Lapeer County Genealogical Society, 921 W. Nepessing St., Lapeer, MI 48446

Lenawee County Historical Society, P.O. Box 511, Adrian, MI 49221

Library (Genealogy), Central Michigan University, Mount Pleasant, MI 48858

Library of Michigan (Genealogy), 717 W. Allegan, Lansing, MI 48909

Livingston County Genealogical Society, P.O. Box 1073, Howell, MI 48844 1073

Lyon Township Genealogical Society, 27025 Milford Rd., New Hudson, MI 48165

Macomb County Genealogical Group, 150 Cass Ave., Mt Clemens, MI 48043

Marquette County Genealogical Society, 217 N. Front St., Marquette, MI 49855

Mason County Genealogical Society, P.O. Box 352, Ludington, MI 49431

Memorial Library (Genealogy), 200 Phelps St., Decatur, MI 49045

Michigan Genealogical Council, P.O. Box 80956, Lansing, MI 48908 0953

Michigan O.G.S., 34233 Shawnee Trail, Westland, MI 48185

Michigan Society S.A.R., 49 Lynwood Dr., Battle Creek, MI 49017

Appendix B: Resources

Mid-Michigan Genealogical Society, P.O. Box 16033, Lansing, MI 48901 6033

Midland County Genealogical Society, 1710 W. St. Andrews Dr., Midland, MI 48640

Muskegon County Genealogical Society, 316 W. Webster, Muskegon, MI 49440

N.E. Mich Genealogical Society, 491 Johnson St., Alpena, MI 49707

Newaygo County Society of Historical & Genealogy, P.O. Box 68, White Cloud, MI 49349

Northville Genealogical Society, 42164 Gladwin Dr., Northville, MI 48167

Oakland County Genealogical Society, P.O. Box 1094, Birmimgham, MI 48012

Oceana County Genealogical Chap, 114 Dryden St., Hart, MI 49420

Ogemaw Genealogical & Historical Society, Public Library, West Branch, MI 48661

Polish Archives (Genealogy), St. Mary's College, Orchard Lake, MI 48323

Polish Genealogical Society of Mich, 3895 Embarcadero Dr., Drayton, MI 48020

Pontiac Area Historical & Genealogical Society, P.O. Box 430901, Pontiac, MI 48343 0901

Public Library (Genealogy), 1840 M Michigan Ste 114, Saginaw, MI 48602 5590

Public Library (Genealogy), 244 W. Michigan Ave., Jackson, MI 49201

Public Library (Genealogy), 5201 Woodward Ave., Detroit, MI 48202

Public Library (Genealogy), N. Nottawa & West St., Sturgis, MI 49091

Public Library (Genealogy), 100 E. Midland St., Bay City, MI 48706

Public Library (Genealogy), 311 Lafayette St., Bay City, MI 48706

Public Library (Genealogy), 107 W. Main, Rose City, MI 48654

Public Library (Genealogy), 845 S. Lapeer Rd., Lake Orion, MI 48359

Public Library (Genealogy), 111 Library St., Grand Rapids, MI 49502

Public Library (Genealogy), 215 S. Michigan, Vicksburg, MI 49097

Public Library (Genealogy), 300 River Ave., Holland, MI 49423

Public Library (Genealogy), 1026 E. Kearsley, Flint, MI 48502

Public Library (Genealogy), 708 Center Ave., Bay City, MI 48706

Public Library (Genealogy), 150 Cass Ave., Mount Clemens, MI 48043

Reed City Area Genealogical Society, 410 W. Upton Ave., Reed City, MI 49677

Roseville Historical & Genealogical Society, 29777 Gratiot Ave., Roseville, MI 48066

Saginaw Genealogical Society, 505 Janes Ave., Saginaw, MI 48607

Seely Genealogical Society, 613 Alendale Ave., Lansing, MI 48910 4616

Shiawasee County Genealogical Society, 1807 James St., Owosso, MI 48867

Southern Michigan Genealogical Society, 239 E. Chicago Rd., Allen, MI 49227

Sterling Hts Genealogical & Historical Society, P.O. Box 1154, Sterling Heights, MI 48311 1154

The Searchers, 140300 V Ave., Vicksburg, MI 49097

Three Rivers Genealogical Society, 13724 Spence Rd., Three Rivers, MI 49093

Tri-State Genealogical Society, P.O. Box 23, Sturgis, MI 49091

Union City Genealogical Society, 221 N. Broadway, Union City, MI 49094

Van Buren Regional Genealogical Society, 200 N. Phelps St., Decatur, MI 49045

Western Mich Genealogical Society, 60 Library Plaza, Grand Rapids, MI 49503

Western Wayne County Genealogical Society, P.O. Box 530063, Livonia, MI 48136 0063

Westland Mich Genealogical Library, P.O. Box 70, Westland, MI 48185

Ypsilanti Historical Society, 220 N. Huron St., Ypsilanti, MI 48197

Anoka County Genealogical Society, 1900 Third Ave., Anoka, MN 55303

Bernadette Library (Genealogy), Gustavus Adolphus College, Saint Peter, MN 56082

Chisago County Genealogical Group, P.O. Box 360, Center City, MN 55012

Appendix B: Resources

Crow Wing Cop Genealogical Society, 2103 Graydon Ave., Brainard, MN 56401

Czechoslovak Genealogical Society, P.O. Box 16225, St. Paul, MN 55116

Dakota County Genealogical Society, P.O. Box 74, South Saint Paul, MN 55075

Dodge County Genealogical Society, Box 683, Dodge Center, MN 55927

Douglas County Genealogical Society, P.O. Box 505, Alexandria, MN 56308

Freeborn County Genealogical Society, P[o Box 403, Albert Lea, MN 56007

Genealogical Roundtable, 160 Johnson St., Winona, MN 55987

Genealogical Society of Carlton Co., P.O. Box 204, Cloquet, MN 55720

Heart O'lakes Genealogical Society, P.O. Box 237, Frazee, MN 56544

Heritage Searchers of Kandiyohi Co., 610 N.E. Hwy 71, Willmar, MN 56201

Irish Genealogical Society, P.O. Box 16585, Saint Paul, MN 55116

Itasca County Genealogical Club, P.O. Box 261, Bovey, MN 55709

Library (Genealogy), University of Minnesota, Minneapolis, MN 55455

Meeker County Genealogical Society, Box 218, Buffalo Lake, MN 55314

Minnesota Genealogical Society, P.O. Box 16069, Saint Paul, MN 55116

Mower County Genealogical Society, Box 145, Austin, MN 55912

Nobles County Genealogical Society, 407 12th St. Ste 2, Worthington, MN 56187 2411

Northfield / Rice County Genealogical Society, 408 Division St., Northfield, MN 55057

Nwtc, P.O. Box 29396, Brooklyn Center, MN 55429 0397

Olmstead County Genealogical Society, P.O. Box 6411, Rochester, MN 55903

Otter Tail County Genealogical Society, 1110 Lincoln Ave. W., Fergus Falls, MN 56537

Pipestone County Genealogical Society, 113 S. Hiawatha, Pipestone, MN 56164

Prairieland Genealogical Society, Historical Center S.W. State University, Marshall, MN 56258

Public Library (Genealogy), Broadway & First Sts. S.E., Rochester, MN 55901

Public Library (Genealogy), 300 Nicolet Ave., Minneapolis, MN 55401

Public Library (Genealogy), 90 W. 4th, Saint Paul, MN 55102

Rainey River Valley Genealogical Society, Box 1032, International Falls, MN 56649

Range Genealogical Society, P.O. Box 388, Chisholm, MN 55719

Renville County Genealogical Society, Box 331, Renville, MN 56284

Rice County Genealogical Society, 408 Division St., Northfield, MN 55057

Rolvaag Library (Genealogy), St. Olaf College, Northfield, MN 55057

South Central Minnesota Genealogical Society, 110 N. Park St., Fairmont, MN 56031

St. Cloud Area Genealogists Inc., P.O. Box 213, Saint Cloud, MN 56302 0213

Traverse-Des-Sioux Genealogical Society, 815 Nicollet Ave., North Mankato, MN 56001

Twin Ports Genealogical Society, P.O. Box 16895, Duluth, MN 55816 0895

Waseca Area Genealogical Society Inc., P.O. Box 264, Waseca, MN 56093

White Bear Lake Genealogical Society, P.O. Box 10555, White Bear Lake, MN 55110

Winona County Genealogical Roundtable, P.O. Box 363, Winona, MN 55987

Wright County Genealogical Society, 911 2nd Ave. S, Buffalo, MN 55313

Yivisaker Library (Genealogy), Concordia College, Moorhead, MN 56560

American Family Records Assn., P.O. Box 15505, Kansas City, MO 64106

Audrian County Area Genealogical Society, 305 W. Jackson St., Mexico, MO 65265

Boone County Historical Society, 3801 Ponderosa Dr., Columbia, MO 65201

Boonslick Reg Library (Genealogy), Kirksville, MO 63501

Cape Girardeau County Genealogical Society, P.O. Box 389, Jackson, MO 63755

Carthage Genealogical Society, Rt. 3, Carthage, MO 64836

County Archives (Genealogy), P.O. Box 99, Liberty, MO 64068

Appendix B: Resources

County Museum (Genealogy), 109 Madison, Jefferson City, MO 65101

Dade County Genealogical Society, P.O. Box 155, Greenfield, MO 65661

Dallas County Historical Society, P.O. Box 594, Buffalo, MO 65622

Excelsior Springs Genealogical Society, P.O. Box 601, Excelsior Springs, MO 64024

Four Rivers Genealogical Society, 314 W. Main St., Washington, MO 63090

Genealogical Friends of the Library, 507 W. Hickory, Neosho, MO 64850

Genealogical Society of Butler County Inc., P.O. Box 426, Poplar Bluff, MO 63901

Genealogical Society of Central Mo, P.O. Box 26, Columbia, MO 65205

Genealogical Society of Liberty, P.O. Box 442, Liberty, MO 64068

Genealogical Society of Pulaski Co., P.O. Box 226, Crocker, MO 65452

Grundy County Genealogical Society, 1715 E. 8th St., Trenton, MO 64683

Grundy County Genealogical Society, 1715 E. 8th St., Trenton, MO 64683

Hamilton National Genealogical Society Inc., 215 W. 20th Terr, Oak Grove, MO 64075

Harrison County Genealogical Society, 2243 Central, Bethany, MO 64424

Heart of America Genealogical Society, 311 E. 12th St., Kansas City, MO 64106

Jackson County Genealogical Society, 420 S. Main St., Independence, MO 64050

Johnson County Historical Society, 135 E. Pine St., Warrensburg, MO 64093

Joplin Genealogical Society, P.O. Box 152, Joplin, MO 64802

Kent Library (Genealogy), S.E. Missouri Stake Coll, Cape Girardeau, MO 63701

Laclede County Genealogical Society, P.O. Box 350, Lebanon, MO 65536

Lincoln County Genealogical Society, P.O. Box 192, Hawk Point, MO 63349

Linn County Genealogical Researchers, 771 Tomahawk, Brookfield, MO 64628

Livingston County Genealogical Society, 450 Locust St., Chillicothe, MO 64601 2597

Mari-Osa Heritage Society, P.O. Box 257, Westphalia, MO 65085

Mercer County Genealogical Society, Princeton, MO 64673

Mid-Continent Public Library (Genealogy), 317 W. 24 Hwy, Independence, MO 64050

Mid-Missouri Genealogical Society Inc., P.O. Box 715, Jefferson City, MO 65102

Mississippi County Genealogical Society, P.O. Box 5, Charleston, MO 63834

Missouri Genealogical Assn., P.O. Box 833, Columbia, MO 65205

Missouri Genealogical Society, P.O. Box 382, Saint Joseph, MO 64502

Missouri Terr Pioneers, 3929 Milton Dr., Independence, MO 64055

Montgomery County Historical Society, 112 W. 2nd St., Montgomery City, MO 63361

Museum Library (Genealogy), 14 N. Main St., Liberty, MO 64068

Musuem Library (Genealogy), 121 N. Washington, Neosho, MO 64850

N.E. Missouri Genealogical Society, 614 Clark St., Canton, MO 63435

Nodaway County Genealogical Society, P.O. Box 214, Matyville, MO 64468

N.W. Missouri Genealogical Society, 412 Felix St., Saint Joseph, MO 64502

Oregon County Genealogical Society, P.O. Box 324, Alton, MO 65606 0324

Ozark County Genealogical Society, H.C. 2 Box 2640, Isabella, MO 65676 9707

Ozarks Genealogical Society Inc., P.O. Box 3494 G S, Springfield, MO 65808

Phelps County Genealogical Society, P.O. Box 571, Rolla, MO 65401

Pike County Genealogical Society, P.O. Box 364, Bowling Green, MO 63334

Platte County Historical Society Inc., P.O. Box 103, Platte City, MO 64079 0103

Public Library (Genealogy), 102 N. Center St., Shelbina, MO 63468

Public Library (Genealogy), 311 E. 12th St., Kansas City, MO 64106

Public Library (Genealogy), 397 E. Central St., Springfield, MO 65801

Public Library (Genealogy), 403 S. Jefferson, Neosho, MO 64850

Appendix B: Resources

Public Library (Genealogy), 901 Maupin, New Haven, MO 63068

Public Library (Genealogy), 110 Bridge St., Keytesville, MO 65261

Public Library (Genealogy), 5th & Main, Maryville, MO 64468

Public Library (Genealogy), 4th & Main Sts., Joplin, MO 64801

Public Library (Genealogy), 601 Grant, Princeton, MO 64673

Public Library (Genealogy), 1301 Olive St., Saint Louis, MO 63103

Public Library (Genealogy), Library Ln, Kirksville, MO 63501

Public Library (Genealogy), Unionville, MO 63565

Public Library (Genealogy), 1007 Main St., Cassville, MO 65625

Public Library (Genealogy), P.O. Box 389, Jackson, MO 63755

Ray County Genealogical Assn., 901 W. Royle St., Richmond, MO 64085 1545

Reynolds County Genealogical & Historical Society, P.O. Box 281, Ellington, MO 63638

S. Vernon Genealogical Society, Rt. 2 Box 280, Sheldon, MO 64784

Santa Fe Trail Research Genealogical Society, Rt. 1, Franklin, MO 65250

Scotland County Genealogical Society, 316 N. Cecil, Memphis, MO 63555

South Central Missouri Genealogical Society, 939 Nichols Dr., West Plains, MO 65775

St. Charles County Genealogical Society, P.O. Box 715, Saint Charles, MO 63301

St. Louis Genealogical Society, 9011 Manchester Rd. #3, St. Louis, MO 63144

State Archives (Genealogy), Secretary of State Capitol Bldg., Jefferson City, MO 65101

State Library (Genealogy), 308 E. High St., Jefferson City, MO 65101

Texas County Genealogical & Historical Society, P.O. Box 12, Houston, MO 65483

Thrailkill Genealogical Society, 2018 Gentry St., North Kansas City, MO 64116

Vernon County Genealogical Society, 225 W. Austin, Nevada, MO 64772

West Central Missouri Genealogical Society, 705 Broad St., Warrensburg, MO 64093

Chickasaw County Historical & Genealogical Society, 101 Tindall Cir., Houston, MS 38851

Genealogical Society of Desoto Co., P.O. Box 303, Hernando, MS 38632

Historical & Genealogical Society of Panola Co., 105 Church St., Batesville, MS 38606

Historic Trails Library, Rt. 1 Box 373, Philadelphia, MS 39350

Itawamba Historical Society, P.O. Box 7, Mantachie, MS 38855

Jackson County Genealogical Society, P.O. Box 984, Pascagoula, MS 39567

L. W. Anderson Genealogical Library, P.O. Box 1647, Gulfport, MS 39501

Library (Genealogy), University of Mississippi, University, MS 38677

McCain Library (Genealogy), University of Southern Mississippi, Hattiesburg, MS 39406

Memorial Library (Genealogy), 5th & 7th Sts., Laurel, MS 39440

Memorial Library (Genealogy), Aberdeen, MS 39730

Mississippi Coast Genealogical & Historical Society, P.O. Box 513, Biloxi, MS 39530

Mississippi Genealogical Society, P.O. Box 5301, Jackson, MS 39216

Mississippi Society S.A.R., 529 Pawnee Way, Madison, MS 39110

N.E. Mississippi Historical & Genealogical Society, P.O. Box 434, Tupelo, MS 38801 0434

Ocean Springs Genealogical Society, P.O. Box 1055, Ocean Springs, MS 39564

Public Library (Genealogy), 3214 Pascagoula St., Pascagoula, MS 39567

Public Library (Genealogy), 401 Bramlett Blvd., Oxford, MS 38655

Public Library (Genealogy), 2517 7th St., Meridian, MS 39301

Public Library (Genealogy), 328 Goodman St., Kosciusko, MS 39090

Public Library (Genealogy), 314 N. 7th St., Columbus, MS 39701

Public Library (Genealogy), 14 St. & 21St Ave., Gulfport, MS 39501

Public Library (Genealogy), 341 Main St., Greenville, MS 38701

Appendix B: Resources

Public Library (Genealogy), 408 W. Washington, Greenwood, MS 38930

Public Library (Genealogy), Vicksburg, MS 39180

Public Library (Genealogy), 1023 Fillmore, Corinth, MS 38834

Public Library (Genealogy), P.O. Box 467, Biloxi, MS 39533

Public Library (Genealogy), 315 E. Main, Marks, MS 38646

Public Library (Genealogy), 106 College St., Batesville, MS 38606

Public Library (Genealogy), P.O. Box 22, New Albany, MS 38652

Skipwith Historical and Genealogical Society, P.O. Box 1382, Oxford, MS 38655

Smith Library (Genealogy), Court Ave. & Main St., New Albany, MS 38652

State Archives (Genealogy), Archives Historical Bldg Capitol Green, Jackson, MS 39205

Tate County Genealogical & Historical Society, P.O. Box 974, Senatobia, MS 38668

Vicksburg Genealogical Society Inc., P.O. Box 1161, Vicksburg, MS 39181 1161

W. Chickasaw County Genealogical & Historical Society, P.O. Box 42, Houston, MS 38851

Big Horn County Genealogical Society, Rt. 1 Box 1166, Hardin, MT 59034

Broken Mts. Genealogical Society, Box 261, Chester, MT 59522

Central Montana Genealogical Society, 701 W. Main St., Lewistown, MT 59457

County Archives (Genealogy), 1400 1St Ave. N., Great Falls, MT 59401

Flathead Valley Genealogical Society, 134 Lawrence Ln, Kalispell, MT 59901

Ft. Assiniboine Genealogical Society, P.O. Box 321, Havre, MT 59501

Galatin Genealogical Society, P.O. Box 1783, Bozeman, MT 59715

Great Falls Genealogical Society, 1400 First Ave. N., Great Falls, MT 59401

Lewis & Clark County Genealogical Society, P.O. Box 5313, Helena, MT 59604

Lewiston Genealogical Society Inc., 701 W. Main, Lewistown, MT 59457

Library (Genealogy), Montana State University, Bozeman, MT 59717

Library (Genealogy), State University, Missoula, MT 59801

Mansfield Library (Genealogy), University of Montana, Missoula, MT 59812

Miles City Genealogical Society, 1 S. 10th, Miles City, MT 59301

Momtana State Genealogical Society, P.O. Box 555, Chester, MT 59522

Montana Historical Society, 225 N. Roberts St., Helena, MT 59601

Montana Society D.A.R., 408 S. Black, Bozeman, MT 59715

Park County Genealogical Society, 228 W. Callender St., Livingston, MT 59047

Powell County Genealogical Society, 912 Missouri Ave., Deer Lodge, MT 59722

Public Library (Genealogy), 106 W. Broadway St., Butte, MT 59701

Public Library (Genealogy), 1 S. 10th, Miles City, MT 59301

Public Library (Genealogy), P.O. Box 1151, Havre, MT 59501

Public Library (Genealogy), Pine & Patee Sts., Missoula, MT 59801

Public Library (Genealogy), Great Falls, MT 59401

Public Library (Genealogy), 510 N. Broadway, Billings, MT 59101

Root Diggers Genealogical Society, P.O. Box 249, Glascow, MT 59230

State Library (Genealogy), 930 E. Lyndale Ave., Helena, MT 59601

Western Montana Genealogical Society, P.O. Box 2714, Missoula, MT 59806 2714

Yellowstone Genealogical Forum, 510 N. Broadway, Billings, MT 59101

Alamance County Genealogical Society, P.O. Box 3052, Burlington, NC 27215 3052

Alexander County Genealogical Society, P.O. Box 241, Hiddenite, NC 28636

Alleghany Historical-Genealogical Society, Box 817, Sparta, NC 28675

Beaufort County Genealogical Society, P.O. Box 1089, Washington, NC 27889 1089

Broad River Genealogical Society, P.O. Box 2261, Shelby, NC 28151 2261

Burke County Genealogical Society, P.O. Box 661, Morgantown, NC 28655

217

Appendix B: Resources

Caldwell County Genealogical Society, Box 2476, Lenoir, NC 28645

Carolinas Genealogical Society, 605 Craig St., Monroe, NC 28110

Catawba County Genealogical Society, P.O. Box 2406, Hickory, NC 28603

Coastal Genealogical Society, P.O. Box 1421, Swansboro, NC 28584

Cumberland County Genealogical Society, P.O. Box 53299, Fayetteville, NC 28305

Davidson County Genealogical Society, P.O. Box 1665, Lexington, NC 27292

Davie County Historical & Genealogical Society, 371 N. Main St., Mocksville, NC 27028

Durham-Orange Genealogical Society, P.O. Box 4703, Chapel Hill, NC 27515 4703

Eastern North Carolina Genealogical Society, P.O. Box 395, New Bern, NC 28560

Forsyth County Genealogical Society, Box 5715, Winston-Salem, NC 27113

Gaston-Lincoln Genealogical Society, P.O. Box 854, Mount Holly, NC 28120

Genealogical Society of Davidson Co., P.O. Box 1665, Lexington, NC 27292

Genealogical Society of Iredell Co., P.O. Box 946, Statesville, NC 28677

Genealogical Society of Old Tryon Co., P.O. Box 938, Forest City, NC 28043

Genealogical Society of Original Wilkes Co., North Wilkesboro, NC 28659

Genealogical Society of Rowan Co., P.O. Box 4305, Salisbury, NC 28144

Guilford County Genealogical Society, P.O. Box 9693, Greensboro, NC 27429 0693

Halifax County Genealogical Society, P.O. Box 447, Halifax, NC 27839

Henderson County Genealogical & Historical Society, 432 N. Main St., Hendersonville, NC 28739

Iredell County Genealogical Society, P.O. Box 946, Statesville, NC 28677

Jewish Genealogical Society of Raleigh, 8701 Sleepy Creek Dr., Raleigh, NC 27612

Johnston County Genealogical Society, 305 Market St., Smithfield, NC 27577

Mecklenburg Genealogical Society, P.O. Box 32453, Charlotte, NC 28232

Moore County Genealogical Society Inc., P.O. Box 56, Carthage, NC 28327

North Carolina Scottish Heritage Society, 1710 Brook Cliff Rd., Sanford, NC 27330

North Carolina Genealogical Society, P.O. Box 1492, Raleigh, NC 27602

North Carolina Society S.A.R., 2221 Oleander Dr., Wilmington, NC 28403

Old Buncombe County Genealogical Society Inc., P.O. Box 2122, Asheville, NC 28802

Old Dobbs County Genealogical Society, P.O. Box 617, Goldsboro, NC 27530

Old New Hanover County Genealogical Society, P.O. Box 2536, Wilmington, NC 28402

Olde Mecklenburg Genealogical Society, P.O. Box 32453, Charlotte, NC 28232

Onslow County Genealogical Society, P.O. Box 1739, Jacksonville, NC 28541 1739

Polk County Genealogical Society, 485 Hunting Country Rd., Tryon, NC 28782

Randolph County Genealogical Society, 201 Worth St., Asheboro, NC 27203

Rockingham County Historical Society, Box 84, Wentworth, NC 27375

Society of Richmond County Desc, P.O. Box 848 Desk 120, Rockingham, NC 28379

Stanley County Genealogical Society, P.O. Box 31, Albermarle, NC 28002

Surry County Genealogical Society, Box 997, Dobson, NC 27017

S.W. North Carolina Genealogical Society, 101 Blumenthal, Murphy, NC 28906

Swain County Genealogical & Historical Society, P.O. Box 267, Bryson City, NC 28713

The North Carolina Genealogical Society, P.O. Box 1492, Raleigh, NC 27602

Toe Valley Genealogical Society, 491 Beaver Creek Rd., Spruce Pine, NC 28777

Wake County Genealogical Society, P.O. Box 17713, Raleigh, NC 27619

Wilkes County Genealogical Society, P.O. Box 1629, North Wilkesboro, NC 28659

Bismark-Mandan Historical & Genealogical Society, Box 485, Bismarck, ND 58501

Appendix B: Resources

Genealogical Guild/Wilkin County MN/Richland County ND, Leach Public Library, Wahpeton, ND 58075

Germans From Russia Heritage Society, 1008 E. Central Ave., Bismarck, ND 58501

Mclean County Genealogical Society, P.O. Box 51, Garrison, ND 58540

Minot Family Historical Center, 62 Western Village, Minot, ND 58701

Mouse River Loop Genealogical Society, Box 1391, Minot, ND 58701

Red River Valley Genealogical Society, P.O. Box 9284, Fargo, ND 58106

Adams County Genealogical Society, P.O. Box 424, Hastings, NE 68902 0424

Cairo Roots, Rt. 1 Box 42, Cairo, NE 68824

Chase County Genealogical Society, P.O. Box 303, Imperial, NE 69033

Cherry County Genealogical Society, Box 380, Valentine, NE 69201

Cheyenne County Genealogical Society, P.O. Box 802, Sidney, NE 69162

Dawson County - Lexington Genealogical Society, Box 778, Lexington, NE 68850

Eastern Nebraska Genealogical Society, 11014 Military Ave., Omaha, NE 68164

Fillmore Heritage Society, Rt. 2 Box 28, Exeter, NE 68351

Frontier County Genealogical Society, P.O. Box 242, Curtis, NE 69025

Ft. Kearney Genealogical Society, Box 22, Kearney, NE 68847

Furnas County Genealogical Society, P.O. Box 391, Beaver City, NE 68926

Genealogical Seekers, 871 W. 6th, Wahoo, NE 68066

Greater Omaha Genealogical Society, P.O. Box 4011, Omaha, NE 68104

Greater York Area Genealogical Society, 6th and Nebraska, York, NE 68467

Holdrege Area Genealogical Club, Box 164, Bertrand, NE 68927

Holt County Genealogical Society, P.O. Box 376, O'neill, NE 68763

Hooker County Genealogical Society, Box 280, Mullen, NE 69152

Lexington Genealogical Society, P.O. Box 778, Lexington, NE 68850 0788

Lincoln-Lancaster County Genealogical Society, P.O. Box 30055, Lincoln, NE 68503

Madison County Genealogical Society, P.O. Box 1031, Norfolk, NE 68701

Madison County Genealogical Society, P.O. Box 347, Norfolk, NE 68701

Nebraska Society S.A.R., 6731 Sumner St., Lincoln, NE 68506

Nebraska State Genealogical Society, P.O. Box 5608, Lincoln, NE 68505 0608

North Central Nebr Genealogical Society, Box 362, O'neill, NE 68763

North Platte Genealogical Society, P.O. Box 1452, North Platte, NE 69101

Northeastern Nebraska Genealogical Society, Box 169, Lyons, NE 68038

Northwest Genealogical Society, P.O. Box 6, Alliance, NE 69301

Orchard Historical Society, Box 56, Orchard, NE 68764

Perkins County Genealogical Society, Box 418, Grant, NE 69140

Plains Genealogical Society, 208 S. Walnut St., Kimball, NE 69145

Platte Valley Kin Seekers, P.O. Box 153, Columbus, NE 68601

Prairie Pioneer Genealogical Society Inc., P.O. Box 1122, Grand Island, NE 68801

Public Library (Genealogy), 202 W. 4th St., Alliance, NE 69301

Public Library (Genealogy), Big Springs, NE 69122

Public Library (Genealogy), Broadwater, NE 69125

Public Library (Genealogy), Bayard, NE 69334

Public Library (Genealogy), Bridgeport, NE 69336

Ravenna Genealogical Society, 105 Alba St., Ravenna, NE 68869

Seward County Genealogical Society, P.O. Box 72, Seward, NE 68434

South Central Genealogical Society, Rt. 2 Box 57, Minden, NE 68959

Southeast Nebr Genealogical Society, P.O. Box 562, Beatrice, NE 68310

Southwest Nebraska Genealogical Society, 1515 W. Fifth, Mccook, NE 69001

Thayer County Genealogical Society, P.O. Box 387, Belvidere, NE 68315

Appendix B: Resources

Thomas County Genealogical Society, Box 136, Thedford, NE 69166

Tri-State Corners Genealogical Society, 120 E. 18th St., Falls City, NE 68355

Valley County Genealogical Society, 619 S. 10th, Ord, NE 68862

Washington County Genealogical Society, Blair Public Library, Blair, NE 68008

Afro-American Historical & Genealogical Society, P.O. Box 668, Manchester, NH 03105

American-Canadian Genealogical Society, P.O. Box 668, Manchester, NH 03105

Carrol County Chapter NHSOG, P.O. Box 250, Freedom, NH 03836

Chesire County Historical Society, 246 Main St., Keene, NH 03431

Hew Hampshire Historical Society, 30 Park St., Concord, NH 03301

Merrimack County Chapter NHSOG, R.R. 1, Contoocook, NH 03229

New Hampshire Society of Genealogy, P.O. Box 6733, Exeter, NH 03833

New Hampshire Society S.A.R., Box 141, Multonboro, NH 03226

North County Chapter NHSOG, P.O. Box 618, Littleton, NH 03561

Rockingham County Chapter NHSOG, P.O. Box 81, Exeter, NH 03833 0081

Westmoreland Historical Society, Box 443 Glebe Rd., Westmoreland, NH 03467

Assn. of Jewish Genealogical Societies, 1485 Teaneck Rd., Teaneck, NJ 07666

Burlington County Genealogical Club, P.O. Box 2449 Rd2, Mount Holly, NJ 08060

Genealogical Club/Metuchen-Edison Historical Society, P.O. Box 61, Metuchen, NJ 08840

Genealogical Society of Bergen Co., P.O. Box 432, Midland Park, NJ 07432

Genealogical Society of Bergen County Nj, P.O. Box 432, Midland Park, NJ 07432

Genealogical Society of New Jersey, P.O. Box 1291, New Brunswick, NJ 08903

Genealogical Society of the West Fields, 550 E. Broad St., Westfield, NJ 07090

Gloucester County Historical Society Library, 17 Hunter St., Woodbury, NJ 08096

Hunterdon County Historical Society, Hiram E. Deats Memorial Library 114 Main St., Flemington, NJ 08822

Jewish Genealogical Society of New Jersey, 1 Bedford Rd., Pompton Lakes, NJ 07442

Matawan Historical Society, P.O. Box 41, Matawan, NJ 07747

Metuchen/Edison Genealogical Club, 48 Elliot Place, Edison, NJ 08817

Monmouth County Historical Assn., 70 Court St., Freehold, NJ 07728

Morris Area Genealogical Society, P.O. Box 105, Convent Station, NJ 07961 0105

New Jersey Society S.A.R., P.O. Box 73, Forked River, NJ 08731

Ocean County Genealogical Society, 444 Longboat Ave., Beachwood, NJ 08722 2452

Ocean County Historical Society, 26 Hadley Ave., Toms River, NJ 08754

Passiac County New Jersey Genealogical Club, 430 Mt. Pleasant Ave., West Paterson, NJ 07424

Salem County Historical Society, 81-83 Market St., Salem, NJ 08079

Artesia Genealogical Society, P.O. Box 803, Artesia, NM 88210

Chaves County Genealogical Society, P.O. Box 51, Roswell, NM 88201

Eddy County Genealogical Society, P.O. Box 461, Carlsbad, NM 88220

Genealogical & Family Historical Comm, 1428 Miracerros S., Santa Fe, NM 87501

Genealogical Club\albuquerque Public Library, 423 Central Ave. N.E., Albuquerque, NM 87102

Lea County Genealogical Society, P.O. Box 1044, Lovington, NM 88260

Los Alamos Family Historical Society, P.O. Box 900, Los Alamos, NM 87544 0900

Los Alamos Genealogical Society, 2161B 36th St., Los Alamos, NM 87544

New Mexico Genealogical Society, P.O. Box 8283, Albuquerque, NM 87198 8283

S.E. New Mexico Genealogical Society, P.O. Box 5725, Hobbs, NM 88240

Sierra County Genealogical Society, P.O. Box 311, Truth Or Consequences, NM 87901

Appendix B: Resources

Southern New Mexico Genealogical Society, 5745 Leasburg Dr., Las Cruces, NM 88005

Totah Tracers Genealogical Society, C/o Salmon Ruin Libr P.O. Box 125, Farmington, NM 87401

Churchill County Historical & Genealogical Society, 1050 S. Main St., Fallon, NV 89406

Clark County Genealogical Society, P.O. Box 1929, Las Vegas, NV 89125 1929

Humboldt County Genealogical Society, 855 E. 5th St., Winnemucca, NV 89445

Jewish Genealogical Society of Las Vegas, P.O. Box 29342, Las Vegas, NV 89126

Nevada Society S.A.R., 309 Duke Cir., Las Vegas, NV 89107

Nevada State Genealogical Society, P.O. Box 20666, Reno, NV 89515

Northeastern Nevada Genealogical Society, P.O. Box 1903, Elko, NV 89801

Adirondack Genealogical/Historical Society, 100 Main St., Saranac Lake, NY 12983

Capital District Genealogical Society, P.O. Box 2174, Albany, NY 12220

Cayuga-Owasco Lakes Historical Society, P.O. Box 241, Moravia, NY 13118

Central New York Genealogical Society, Box 104 Colvin Station, Syracuse, NY 13205

Chautauqua County Genealogical Society, P.O. Box 404, Fredonia, NY 14063

Colonial Dames of America, 421 E. 61St St., New York, NY 10021

Creole-American Genealogical Society Inc., P.O. Box 2666, New York, NY 10008

Dutchess County Genealogical Society, P.O. Box 708, Poughkeepsie, NY 12602

Finger Lakes Genealogical Society, P.O. Box 47, Seneca Falls, NY 13148

Genealogical Conference of New York Inc., Interlaken, NY 14847

Genealogical Workshop Brooklyn Historical Society, 128 Pierrepont St., Brooklyn, NY 11201

Genealogical Workshop Huntington Historical Society, 209 Main St., Huntington, NY 11743

General Society of Colonial Wars, 122 58th St., New York, NY 10022

Heritage & Genealogical Society Montgomery Co., P.O. Box 1500, Fonda, NY 12068 1500

Historical & Genealogical Dept, Elting Library 93 Main St., New Paltz, NY 12561

Jewish Genealogical Society Inc., P.O. Box 6398, New York, NY 10128

Jewish Genealogical Society of Capital District, 55 Sycamore St., Albany, NY 12208

Jewish Genealogical Society of Long Island, 37 W. Cliff Dr., Dix Hills, NY 11746

Jewish Genealogical Society/Greater Buffalo, 174 Peppertree Dr # 7, Amherst, NY 14228

Kodak Genealogical Club, Kodak Park Activities Assn., Rochester, NY 14650

Livingston-Steuben County Genealogical Society, 9297 Shaw Rd. Rt. 1 Box 313, Nunda, NY 14517

Montgomery County Dept. of Historical & Archives, Old Courthouse, Fonda, NY 12068

Nassau Genealogical Workshop, 1101 Candlewood Rd., Brentwood, NY 11717

New York Genealogical and Biographical Society, 122-126 E. 58th St., New York, NY 10022 1939

Niagra County Genealogical Society, 2650 Hess Rd., Appleton, NY 14008

North NY American-Canadian Genealogical Society, P.O. Box 1256, Plattsburgh, NY 12901

Nyando Roots Genealogy Society, P.O. Box 175, Massena, NY 13662

Oneida County Historical Society, 1608 Genesee St., Utica, NY 13502

Ontario County Genealogical Society, 55 N. Main St., Canandaigua, NY 14424

Orange County Genealogical Society, 101 Main St., Goshen, NY 10924

Rochester Genealogical Society, P.O. Box 10501, Rochester, NY 14610

Roswell Flower Genealogical Library, 229 Washington St., Watertown, NY 13601

Southern Tier Genealogical Club, P.O. Box 680, Vestal, NY 13851 0680

St. Lawrence Valley Genealogical Society, P.O. Box 341, Colton, NY 13625 0341

Twin Tiers Genealogical Society, P.O. Box 763, Elmira, NY 14902

Appendix B: Resources

Ulster County Genealogical Society, P.O. Box 333, Hurley, NY 12443

W. New York Genealogical Society, P.O. Box 338, Hamburg, NY 14075

Westchester County Genealogical Society, P.O. Box 518, White Plains, NY 10603

Yates County Genealogical & Historical Society, 200 Main St., Penn Yan, NY 14527

Adams County Genealogical Society, P.O. Box 231, West Union, OH 45693

Allen County Chapter O.G.S., 620 W. Market St., Lima, OH 45801

Alliance Genealogical Society Chapter O.G.S., P.O. Box 3630, Alliance, OH 44601

American Society of Genealogy, 1328 Stimmel Rd., Columbus, OH 43223 2917

Ashland County Chapter O.G.S., Box 681, Ashland, OH 44805

Ashtabula County Chapter O.G.S., 54 E. Jefferson St., Jefferson, OH 44047

Athens County O.G.S., 65 N. Court St., Athens, OH 45701 2506

Auglaise County Chapter O.G.S., P.O. Box 2021, Wapakoneta, OH 45895

Belmont County Chapter O.G.S., 361 S. Chestnut St., Barnesville, OH 43713

Brown County Chapter O.G.S., P.O. Box 83, Georgetown, OH 45121

Butler County Chapter O.G.S., Box 2011, Middletown, OH 45044

Carroll County Chapter O.G.S., 59 3rd St. N.E., Carrollton, OH 44615

Champaign County Chapter O.G.S., P.O. Box 680, Urbana, OH 43078

Cincinnati Historical Society, 1301 Western Ave., Cincinnati, OH 45203

Clark County Chapter O.G.S., P.O. Box 1412, Springfield, OH 45501

Clermont County Chapter O.G.S., P.O. Box 394, Batavia, OH 45103

Clinton County O.G.S., P.O. Box 529, Wilmington, OH 45177

Columbiana County Chapter O.G.S., P.O. Box 861, Salem, OH 44460

Coshocton County Chapter O.G.S., P.O. Box 117, Coshocton, OH 43812

Council of OH Genealogists, P.O. Box 119, Washington Court House, OH 43160

Crawford County Chapter O.G.S., P.O. Box 92, Galion, OH 44833

Cuyahoga Valley Chapter O.G.S., P.O. Box 41414, Brecksville, OH 44141 0414

Cuyahoga West Chapter O.G.S., P.O. Box 26196, Fairview Park, OH 44126

Darke County Chapter O.G.S., P.O. Box 908, Greenville, OH 45331

Defiance County Chapter O.G.S., P.O. Box 675, Defiance, OH 43512

Delaware County Chapter O.G.S., P.O. Box 1126, Delaware, OH 43015

East Cuyahoga Chapter O.G.S., P.O. Box 24182, Lyndhurst, OH 44124

Erie County Chapter O.G.S., P.O. Box 1301, Sandusky, OH 44870

Fairfield County Chapter O.G.S., P.O. Box 1470, Lancaster, OH 43130

Fayette County Chapter O.G.S., P.O. Box 342, Washington Court House, OH 43160

Franklin County Chapter O.G.S., P.O. Box 2503, Columbus, OH 43216

Fulton County Chapter O.G.S., P.O. Box 337, Swanton, OH 43558

Gallia County Chapter O.G.S., P.O. Box 295, Gallipolis, OH 45631

Geauga County Chapter O.G.S., 110 E. Park St., Chardon, OH 44024

German Genealogical Society, 162 Burbridge Ave., Chillicothe, OH 45601

Greater Cleveland Chapter O.G.S., P.O. Box 40254, Cleveland, OH 44140

Greene County Chapter O.G.S., P.O. Box 706, Xenia, OH 45385

Guernsey County Chapter O.G.S., 836 Steubenville Ave. # B, Cambridge, OH 43725 2368

Hacker's Creek Pioneer Desc, 321 Highland Ave. S.W., Massillon, OH 44646

Hamilton County Chapter O.G.S., P.O. Box 15815, Cincinnati, OH 45215

Hancock County Chapter O.G.S., P.O. Box 672, Findlay, OH 45839

Hardin County Chapter O.G.S., P.O. Box 520, Kenton, OH 43326

Harrison County Chapter O.G.S., 45507 Unionvale Rd., Cadiz, OH 43907 9723

Henry County Chapter O.G.S., 208 N. East Ave., Deshler, OH 43516

Appendix B: Resources

Hocking County O.G.S., P.O. Box 115, Rockbridge, OH 43149 0115

Holmes County Chapter O.G.S., P.O. Box 136, Millersburg, OH 44654 0136

Hudson O.G.S., 22 Aurora St. #G, Hudson, OH 44236

Huron County Chapter O.G.S., P.O. Box 923, Norwalk, OH 44857

Intnl Society for British Genealogy, P.O. Box 20425, Cleveland, OH 44120

Jackson County Chapter O.G.S., P.O. Box 807, Jackson, OH 45640

Jefferson County Chapter O.G.S., P.O. Box 4712, Steubenville, OH 43952

Jewish Genealogical Society of Cleveland, 996 Eastlawn Dr., Highland Heights, OH 44143

Jewish Genealogical Society of Dayton, P.O. Box 338, Dayton, OH 45406

Johnstown Genealogical Society, P.O. Box 345, Mount Vernon, OH 43050

Knox County O.G.S., P.O. Box 1098, Mount Vernon, OH 43050 1098

Lake County Genealogical Society, 184 Phelps St., Painesville, OH 44077

Lawrence County Genealogical Society, P.O. Box 945, Ironton, OH 45638

Licking County Chapter O.G.S., P.O. Box 4037, Newark, OH 43055

Logan County Genealogical Society, P.O. Box 36, Bellefontaine, OH 43311

Lorain County Chapter O.G.S., P.O. Box 865, Elyria, OH 44036

Lucas County Chapter O.G.S., 325 N. Michigan St., Toledo, OH 43624

Madison County Chapter O.G.S., P.O. Box 102, London, OH 43140

Mahoning County Chapter O.G.S., 3430 Rebecca Dr., Canfield, OH 44406

Marion Area Chapter O.G.S., P.O. Box 844, Marion, OH 43302

Medina County Chapter O.G.S., P.O. Box 804, Medina, OH 44258

Meigs County Chapter O.G.S., Box 346, Pomeroy, OH 45769

Mennonite Historical Library, Bluffton College, Bluffton, OH 45817

Mercer County Chapter O.G.S., P.O. Box 437, Celina, OH 45822

Miami County Chapter O.G.S., P.O. Box 305, Troy, OH 45373

Miami Valley Chapter O.G.S., P.O. Box 1364, Dayton, OH 45401

Monroe County Chapter O.G.S., Box 641, Woodsfield, OH 43793

Montgomery County Chapter O.G.S., P.O. Box 1584, Dayton, OH 45401

Morgan County Chapter O.G.S., P.O. Box 418, Mcconnelsville, OH 43756

Morrow County Chapter O.G.S., P.O. Box 401, Mount Gilead, OH 43338

Muskingum County Chapter O.G.S., P.O. Box 3066, Zanesville, OH 43701

Noble County Chapter O.G.S., P.O. Box 444, Caldwell, OH 43724

N.W. Ohio Genealogical Society, P.O. Box 17066, Toledo, OH 43615

Ohio Genealogical Society, P.O. Box 2625, Mansfield, OH 44906

Ohio Historical Society Library, 1982 Velma Ave., Columbus, OH 43211

Ohio Society S.A.R., 2170 Brookridge Dr., Dayton, OH 45431

Ottawa County Chapter O.G.S., P.O. Box 193, Port Clinton, OH 43452

Parma Cuyahoga Chapter O.G.S., 6428 Nelwood Rd., Parma Hts, OH 44130

Paulding County Chapter O.G.S., 205 S. Main St., Paulding, OH 45879

Perry County Chapter O.G.S., P.O. Box 275, Junction City, OH 43748

Pike County Chapter O.G.S., P.O. Box 224, Waverly, OH 45690

Portage County Chapter O.G.S., 6252 N. Spring St., Ravenna, OH 44266

Preble County Chapter O.G.S., 301 N. Barron St., Eaton, OH 45320

Putnam County Chapter O.G.S., Box 403, Ottawa, OH 45875

Richland County Chapter O.G.S., P.O. Box 3823, Lexington, OH 44904

Richland-Shelby Genealogical Society, 6644 Baker Rd. #47, Shelby, OH 44875

Ross County Chapter O.G.S., P.O. Box 6352, Chillicothe, OH 45601

Sandusky County Chapter O.G.S., 1337 Hayes Ave., Fremont, OH 43420

Appendix B: Resources

Scioto County Chapter O.G.S., P.O. Box 812, Portsmouth, OH 45662

Seneca County Chapter O.G.S., P.O. Box 841, Tiffin, OH 44883 0157

Shelby Genealogical Society, 65 Marvin Ave., Shelby, OH 44875

Southern Ohio Genealogical Society, P.O. Box 414, Hillsboro, OH 45133

Southwest Cuyahoga Chapter O.G.S., 18631 Howe Rd., Strongsville, OH 44136

Stark County Chapter O.G.S., 7300 Woodcrest N.E., Canton, OH 44721

Summit County Chapter O.G.S., P.O. Box 2232, Akron, OH 44309

Tri County Lineage Research Society, Kaubisch Library, Fostoria, OH 44830

Trumbull County Chapter O.G.S., P.O. Box 309, Warren, OH 44483

Tuscarawas County Chapter O.G.S., P.O. Box 141, New Philadelphia, OH 44663

Union County Chapter O.G.S., P.O. Box 438, Marysville, OH 43040

Van Wert County Chapter O.G.S., P.O. Box 485, Van Wert, OH 45891

Vinton County Chapter O.G.S., P.O. Box 306, Hamden, OH 45634 0306

Warren County Chapter O.G.S., 300 E. Silver St., Lebanon, OH 45036

Washington County Chapter O.G.S., P.O. Box 2174, Marietta, OH 45750

Wayne County Chapter O.G.S., 546 E. Bowman St., Wooster, OH 44691

Wellington Genealogical Workshop, P.O. Box 224, Wellington, OH 44090

Williams County Chapter O.G.S., P.O. Box 293, Bryan, OH 43506

Wood County Chapter O.G.S., P.O. Box 722, Bowling Green, OH 43402

Wyandot County Chapter O.G.S., P.O. Box 414, Upper Sandusky, OH 43351

Atoka County Genealogical Society, P.O. Box 83, Atoka, OK 74525

Bartlesville Genealogical Society, Sixth & Johnstone, Bartlesville, OK 74003

Broken Arrow Genealogical Society, P.O. Box 1244, Broken Arrow, OK 74013

Bryan County Heritage Society, P.O. Box 153, Calera, OK 74730

Cleveland County Genealogical Society, P.O. Box 6176, Norman, OK 73070

Cushing Genealogical Society, P.O. Box 551, Cushing, OK 74023

Federation of Oklahoma Genealogical Society, P.O. Box 26151, Oklahoma City, OK 73126

Ft. Gibson Genealogical & Historical Society, P.O. Box 416, Fort Gibson, OK 74434

Garfield County Genealogical Inc., P.O. Box 1106, Enid, OK 73702

Grady County Genealogical Society, P.O. Box 792, Chickasha, OK 73023

Haskell County Genealogical Society, 408 N.E. 6th St., Stigler, OK 74462

Logan County Genealogical Society, P.O. Box 1419, Guthrie, OK 73044

Major County Genealogical Society, Box 24 Rt. 2, Okeene, OK 73763

Mayes County Genealogical Society, P.O. Box 924, Chouteau, OK 74337

Mcclain County Historical & Genealogical Society, 203 Washington St., Purcell, OK 73080

Mccurtain County Genealogical Society, P.O. Box 1832, Idabel, OK 74745

Muldrow Genealogical Society, P.O. Box 1253, Muldrow, OK 74948

Muskoge County Genealogical Society, 801 W. Okmulgee, Muskogee, OK 74401

N.E. Oklahoma Genealogical Society, P.O. Box 484, Vinita, OK 74301

N.W. Oklahoma Genealogical Society, P.O. Box 834, Woodward, OK 73801

Oklahoma Society S.A.R., P.O. Box 715, Sapulpa, OK 74066

Oklahoma Yesterday Publications, 8745 E. 9th St., Tulsa, OK 74112

Okmulgee County Genealogical Society, P.O. Box 805, Okmulgee, OK 74447

Ottawa County Genealogical Society, Box 1383, Miami, OK 74355

Pawhuska Genealogical Society, P.O. Box 807, Pawhuska, OK 74056

Payne County Genealogical Society, 206 W. 6th, Stillwater, OK 74074

Pioneer Genealogical Society, P.O. Box 1965, Ponca City, OK 74602

Appendix B: Resources

Pittsburg County Genealogical & Historical Society, 113 E. Carl Albert Pkwy, Mcalester, OK 74501

Pocahontas Trails Genealogical Society, Rt. 2 Box 40, Mangum, OK 73554

Pontotoc County Historical & Genealogical Society, 221 W. 16th St., Ada, OK 74820

Poteau Valley Genealogical Society, P.O. Box 1031, Poteau, OK 74953

Sequoyah, P.O. Box 1112, Sallisaw, OK 74955

Southwest Oklahoma Genealogical Society, P.O. Box 148, Lawton, OK 73502

Stephens County Genealogical Society, 301 N. 8th, Duncan, OK 73533

Three Forks Genealogical Society, 102 1/2 S. State St., Wagoner, OK 74467

Tulsa Genealogical Society, P.O. Box 585, Tulsa, OK 74101

Western Plains Weatherford Genealogical Society, P.O. Box 1672, Weatherford, OK 73096

Western Trails Genealogical Society, P.O. Box 70, Altus, OK 73522

Woods County Genealogists, P.O. Box 234, Alva, OK 73717

Alsi Historical & Genealogical Society Inc., P.O. Box 822, Waldport, OR 97394

Blue Mountain Genealogical Society, P.O. Box 1801, Pendleton, OR 97801

Caltsop County Genealogical Society, 450 10th St., Astoria, OR 97103

Clackamas County Family Historical Society, P.O. Box 995, Oregon City, OR 97045

Columbia Gorge Genealogical Society, 722 Court St., The Dalles, OR 97058

Cottage Grove Genealogical Society, P.O. Box 388, Cottage Grove, OR 97424

Deschutes County Historical & Genealogical Society, P.O. Box 5252, Bend, OR 97708

Genealogical Council of Oregon Inc., P.O. Box 15169, Portland, OR 97215

Genealogical Forum of Portland, 1410 S.W. Morrison Rm 812, Portland, OR 97205

Genealogical Heritage Council, P.O. Box 628, Ashland, OR 97520 0021

Genealogical Society of Douglas Co., P.O. Box 579, Roseburg, OR 97470

Grants Pass Genealogical Society, P.O. Box 1834, Grants Pass, OR 97526

Jewish Genealogical Society of Or, 6651 Capitol Hwy, Portland, OR 97219

Klamath Basin Genealogical Society, 1555 Hope St., Klamath Falls, OR 97603

Lapine Genealogical Society, P.O. Box 2081, La Pine, OR 97739

Lebanon Genealogical Society, 626 2nd St., Lebanon, OR 97355

Linn Genealogical Society, P.O. Box 1222, Albany, OR 97321

Mid-Columbia Genealogical Society, 722 Court St., The Dalles, OR 97058

Mid-Valley Genealogical Society, 3960 N.W. Elizabeth Place, Corvallis, OR 97330

Milton-Freewater Genealogical Club, 127 S.E. 6th St., Milton-Freewater, OR 97862

Oregon Genealogical Society, P.O. Box 10306, Eugene, OR 97440

Pocahontas Trails Genealogical Society, 537 N.E. Locust St., Oakland, OR 97462

Polk County Genealogical Society, 535 S.E. Ash St., Dallas, OR 97338

Point Orford Genealogical Society, 555 W. 20th St., Port Orford, OR 97465

Rogue Valley Genealogical Society, 125 S. Central Ave. #204, Medford, OR 97501

Siuslau Genealogical Society, P.O. Box 1540, Florence, OR 97439

Sweet Home Genealogical Society, 13th & Kalmia Sts., Sweet Home, OR 97386

Tillamook County Historical Society, P.O. Box 123, Tillamook, OR 97141

Willamette Valley Genealogical Society, P.O. Box 2083, Salem, OR 97308

Woodburn Genealogical Club, 2220 Oregon Ct, Woodburn, OR 97071

Yamhill County Genealogical Society, P.O. Box 568, Mcminnville, OR 97128

Beaver County Genealogical Society, 1301 7th Ave., Beaver Falls, PA 15010

Berks County Genealogical Society, P.O. Box 14774, Reading, PA 19612

Blair County Genealogical Society, P.O. Box 855, Altoona, PA 16603

Bucks County Genealogical Society, P.O. Box 1092, Doylestown, PA 18901

Capital Area Genealogical Society, P.O. Box 4502, Harrisburg, PA 17111 4502

Appendix B: Resources

Centre County Genealogical Society, P.O. Box 1135, State College, PA 16801

Chester County Historical Society, 225 N. High St., West Chester, PA 19083

Clearfield County Historical Society - Genealogical, 104 E. Pine St., Clearfield, PA 16830

Cornerstone Genealogical Society, P.O. Box 547, Waynesburg, PA 15370

Crawford County Genealogical Society, 848 N. Main St., Meadville, PA 16335

Elk County Genealogical Society, P.O. Box 142, Johnsonburg, PA 15845

Erie Society for Genealogical Research, P.O. Box 1403, Erie, PA 16512

Fayette County Genealogical Society, 24 Jefferson St., Uniontown, PA 15401

Friends Historical Assn., Haverford College, Haverford, PA 19041

Genealogical Society of Pa, 1300 Locust St., Philadelphia, PA 19107

Genealogical Society of S.W. Pennsylvania, P.O. Box 894, Washington, PA 15301

Heritage Society of Pennsylvania, P.O. Box 146, Laughlintown, PA 15655

Historical & Genealogical Society of Indiana Co., Sixth St. & Wayne Ave., Indiana, PA 15701

Jewish Genealogical Society of Pittsburgh, 2131 Fifth Ave., Pittsburgh, PA 15219

Jewish Genealogical Society of Philadelphia, 332 Harrison Ave., Elkins Park, PA 19117

Lycoming County Genealogical Society, P.O. Box 3625, South Williamsport, PA 17701

Mckean County Genealogical Society, P.O. Box 207A, Derrick City, PA 16727

Mercer County Genealogical Society, Box 812, Sharon, PA 16146

Northampton County Historical & Genealogical Society, 101 S. 4th St., Easton, PA 18042

Oil City Heritage Society, P.O. Box 962, Oil City, PA 16301

Old York Road Genealogical Society, 1030 Old York Rd., Abington, PA 19001

Pennsylvania Genealogical Society, 1300 Locust St., Philadelphia, PA 19107

Pennsylvania Society S.A.R., R.R. 1 Box 422, Monongahela, PA 15063

Perry Historical Genealogical Society, P.O. Box 73, Newport, PA 17074

South Central Pennsylvania Genealogical Society, P.O. Box 1824, York, PA 17405

Tarentum Genealogical Society, 315 E. Sixth Ave., Tarentum, PA 15084

Venago County Genealogical Club, P.O. Box 811, Oil City, PA 16301

Warren County Genealogical Society, 230 Oneida Ave., Warren, PA 16365 2253

Washington County Historical Society, 49 E. Maiden St., Washington, PA 15301

Western Pennsylvania Genealogical Society, 4338 Bigelow Blvd., Pittsburgh, PA 15213

Windbar-Johnstown Area Genealogical Society, P.O. Box 3308, Johnstown, PA 15904

Wyoming Historical & Genealogical Society, 69 S. Franklin St., Wilkes-Barre, PA 18701

York County Historical Society Library, 250 E. Market St., York, PA 17403

American-French Genealogical Society, P.O. Box 2113, Pawtucket, RI 02861

Newport Historical Society, 82 Touro St., Newport, RI 02840

Rhode Island Mayflower Desc, 128 Massasoit, Warwick, RI 02888

Rhode Island Society S.A.R., P.O. Box 137, East Greenwich, RI 02818

Rhode Island State Historical Society, 52 Power St., Providence, RI 02906

Abbeville-Greenwood Regional Library, N. Main St., Greenwood, SC 29646

Catawba-Wateree Genealogical Society, 1314 Broad St., Camden, SC 29020

Charleston Chapter South Carolina Genealogical Society, 1300 N. Edgewater, Charleston, SC 29407

Chester County Genealogical Society, P.O. Box 336, Richburg, SC 29729

Columbia Chapter South Carolina Genealogical Society, P.O. Box 11353, Columbia, SC 29211

Dutch Fork Genealogical Society, P.O. Box 481, Chapin, SC 29036

Edgefield District Genealogical Society, P.O. Box 468, Edgefield, SC 29824

Appendix B: Resources

Greenville Genealogical Society, P.O. Box 16236, Greenville, SC 29606

Hilton Head Island Genealogical Society, P.O. Box 5492, Hilton Head Island, SC 29938 5492

Laurens District Genealogical Society, P.O. Box 1217, Laurens, SC 29360

Lexington County Genealogical Assn., P.O. Box 1442, Lexington, SC 29072

Old 96 District Genealogical Society, P.O. Box 3468, Greenwood, SC 29648

Old Darlington District Genealogical Society, P.O. Box 10, Lydia, SC 29079

Old Pendleton District Genealogical Society, 101 Cherokee Rd., Clemson, SC 29631

Orangeburg German-Swiss Genealogical Society, P.O. Box 974, Orangeburg, SC 29116 0974

Pee Dee Chapter South Carolina Genealogical Society, P.O. Box 236, Latta, SC 29565

Pickney District Chapter South Carolina Genealogical Society, P.O. Box 5281, Spartanburg, SC 29304

South Carolina Historical Society, 100 Meeting St., Charleston, SC 29401

Sumter County Genealogical Society, P.O. Box 2543, Sumter, SC 29151

York County Genealogical & Historical Society, P.O. Box 3061 Crs, Rock Hill, SC 29731

Aberdeen Area Genealogical Society, 519 S. Kline St., Aberdeen, SD 57401

Brookings Area Genealogical Society, 524 Fourth St., Brookings, SD 57006

East River Genealogical Society Forum, R.R. 2 Box 148, Wolsey, SD 57384

Lake County Genealogical Society, Karl Mundt Library Dakota St. Coll, Madison, SD 57042

Lyman-Brule Genealogical Society, Box 555, Chamberlain, SD 57325

Mitchell Area Genealogical Society, 1300 Palmer Place, Mitchell, SD 57301 3137

Pierre-Ft. Pierre Genealogical Society, P.O. Box 925, Pierre, SD 57501

Rapid City Society for Genealogical Research, P.O. Box 1495, Rapid City, SD 57701

Sioux Valley Genealogical Society, 200 W. 6th St., Sioux Falls, SD 57102 0302

South Dakota Genealogical Society, Box 490, Winner, SD 57580

South Dakota Society S.A.R., P.O. Box 2800, Rapid City, SD 57709

Tri State Genealogical Society, 905 5th Ave., Belle Fourche, SD 57717

Bedford County Historical Society Inc., 250 Riverbend Rd., Shelbyville, TN 37160

Blount County Genealogical & Historical Society, P.O. Box 653, Maryville, TN 37803

Bradley County Historical Society, P.O. Box 4845, Cleveland, TN 37320 4845

Campbell County Genealogical Society, 109 Crestview Dr., La Follette, TN 37766

Claiborne County Historical Society, P.O. Box 32, Tazewell, TN 37879

Coffee County Historical Society, P.O. Box 524, Manchester, TN 37355

East Tennesse Historical Society, 500 W. Church Ave., Knoxville, TN 37902 2505

Fentress County Genealogical Society, P.O. Box 178, Jamestown, TN 38556

Franklin County Historical Society, P.O. Box 130, Winchester, TN 37398

Giles County Historical Society, P.O. Box 693, Pulaski, TN 38478

Greene County Genealogical Society, 1324 Mt. Bethel Rd., Greeneville, TN 37743

Hamblen County Genealogical Society, P.O. Box 1213, Morristown, TN 37816 1213

Hancock County Historical & Genealogical Society, P.O. Box 277, Sneedville, TN 37869

Hawkins County Genealogical Society, P.O. Box 439, Rogersville, TN 37857

Jefferson County Genealogical Society, P.O. Box 267, Jefferson City, TN 37760

Macon County Historical Society, Rt. 3, Lafayette, TN 37083

Marion County Tn Genealogical Group, R.R. 5 Box 224, Whitwell, TN 37397

Marshall County Historical Society, 224 3rd Ave. N., Lewisburg, TN 37091

Maury County Historical Society, P.O. Box 147, Columbia, TN 38401

Mid-West Tennessee Genealogical Society, P.O. Box 3343, Jackson, TN 38303

227

Appendix B: Resources

Morgan County Genealogical & Historical Society, Rt. 2 Box 992, Wartburg, TN 37887

Obion County Genealogical Society, P.O. Box 241, Union City, TN 38261

Old James County Historical Society, P.O. Box 203, Ooltewah, TN 37363

Pellissippi Genealogical & Historical Society, 118 S. Hicks, Clinton, TN 37716

Roane County Genealogical Society, P.O. Box 297, Kingston, TN 37763 0297

Signal Mt. Genealogical Society, 103 Florida Ave., Signal Mountain, TN 37377

Tenn Genealogical Library, 3340 Poplar Ave., Memphis, TN 38111

Tennessee Genealogical Society, P.O. Box 111249, Memphis, TN 38111 1249

Tennessee Society S.A.R., 1712 Natchez Trace, Nashville, TN 37212

Union County Historical Society, P.O. Box 95, Maynardville, TN 37807

Upper Cumberland Genealogical Assn., 48 E. Broad St., Cookeville, TN 38501

Van Buren County Historical Society, P.O. Box 126, Spencer, TN 38585

Watauga Assn.. of Genealogy, P.O. Box 117, Johnson City, TN 37605 0117

Wayne County Historical Society, P.O. Box 866, Waynesboro, TN 38485

Weakley County Genealogical Society, P.O. Box 894, Martin, TN 38237

Amarillo Genealogical Society, P.O. Box 2171, Amarillo, TX 79189

Anderson County Genealogical Society, P.O. Box 2045, Palestine, TX 75802

Arlington Genealogical Society, 101 E. Abram St., Arlington, TX 76010

Armstrong County Historical Assn., R.R. 1 Box 241 E., Claude, TX 79019

Atascosito Historical Society, P.O. Box 310, Liberty, TX 77575 0310

Athens Genealogical Organization, 121 Prairieville St., Athens, TX 75751

Austin Genealogical Society, P.O. Box 1507, Austin, TX 78767

Austin Jewish Genealogical Society, 1301 W. Lynn #202, Austin, TX 78703

Bandera Chapter D.A.R., H.C. 1 Box 59, Bandera, TX 78003

Bay Area Heritage Society, P.O. Box 4161, Baytown, TX 77520

Baytown Genealogical Society, P.O. Box 2486, Baytown, TX 77522

Beaumont Heritage Society, 2985 French Rd., Beaumont, TX 77706

Bellville Historical Society, P.O. Box 67, Bellville, TX 77418

Big Thicket Genealogical Club, P.O. Box 1260, Kountze, TX 77625

Boerne Area Historical Society, Box 178, Boerne, TX 78006

Bosque Valley Heritage Society, Box 168, Valley Mills, TX 76689

Brazos Genealogical Assn., P.O. Box 5493, Bryan, TX 77805 5493

Brazosport Genealogical Society, P.O. Box 813, Lake Jackson, TX 77566

Brown County Historical Society, P.O. Box 146, Brownwood, TX 76801

Burkburnett Genealogical Society, 215 E. Fourth St., Burkburnett, TX 76354

Burnet County Genealogical Society, 100 E. Washington St., Burnet, TX 78611

Caldwell County Historical Genealogical Society, 215 S. Pecan Ave., Luling, TX 78648

Calhoun County Genealogical Society, P.O. Box 1150, Port Lavaca, TX 77979

Cass County Genealogical Society, P.O. Box 541, Atlanta, TX 75551

Castro County Genealogical Society, P.O. Box 911, Dimmitt, TX 79027

Center for Genealogical Research, 5300 Caroline, Houston, TX 77004

Central Texas Genealogical Society, 1717 Austin Ave., Waco, TX 76701

Chambers County Heritage Society, P.O. Box 870, Mont Belvieu, TX 77580

Chaparral Genealogical Society, P.O. Box 606, Tomball, TX 77375

Cherokee County Genealogical Society, P.O. Box 1332, Jacksonville, TX 75766

Childress Genealogical Society, 117 Ave. B N.E., Childress, TX 79201

Cleveland Area Genealogical Ent., 220 S. Bonham, Cleveland, TX 77327

Appendix B: Resources

Coastal Bend Genealogical Society, 402 Chase Dr., Corpus Christi, TX 78400

Coastal Bend Genealogical Society, P.O. Box 2711, Corpus Christi, TX 78403

Collin County Genealogical Society, P.O. Box 865052, Plano, TX 75086 5052

Comal County Genealogical Society, P.O. Box 310583, New Braunfels, TX 78130 0583

Cooke County Heritage Society, P.O. Box 150, Gainesville, TX 76240

Coryell County Genealogical Society, 811 Main St., Gatesville, TX 76528

Cottle County Genealogical Society, Box 1005, Paducah, TX 79248

Crockett County Historical Society, P.O. Box B, Ozona, TX 76943

Cross Timbers Genealogical Society, P.O. Box 197, Gainesville, TX 76240

Cypress Basin Genealogical & Historical Society, P.O. Box 403, Mount Pleasant, TX 75455

Czech Heritage Society Texas, 9174 Westview, Houston, TX 77055

Dallas County E. Genealogical Society, 7637 Mary Dan Dr., Dallas, TX 75217 4603

Dallas Genealogical Society, P.O. Box 12648, Dallas, TX 75225

Deaf Smith County Genealogical Society, 211 E. 4th St., Hereford, TX 79045

Denton County Genealogical Society, P.O. Box 23322 Twu Stn, Denton, TX 76204

Descendants of Mexican War Vets, 1114 Pacific Dr., Richardson, TX 75081

Donley County Genealogical Society, Box 116, Clarendon, TX 79226

East Texas Genealogical Society, P.O. Box 6967, Tyler, TX 75711

El Paso Genealogical Library, 3651 Douglas, El Paso, TX 79903

El Paso Genealogical Society, 501 N. Oregon St., El Paso, TX 79901

Ellis County Genealogical Society, P.O. Box 385, Waxahachie, TX 75165

Forney Heritage Society, 98 F.M. 2757, Forney, TX 75126

Freestone County Genealogical Society, P.O. Box 14, Fairfield, TX 75840

Ft. Bend County Genealogical Society, P.O. Box 274, Richmond, TX 77469

Ft. Brown County Genealogical Society, 608 E. Adams, Brownsville, TX 78520

Ft. Clark Historical Society, P.O. Box 1061, Brackettville, TX 78832

Ft. Worth Genealogical Society, P.O. Box 9767, Fort Worth, TX 76107 2767

Galveston County Genealogical Society, 2310 Sealy, Galveston, TX 77550

Genealogical & Historical Society Caldwell Co., 215 S. Pecan Ave., Luling, TX 78648

Genealogical Research Center, Rt. 1 Box 405, Kountze, TX 77625

Genealogical Society / Big Spring, Howard County Library, Big Spring, TX 79720

Genealogical Society Kendall Co., P.O. Box 623, Boerne, TX 78006

Genealogical Society N.E. Texas, 2400 Clarksville St., Paris, TX 75460

German-Texas Heritage Society, 507 E. 10th St., Austin, TX 78768

Gillespie County Historical Society, P.O. Box 542, Longview, TX 75606

Grand Prairie Genealogical Society, P.O. Box 532026, Grand Prairie, TX 75053

Grayson County Genealogical Society, 421 N. Travis, Sherman, TX 75090

Gregg County Historical & Genealogical Society, P.O. Box 542, Longview, TX 75606

Gromes County Heritage Assn., 1215 E. Washington Ave., Navasota, TX 77868

Guadalupe Victoria Chapter D.A.R., 707 E. College St., Seguin, TX 78155

Gulf Coast Ancestral Research, P.O. Box 157, Wallisville, TX 77597

Harris County Genealogical Society, P.O. Box 391, Pasadena, TX 77501

Heart of Texas Genealogical Society, P.O. Box 133, Rochelle, TX 76872

Hemphill County Historical & Genealogical Society, Rt. 2, Canadian, TX 79014

Henderson County Historical Society, P.O. Box 943, Athens, TX 75751

Heritage Assn. San Marcos, P.O. Box 1806, San Marcos, TX 78666

Heritage Society Washington Co., P.O. Box 1123, Brenham, TX 77833

Hi Plains Genealogical Society, 825 Austin, Plainview, TX 79072

Appendix B: Resources

Hill County Genealogical Society, P.O. Box 72, Brandon, TX 76628

Hill Country Genealogical Society, Prairie Mt. Rt., Llano, TX 78643

Hillsboro Heritage League, P.O. Box 2, Hillsboro, TX 76645

Hispanic Genealogical Society, 2932 Barksdale, Houston, TX 77093

Hood County Genealogical Society, P.O. Box 1623, Granbury, TX 76048

Hopkins County Genealogical Society, P.O. Box 624, Sulphur Springs, TX 75482

Houston Area Genealogical Assn., 2507 Tannehill, Houston, TX 77008 3052

Houston Genealogical Forum, P.O. Box 271466, Houston, TX 77277 1466

Humble Genealogical Society, P.O. Box 2723, Humble, TX 77338

Hunt County Genealogical Society, P.O. Box 398, Greenville, TX 75401

Hutchinson County Genealogical Society, 625 Weatherly St., Borger, TX 79007

Johnson County Genealogical Society, P.O. Box 10246, Cleburne, TX 76033 5246

Karnes County Historical Society, Box 162, Karnes City, TX 78118

Kaufman County Genealogical Society, Box 337, Terrell, TX 75160

Kent County Genealogical & Historical Society, Box 414, Jayton, TX 79528

Kerrville Genealogical Society, 505 Water St., Kerrville, TX 78028

Lake Cities Historical Society, P.O. Box 1222, Lake Dallas, TX 75065

Lamesa Area Genealogical Society, Box 1264, Lamesa, TX 79331

Lee County Genealogical Society, Rt. 1 Box 8D, Ledbetter, TX 78946

Leon County Genealogical Society, P.O. Box 500, Centerville, TX 75833

Limestone County Genealogical Society, 350 E. Rusk St., Mexia, TX 76667

Lubbock Heritage Society, P.O. Box 5443, Lubbock, TX 79417

Lufkin Genealogical & Historical Society, P.O. Box 150631, Lufkin, TX 75915 0631

Madison County Genealogical Society, Box 26, Madisonville, TX 77864

Matagorda County Genealogical Society, P.O. Box 264, Bay City, TX 77404

Mcallen Genealogical Society, 601 N. Main St., Mcallen, TX 78501

Mesquite Historical & Genealogical Society, P.O. Box 165, Mesquite, TX 75149

Mid Cities Genealogical Society, P.O. Box 407, Bedford, TX 76095 0407

Midland Genealogical Society, P.O. Box 1191, Midland, TX 79702

Montague County Genealogical Society, P.O. Box 795, Bowie, TX 76230

Montgomery County Genealogical & Historical Society, P.O. Box 751, Conroe, TX 77305 0751

Nacogdoches Genealogical Society, P.O. Box 4634, Nacogdoches, TX 75962

Navarro County Genealogical Society, P.O. Box 2278, Corsicana, TX 75151

New Boston Genealogical Society, P.O. Box 404, New Boston, TX 75570

North Texas Genealogical & Historical Assn., Box 4602, Wichita Falls, TX 76308

Orange County Historical Society, P.O. Box 1345, Orange, TX 77630

Pampa Genealogical & Historical Society, 430 N. Summer St., Pampa, TX 79065

Panhandle-Plains Historical Society, Box 967 Wt Stn, Canyon, TX 79016

Parker County Genealogical Society, 1214 Charles St., Weatherford, TX 76086

Pecan Valley Genealogical Society, 600 Carnegie Blvd., Brownwood, TX 76801

Permian Basin Genealogical Society, 321 W. 5th St., Odessa, TX 79761

Plano Heritage Assn., 1900 W. 15th St., Plano, TX 75075

Polish Genealogical Society of Texas, 218 Beaver Bend, Houston, TX 77037

Polk County Heritage Society, 207 N. Beatty St., Livingston, TX 77351

Public Library (Genealogy), 622 N. Lee St., Odessa, TX 79761

Public Library (Genealogy), 3716 Lee St., Greenville, TX 75401

Public Library (Genealogy), 421 N. Travis, Sherman, TX 75090

230

Appendix B: Resources

Red River Genealogical Society, Box D, Clarksville, TX 75426

Refugio County Historical Society, 102 West St., Refugio, TX 78377

Salado Historical Society, P.O. Box 251, Salado, TX 76571

San Angelo Genealogical & Historical Society, P.O. Box 3453, San Angelo, TX 76901

San Antonio Genealogical & Historical Society, P.O. Box 17461, San Antonio, TX 78217 0461

San Jacinto County Heritage Society, P.O. Box 505, Coldspring, TX 77331

San Marcos/hays County Genealogical Society, P.O. Box 503, San Marcos, TX 78666

Scarborough Library of Genealogy, Mcmurry College Library Mcmurry Stn, Abilene, TX 79605

Schleicher County Historical Society, Box 473, Eldorado, TX 76936

S.E. Texas Genealogical & Historical Society, P.O. Box 3827, Beaumont, TX 77704

Smith County Historical Society, 125 S. College Ave., Tyler, TX 75702

Southern Plains Genealogical Society, 4215 University Ave., Lubbock, TX 79408

Southern Texas Genealogical Society, P.O. Box 754, Beeville, TX 78104

Soc Desc of Mex War Vets, 1114 Pacific, Richardson, TX 75081

Southwest Genealogical Society, 1300 San Pedro Ave., San Antonio, TX 78212

Stephens County Genealogical Society, P.O. Box 350, Breckenridge, TX 76424

S.W. Texas Genealogical Society, P.O. Box 295, Uvalde, TX 78802

Tarrant County Black Historical & Genealogical Society, 1020 E. Humboldt St., Fort Worth, TX 76104

Taylor Heritage Society, P.O. Box 385, Taylor, TX 76574

Tex Wendish Heritage Society, R.R. 2 Box 155, Giddings, TX 78942

Texarkana Historical Museum (Genealogy), 219 State Line, Texarkana, TX 75501

Texarkana USA Genealogical Society, P.O. Box 2323, Texarkana, TX 75504

Texas Society S.A.R., 3342 Dartmoor Dr., Dallas, TX 75229

Texas State Genealogical Society, Rt. 4 Box 56, Sulphur Springs, TX 75482

Timspon Area Genealogical & Heritage Society, P.O. Box 726, Timpson, TX 75975

Tip o'Texas Genealogical Society, Public Library, Harlingen, TX 78550

Val Verde County Genealogical Society, P.O. Box 442052, Del Rio, TX 78842

Van Zandt County Genealogical Society, P.O. Box 716, Canton, TX 75103

Victoria County Genealogical Society, 302 N. Main St., Victoria, TX 77901

Walker County Genealogical Society, P.O. Box 1295, Huntsville, TX 77342 1295

Waller County Historical Society, P.O. Box 235, Brookshire, TX 77423

Wallisville Heritage, P.O. Box 16, Wallisville, TX 77597 0016

Ward County Genealogical Society, 400 E. Fourth St., Monahans, TX 79756

West Bell Genealogical Society, P.O. Box 851, Killeen, TX 76540

West Texas Genealogical Society, P.O. Box 2307, Abilene, TX 79604

Wetsern Plains-Weatherford Genealogical Society, P.O. Box 1672, Weatherford, TX 76086

Williamson County Genealogical Society, P.O. Box 585, Round Rock, TX 78680

Winkler County Genealogical Society, P.O. Box 1028, Kermit, TX 79745

Wise County Genealogical Society, P.O. Box 126, Rhome, TX 76078

Wood County Genealogical Society, P.O. Box 832, Quitman, TX 75783

Yorktown Historical Society, P.O. Box 884, Yorktown, TX 78164

Assn. of Professional Genealogists, P.O. Box 11601, Salt Lake City, UT 84147

Byu Library, Provo, UT 84601

Dixie Genealogical Library, 410 S. 200 E., Saint George, UT 84770

Early Mormon Research Institute, P.O. Box 2650, Salt Lake City, UT 84110

Family Historical Library, 35 N. W. Temple St., Salt Lake City, UT 84150

International PAF, 2463 Ledgewood Dr., West Jordan, UT 84084

Appendix B: Resources

Jewish Genealogical Society of S.L.C., 3510 Fleetwood Dr., Salt Lake City, UT 84109

St. George Genealogical Club, P.O. Box 184, Saint George, UT 84770

Temple Area Genealogical Library, Manti, UT 84642

Utah Genealogical Assn., P.O. Box 1144, Salt Lake City, UT 84110

Utah Society S.A.R., 5539 Capital Reef Dr., West Jordan, UT 84084

Albermarle County Historical Society, 220 Court Sq, Charlottesville, VA 22901

Augusta County Historical Society, P.O. Box 686, Staunton, VA 24401

Bath County Historical Society, P.O. Box 212, Warm Springs, VA 24484

Bedford Historical Society, P.O. Box 602, Bedford, VA 24523

Central Virginia Genealogical Assn., P.O. Box 39, Crozet, VA 22932

Chesterfield Historical Society, P.O. Box 40, Culpeper, VA 22701

Claiborne County Historical Society, Rt. 1 Box 589, Jonesville, VA 24263

Clarke County Historical Assn., P.O. Box 306, Berryville, VA 22611

Culpeper Historical Society, P.O. Box 785, Culpeper, VA 22701

Cumberland County Historical Society, Box 88, Cumberland, VA 23040

Fairfax Genealogical Society, P.O. Box 2344, Merrifield, VA 22116

Genealogical Research Institute of Va, P.O. Box 29178, Richmond, VA 23242 0178

Genealogical Society of Page Co., P.O. Box 734, Luray, VA 22835 0734

Giles County Virginia Historical Society, Box 404, Perisburg, VA 24134

Goochland County Historical Society, Box 602, Goochland, VA 23063

Greene County Historical Society, P.O. Box 185, Stanardsville, VA 22973

Harrisonburg-Rockingham Historical Society, P.O. Box 716, Dayton, VA 22821

Historical Society of Washington Co., Box 484, Abingdon, VA 24210

Holston Terr Genealogical Society, P.O. Box 433, Bristol, VA 24203

Jewish Genealogical Society of Greater Washington, P.O. Box 412, Vienna, VA 22183 0412

King & Queen Historical Society, Newtown, VA 23126

Loudoun Genealogical Club, P.O. Box 254, Leesburg, VA 22075

National Genealogical Society, 4527 17th St. N., Arlington, VA 22207 2399

Norfolk Genealogical Society, P.O. Box 12813, Norfolk, VA 23502

Northern Neck Historical Society, P.O. Box 716, Montross, VA 22520

Northumberland County Historical Society, P.O. Box 221, Heathsville, VA 22473

Pittsylvania Historical Society, P.O. Box 846, Chatham, VA 24531

Prince William County Genealogical Society, 9400 Blackstone Rd., Manassas, VA 22110

Roanoke Valley Historical Society, P.O. Box 1904, Roanoke, VA 24008

S.W. Virginia Genealogical Society, P.O. Box 12485, Roanoke, VA 24026

Tidewateer Genealogical Society, P.O. Box 76, Hampton, VA 23669

Virginia Genealogical Society, P.O. Box 7469, Richmond, VA 23221

VA-NC Piedmont Genealogical Society, P.O. Box 2272, Danville, VA 24541

Virginia Beach Genealogical Society, P.O. Box 62901, Virginia Beach, VA 23462

Virginia Society S.A.R., 7214 Regent Dr., Alexandria, VA 22307

Winchester-Frederick Historical Society, P.O. Box 97, Winchester, VA 22601

Genealogical Society of Vermont, 46 Chestnut St., Brattleboro, VT 05301 3152

Genealogical Library, Bennington Museum, Bennington, VT 05201

Vermont Society S.A.R., R.R. Box 18, Norwich, VT 05055

Vt Genealogical Society, P.O. Box 422, Pittsford, VT 05763

Welsh-American Genealogical Society, R.R. 2 Box 516, Poultney, VT 05764

Clallam County Genealogical Society, 223 E. Fourth St., Port Angeles, WA 98362

Clark County Genealogical Society, P.O. Box 2728, Vancouver, WA 98668

Appendix B: Resources

Douglas County Genealogical Society, P.O. Box 580, Waterville, WA 98858

Eastern Washington Genealogical Society, Box 1826, Spokane, WA 99210 1826

Eastside Genealogical Society, P.O. Box 374, Bellevue, WA 98009

Ellensburg Genealogical Group, 507 E. Tacoma St., Ellensburg, WA 98926

Ft. Vancouver Historical Society, Box 1834, Vancouver, WA 98663

Genealogical Society of Pierce Co., P.O. Box 98634, Tacoma, WA 98498 0634

Grant County Genealogical Society, 339 1St Ave. S.W., Ephrata, WA 98823

Grays Harbor Genealogical Society, P.O. Box 867, Cosmopolis, WA 98537

Heritage League Pierce Co., 4010 North 36th, Tacoma, WA 98407

Jefferson County Genealogical Society, 210 Madison, Port Townsend, WA 98368

Kitsap County Genealogical Society, 4305 Lakeview Dr S.E., Port Orchard, WA 98366

Lower Columbia Genealogical Society, P.O. Box 472, Longview, WA 98632

Maple Valley Historical Society, P.O. Box 123, Maple Valley, WA 98038

Metis Genealogical Society, N. 6206 Washington, Spokane, WA 99208

N Central Wash Genealogical Society, P.O. Box 613, Wenatchee, WA 98801

N.E. Washington Genealogical Society, 195 S. Oak, Colville, WA 99114

Okanogan County Genealogical Society, R.R. 1 Box 323, Omak, WA 98841

Olympia Genealogical Society, P.O. Box 1313, Olympia, WA 98507

Pacific County Genealogical Society, P.O. Box 843, Ocean Park, WA 98640

Puget Sound Genealogical Society, P.O. Box 601, Tracyton, WA 98393 0601

S.E. Lincoln County Historical Society, Sprague, WA 99032

Seattle Genealogical Society, P.O. Box 1708, Seattle, WA 98111 1708

Skagit Valley Genealogical Society, P.O. Box 715, Conway, WA 98238

Sno-Isle Genealogical Society, P.O. Box 63, Edmonds, WA 98020

South King County Genealogical Society, P.O. Box 3174, Kent, WA 98032

Stillagaumish Valley Genealogical Society, P.O. Box 34, Arlington, WA 98223

Tacoma-Pierce County Genealogical Society, P.O. Box 1952, Tacoma, WA 98401

The Tacoma Genealogical Society, P.O. Box 1952, Tacoma, WA 98401

Tonasket Genealogical Society, P.O. Box 84, Tonasket, WA 98855

Tri-City Genealogical Society, P.O. Box 1410, Richland, WA 99352 1410

Walla Walla Valley Genealogical Society, P.O. Box 115, Walla Walla, WA 99362

Washington Society S.A.R., 12233 9th Ave. N.W., Seattle, WA 98177

Washington State Genealogical Society, P.O. Box 1422, Olympia, WA 98507

Whatcom Genealogical Society, P.O. Box 1493, Bellingham, WA 98227

Whitman County Genealogical Society, P.O. Box 393, Pullman, WA 99163

Yakima Valley Genealogical Society, P.O. Box 445, Yakima, WA 98907

Ashland County Historical Society, Box 433, Ashland, WI 54806

Bay Area Genealogical Society, P.O. Box 283, Green Bay, WI 54305

Bayfield County Genealogical Society, Rt. 1 Box 139, Mason, WI 54856

Chippewa County Genealogical Society, 1427 Hilltop Blvd., Chippawa Falls, WI 54729

County Library (Genealogy), 515 Pine St., Green Bay, WI 54301

Fond Du Lac County Genealogical Society, 719 Wisconsin Ave., Fond Du Lac, WI 54935

Fox Valley Genealogical Society, P.O. Box 1592, Appleton, WI 54913 1592

French-Canadian/Acadian Genealogical Soc. of Wisc., 4624 W. Tesch Ave., Greenfield, WI 53220

Genealogical Research Society Eau Claire, P.O. Box 1204, Eau Claire, WI 54702

Genealogical Workshop, Rt. 3 Box 253, Black River Falls, WI 54615

Appendix B: Resources

Grant County Genealogical Society, 955 Williams St., Platteville, WI 53818

Hartford Genealogical Society, W720 Buchanan Rd., Hartford, WI 53027

Heart o'Wisconsin Genealogical Society, 490 E. Grand Ave., Wisconsin Rapids, WI 54494

Historical Society of Wisconsin, 816 State St., Madison, WI 53706 1482

Juneau County Genealogical Society, 511 Grayside, Mauston, WI 53948

Kenosha County Genealogical Society, 4902 52nd St., Kenosha, WI 53142

Lafayette County Genealogical Society Workshop, P.O. Box 443, Shullsburg, WI 53586

Manitowoc County Genealogical Society, P.O. Box 1745, Manitowoc, WI 54221

Marathon County Genealogical Society, P.O. Box 1512, Wausau, WI 54401

Marshfield Area Genealogical Group, P.O. Box 337, Marshfield, WI 54449

Menomonee Falls Historical Society, Box 91, Menomonee Falls, WI 53051

Milwaukee County Genealogical Society, P.O. Box 27326, Milwaukee, WI 53227

North Wisconsin Genealogists, P.O. Box 321, Shawano, WI 54166

Northwoods Genealogical Society, P.O. Box 1132, Rhinelander, WI 54501

Oconomowoc Genealogical Club, 733 E. Sherman Ave., Oconomowoc, WI 53066

Plymouth Genealogical Society, 130 Division St., Plymouth, WI 53073

Polish Genealogical Society Wisc, P.O. Box 37476, Milwaukee, WI 53237

Rock County Genealogical Society, P.O. Box 711, Janesville, WI 53547

Sheboygan County Genealogical Society, 518 Water St., Sheboygan Falls, WI 53085

St. Croix County Genealogical Society, Box 396, River Falls, WI 54022

Stevens Point Area Genealogical Society, 1325 Church St., Stevens Point, WI 54481

Washburn County Genealogical Society, P.O. Box 366, Shell Lake, WI 54871

Watertown Genealogical Society, P.O. Box 91, Watertown, WI 53094 0091

Waukesha County Genealogical Society, 17020 Patricia Ln, Brookfield, WI 53005

White Pine Genealogical Society, P.O. Box 512, Marinette, WI 54143

Winnebagoland Genealogical Society, 106 Washington Ave., Oshkosh, WI 54901 4985

Wisconsin Genealogical Council Inc., 6083 County Trunk S, Wisconsin Rapids, WI 54494 9212

Wisconsin State Genealogical Society, 2109 20th Ave., Monroe, WI 53566 3426

Wisconsin Society S.A.R., 3230 Meachem Rd., Racine, WI 53405

Wisconsin State Old Cemetery Society, 1562 N. 119 St., Wauwatosa, WI 53213

Berkeley County Genealogical Historical Society, P.O. Box 679, Martinsburg, WV 25401

Boone County Genealogical Society, P.O. Box 306, Madison, WV 25130

Brooke County Genealogical Historical Society, 1200 Pleasant Ave., Wellsburg, WV 26070

Calhoun Historical & Genealogical Society, P.O. Box 242, Grantsville, WV 26147

Doddridge County Historical Society, Box 23, West Union, WV 26456

Genealogical Society of Fayette & Raleigh Cos, P.O. Box 68, Oak Hill, WV 25901

Gilmer County Historical Society, 706 Mineral Rd., Glenville, WV 26351

Grant County Genealogical Historical Society, Lahmansville, WV 26731

Hamilton National Genealogical Society, P.O. Box 8636, Charleston, WV 25302

Hancock County Genealogical Historical Society, 103 Bell St., Weirton, WV 26067

Hardy County Genealogical Historical Society, Moorefield, WV 26836

Jackson County Historical Society, P.O. Box 22, Ripley, WV 25271

Kanawha Valley Genealogical Society, P.O. Box 8555, South Charleston, WV 25303

Kyowva Genealogical Society, P.O. Box 1254, Huntington, WV 25715

Appendix B: Resources

Lewis County Genealogical Historical Society, 252 Main Ave., Weston, WV 26452

Lincoln County Genealogical Society, P.O. Box 92, Griffithsville, WV 2552

Logan County Genealogical Society, P.O. Box 1959, Logan, WV 25601

Marion County Genealogical Club, County Library Monroe St., Fairmont, WV 26554

Mason County Genealogical Historical Society, H.C. 89 Box 25, Henderson, WV 25106

Mercer County Historical Society Inc., P.O. Box 5012, Princeton, WV 24740

Mineral County Genealogical Historical Society, 107 Orchard St., Keyser, WV 26726

Mingo County Genealogical Society, Box 2581, Williamson, WV 25661

Monroe County Historical Society, P.O. Box 465, Union, WV 24983

Morgan County Historical & Genealogical Society, Box 52, Berkeley Springs, WV 25411

Pendleton County Historical Society, Main St., Franklin, WV 26807

Ritchie County Historical Society, 200 S. Church St., Harrisville, WV 26362

Tyler County Heritage & Historical Society, P.O. Box 317, Middlebourne, WV 26149

Tyler County Historical Society, Box 317, Middlebourne, WV 26149

West Augusta Historical & Genealogical Society, 2515 10th Ave., Parkersburg, WV 26101

West Virginia S.A.R., 132 N. Court St., Lewisburg, WV 24901

Wetzel County Genealogical Society, P.O. Box 464, New Martinsville, WV 26155 0464

Wheeling Area Genealogical Society, 2237 Marshall Ave., Wheeling, WV 26003

W.V. Genealogical Society, P.O. Box 249, Elkview, WV 25071

Wyoming County Genealogical Society, P.O. Box 1456, Pineville, WV 24874

Cheyenne Genealogical Society, Laramie County Library Central Ave., Cheyenne, WY 82001

Converse County Genealogical Society, 119 N. 9th St., Douglas, WY 82633

Fremont County Genealogical Society, 1330 West Park, Riverton, WY 82501

Laramie Peekers Genealogical Society, 1108 21 St. St., Wheatland, WY 82201

Natrona County Genealogical Society, P.O. Box 9244, Casper, WY 82609

Park County Genealogical Society, P.O. Box 3056, Cody, WY 82414

Powell Valley Genealogical Club, P.O. Box 184, Powell, WY 82435

Sheridan Society for Genealogical Research, 1704 Big Horn Ave., Sheridan, WY 82801

Sublette County Genealogical Society, P.O. Box 1186, Pinedale, WY 82941

Wyoming Society S.A.R., 1040 S. Thurmond, Sheridan, WY 82801

Your Family Tree
Index

A

Abstract 185
AGLL web site 66
Ahnentafel 185
Ahnentafel numbering system 185
America Online 34, 42–54
    AOL Genealogy Forum 42–48
    PictureWeb Forum 87
Ancestor 185
Ancestor (or pedigree) chart 185
Ancestor Publishers web site 66
Ancestral file 185
Ancestry web site 67
AOL
    See America Online
Archives 185

B

Barrel of Genealogy Links web site 67
Bequeath 186
Bibliography 186
Birth certificate 186
Brother's Keeper 126–132
Building a family web site 142–144

C

Canan 186
Census 186
Church of Jesus Christ of Latter-day
Saints (The M 188
CIS
    See CompuServe
Citation 186
Civil 186
Collateral 186
COMMSOFT web site 68
Companion CD-ROM 159–182
    ADOBE 161
    Best Genealogy Sites Folder 169
    BK5STEED 162
    Bookmark List 169
    Calendar Explorer 178–179
    CATALOGS 165
    Contents 160–166
    EASY PHOTO DEMO 176–177
    Family Calendar for Windows 179–180
    Family Origins Demo web site 168
    Famtree.htm file 171
    Famtree.htm file (installing) 174–176
    FORMS 182
    FOW5DEMO 162–163
    FT4WIN 164
    FTMDEMO 163
    GED2HTML 168
    Graphic Work Shop 181
    NavRoad Web Browser 166
    R4DEMO 164
    SEATTLE FILMWORKS DEMO 177
    Sprynet homepage 167
    ThumbsUp! 181
    WINMORET 180
CompuServe 34–36, 48–54
    Genealogy Forum 48–54
    Genealogy Support Forum 49–54
    Photography forums 87
CompuServe Information Services
    See CompuServe
Cyndi's List of Genealogy Sites web site
.... 68

Index

D

Death certificate 186
Deed 186
Deja News web site 69
Descendancy chart 186
Descendant 186
Digital cameras 84–85
Digitizing family photos 83–108
Digitizing photographs
　See Photographs
Direct line 186

E

E-mail 39–42
EasyPhoto Scanner 90–91
Emigrant 186
Estate 187
Everton web site 69

F

Family group sheet 187
Family history 187
Family History Centers 187
Family History Library 187
Family Origins for Windows 132–142
Family Tree Maker for Windows 146–155
Family Tree Maker web site 70
Family web site 142
FamilySearch 187

G

GEDCOM 187
GEDCOM-L 59
GEN-NEWBIE-L 59
Genealogical Journeys In Time web site
.... 73
Genealogical Publishing Co. web site . 72
Genealogy 187
Genealogy Home Page web site 72
Genealogy newsletters 61–62
Genealogy research
　See Research

Genealogy SF web site 70
Genealogy software 11–12, 123–155
　Brother's Keeper for MS-DOS 126–132
　Family Origins for Windows 132–142
　Family Tree Maker for Windows 146–155
Genealogy Software Distribution System
　See GSDS
Genealogy Toolbox web site 71
GENMTD-L 59
GENSERV 61
GENWEB 61
Given name 187
Glossary 185–189
Grantee 187
Grantor 187
Graphic files
　Paint Shop Pro 90

H

Hearthstone Bookshop web site 73–74
Heritage Books web site 74

I

Immigrant 188
Index 188
International Genealogical Index (IGI) ...
.... 188
International sources 27

J

Journal of Online Genealogy (JOG) web
site 77

L

LDS 188
Library of Congress web site 75
Lineages web site 74
Local government sources 22–24

Index

M

Maiden name 188
Mailing lists 58–60
    GEDCOM-L 59
    GEN-NEWBIE-L 59
    GENMTD-L 59
    MAUCK 59–60
    ROOTS-L 59
Manipulating photographs 92–108
    Paint Shop Pro 92–102
MapQuest! 103
MapQuest! web site 75
Maps and map software 102–108
    DeLorme's Street Atlas USA 103
    Manipulating with Paint Shop Pro . 104–108
    MapQuest! 103
Maternal 188
MAUCK 59–60
Media Player 105–108
Microfiche 188
Microfilm 188
Microsoft Publisher 116–120
Microsoft Word 111–115
Modified register 188

N

National Archives and Records Administration web s 76
National Genealogical Society web site 77
Naturalization 188
New England Historical Genealogical Society web s 76
Newsgroups 36, 54–58
    GeneSplicer 57
    GSDS 57–58
    See also Usenet newsgroups
Newsletters
    Online electronic genealogy newsletters 61–62
Non-commercial BBSs 33
Note 188

O

Obituary 188
On-line research 33–80
    Accessing information 33–38
    America Online 34, 42–54
    CompuServe 34–36
    E-mail 39–42
    GEDCOM-L 59
    GEN-NEWBIE-L 59
    GeneSplicer 57
    GENMTD-L 59
    GENSERV 61
    GENWEB 61
    GSDS 57–58
    Mailing lists 58–60
    MAUCK 59–60
    Newsgroups 36, 54–58
    Non-commercial BBSs 33
    On-line services 34–36
    Online electronic genealogy newsletters ....
    61–62
    ROOTS-L 59
    ROOTSWEB 60
    Usenet newsgroups 36, 54–58
    World Wide Web 36–38, 62–65
    World Wide Web bookmarks 62–65
    World Wide Web web sites 65–80
    World Wide Web websites 65–80
On-line services 34–36
    Developing/copying photographs ... 87–102
Online electronic genealogy newsletters
.... 61–62

P

Paint Shop Pro
    Manipulating maps and map software ....
    104–108
    To manipulate photographs 92–102
Parsons Genealogy Section web site 78
Passenger list 188
Paternal 188
Pedigree (or ancestor) chart 189
Photo CD (TM) service company ... 84–85

239

Index

Photographs 83–108
    Digital cameras 84–85
    Digitizing 84–91
    EasyPhoto Scanner 90–91
    Manipulating 92–108
    Manipulating with Paint Shop Pro ... 92–102
    On-line services & develop/copy photo-
        graphs 87
    Photo CD (TM) service company 84–85
    Photos on Disk Services 86
    Scanning your photographs 86
    Seattle Filmworks' PhotoWorks 87–90
Photographs (manipulating)
    See Manipulating photographs
Photos on Disk Services 86
PictureWeb Forum 87
Prefix title 189
Primary record or evidence 189
Probate 189

R

Research 3–12
    International sources 27
    Local government sources 22–24
    National resources 24–27
    On-line research 33–80
    Planning 3–12
    Starting 17–29
    State government sources 24
    Tools you'll need 4–12
Resource lists 191–235
Resources 17–29
    International sources 27
    Local government sources 22–24
    National resources 24–27
    State government sources 24
Roots Computing Genealogy Home Page
    web site 78
ROOTS-L 59
ROOTS-L web site 79
ROOTSWEB 60
RootsWeb Genealogical Data Coopera-
    tive web site 79

S

Scanning your photographs 86
Seattle Filmworks' PhotoWorks 87–90
Secondary record 189
Social Security Death Index (SSDI) ... 189
Software 11–12
    See also Genealogy software
Sound 83–108
Sound capabilities 105–108
Sound cards 105–108
Soundex 189
Source 189
State government sources 24
    National resources 24–27
Street Atlas USA (DeLorme) 103
Suffix title 189
Surname 189
Switchboard Home Page web site 80

T

Tools for research 4–12
Treasure Maps web site 80

U

Usenet newsgroups 36, 54–58
    GeneSplicer 57
    GSDS 57–58
USGenWeb Project web site 71

W

Web sites
    Building a family web site 142–144
World Wide Web 33–38, 65–80
    Building a family web site 142–144
    Saving time 62–65
    Web sites 65–80
World Wide Web bookmarks 62–65
World Wide Web web sites 65–80
    AGLL 66
    Ancestor Publishers 66
    Ancestry 67
    Barrel of Genealogy Links 67

Index

COMMSOFT 68
Cyndi's List of Genealogy Sites 68
Deja News 69
Everton 69
Family Tree Maker 70
Genealogical Journeys In Time 73
Genealogical Publishing Co. 72
Genealogy Home Page 72
Genealogy SF 70
Genealogy Toolbox 71
Hearthstone Bookshop 73–74
Heritage Books 74
Journal of Online Genealogy (JOG) 77
Library of Congress 75
Lineages 74
MapQuest! 75
National Archives and Records Administration 76
National Genealogical Society 77
New England Historical Genealogical Society 76
Parsons Genealogy Section 78
Roots Computing Genealogy Home Page 78
ROOTS-L 79
RootsWeb Genealogical Data Cooperative. 79
Switchboard Home Page 80
Treasure Maps 80
USGenWeb Project 71

241

PC catalog

Order Toll Free 1-800-451-4319
Books and Software

Includes CD-ROM with Sample Programs

Abacus

To order direct call Toll Free 1-800-451-4319

In US and Canada add $5.00 shipping and handling. Foreign orders add $13.00 per item.
Michigan residents add 6% sales tax.

Developers Series books are for professional software dovelopers who require in-depth technical information and programming techniques.

PC Intern—6th Edition
The Encyclopedia of System Programming

Now in its 6th Edition, more than 500,000 programmers worldwide rely on the authoritative and eminently understandable information in this one-of-a-kind volume. You'll find hundreds of practical, working examples written in assembly language, C++, Pascal and Visual Basic—all professional programming techniques which you can use in your own programs. PC INTERN is a literal encyclopedia for the PC programmer. PC INTERN clearly describes the aspects of programming under all versions of DOS as well as interfacing with Windows.

Includes CD-ROM with Sample Programs

Some of the topics include:
- Memory organization on the PC
- Writing resident TSR programs
- Programming graphic and video cards
- Using extended and expanded memory
- Handling interrupts in different languages
- Networking programming NetBIOS and IPX/SPX
- Win95 virtual memory and common controls
- IRQs—programming interrupt controllers
- Understanding DOS structures and function
- Using protected mode, DOS extenders and DPMI/VCPI multiplexer
- Programming techniques for CD-ROM drives
- Programming Sound Blaster and compatibles

The companion CD-ROM transforms PC INTERN from a book into an interactive reference. You can search, navigate and view the entire text of the book and have instant access to information using hypertext links. Also included on the CD-ROM are hundreds of pages of additional programming tables and hard-to-find material.

Author: Michael Tischer and Bruno Jennrich
Order Item: #B304
ISBN: 1-55755-304-1
SRP: $69.95 US/$99.95 CAN with companion CD-ROM

To order direct call Toll Free 1-800-451-4319

In US and Canada add $5.00 shipping and handling. Foreign orders add $13.00 per item. Michigan residents add 6% sales tax.

Productivity Series books are for users who want
to become more productive with their PC.

Upgrading and Maintaining Your PC
New 4th Edition

Buying a personal computer is a major investment. Today's ever-changing technology requires that you continue to upgrade if you want to maintain a state of the art system. Innovative developments in hardware and software drive your need for more speed, better hardware, and larger capacities. **Upgrading and Maintaining Your PC** gives you the knowledge and skills that help you upgrade or maintain your system. You'll save time and money by being able to perform your own maintenance and repairs.

How to upgrade, repair, maintain and more:
- Hard drives, Memory and Battery Replacement
- Sound & Video Cards, CD-ROM's
- Pentium Powerhouses 60 - 133 *MHz*, overdrive processor
- Large Capacity Hard Drives
- Quad Speed CD-ROM Drives
- Sound Cards - 64-bit and Wave Table
- Modems/Fax Cards, ISDN
- AMD, Cyrix, AMI and Intel Processors
- Operating Systems - DOS 6.22, Novell DOS, IBM PC DOS 6.3, OS/2 Warp & Windows 3.1 to Windows 95

On the CD-ROM!

System Sleuth Analyzer from Dariana ($99.95 value) - A toolbox of valuable PC diagnostic aids rolled into a single, easy-to-use software utility. It lets you explore exacting details of your PC without fear of accidental, unrecoverable modifications to a particular subsystem.

Cyrix Upgrade Compatibility Test - Run "Cyrix's" own test to see if you can upgrade with one of their new 486 chips!

Intel's Pentium Chip Test - calculate the now famous "math problem" on your own system!

Authors: H. Veddeler & U. Schueller
Order Item:#B300
ISBN: 1-55755-300-9
Suggested retail price: $34.95 US / $46.95 CAN with CD-ROM

To order direct call Toll Free 1-800-451-4319

In US and Canada add $5.00 shipping and handling. Foreign orders add $13.00 per item.
Michigan residents add 6% sales tax.

**Productivity Series books are for users who want
to become more productive with their PC.**

Win95 Rx
**Solve Your Own Windows 95
Computing Problems Easily**

Solve all of your computing problems once and for all. Here's an easy-to-follow troubleshooting guide that will save you time, money and headaches. Learn how to identify and fix problems yourself instead of having to endlessly wait for vague, unclear answers from those so-called "expert" tech support lines. Do it right. Do it yourself!

What's inside the book:
- Preparing your system for Windows 95
- Installing new or additional hardware
- Tips for working with the new desktop
- Protecting your valuable data – backup and viruses
- Tune up your hard drive for peak performance
- Multimedia setup and software
- Running your existing DOS and Win 3.X programs
- Running your DOS games without the nightmares

Win95 Rx includes a companion CD-ROM filled with useful tools for testing and configuring your entire PC system.

Author: Kober, Buechel & Baecker
Order Item: #B297
ISBN: 1-55755-297-5
Suggested retail price: $34.95 US/ $46.95 with CD-ROM

To order direct call Toll Free 1-800-451-4319

In US and Canada add $5.00 shipping and handling. Foreign orders add $13.00 per item.
Michigan residents add 6% sales tax.

Developers Series books are for professional software developers who require in-depth technical information and programming techniques.

Win95 Game Programming
Hard Core Gamewriter's Guide

Windows 95 is going to revolutionize the way programmers code graphics, sound and music. The new 32-bit WinG Library from Microsoft is a giant toolbox of graphics capabilities that insulate the gamewriter from the hardware, yet delivers the performance that you need to write fast, responsive games and animations.

Win95 Game Programming introduces you to WinG with practical, working examples. You'll learn about "Windowing" with APIs, creating graphic effects with multichannel sound (MIDI and Wave files), applying texture mapping, light and shadow effects and more! The book takes you through three complete projects to demonstrate the graphical programming techniques.

Game Programming Projects in this book:
- Jump - A Classic in New Clothing
- Space Flight Simulator - From the Virtual World to the Screen
- Underworld - A DOOM™-like game
- Underground Designs & Descent into the Caves

You'll find all the source code to these exciting game programs on the CD! Written in Pascal and C, you can use this code to work on your own graphic projects and games.

Author: Matthias Rasch
Order Item: #B294
ISBN: 1-55755-294-0
Suggested retail price: $44.95 US/ $59.95 with CD-ROM

To order direct call Toll Free 1-800-451-4319

In US and Canada add $5.00 shipping and handling. Foreign orders add $13.00 per item. Michigan residents add 6% sales tax.

Multimedia Presentation

PC Photography Book

The PC Photography Book is for all camera buffs, home users, hobbyists, desktop publishers, graphic artists, marketing communication professionals and multimedia enthusiasts.

Many companies, including Kodak, Seattle Film Works, Storm Software, Delrina, Hewlett-Packard and others, are pioneering a new consumer level technology which lets you move common photos or snap shots onto your PC. Digital imaging software and graphic gear is easier to use, more affordable and the quality of output excellent.

PC Photography starts with the basics of image processing and taking quality photos. A special treatment is given to Kodak's photo CD format that allows anyone to put photos on CD-ROM. The technology and process are both explained in depth. It then moves on to examine how today's hardware and software work—both the digital camera and the photo reader.

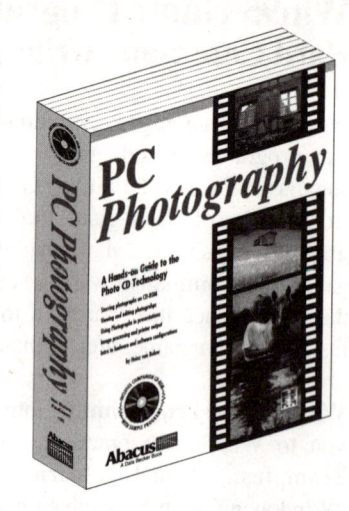

Learn how to work with: Micrografx PhotoMagic, Microsoft Publisher, CorelDraw, Aldus Freehand and Photostyler, and Adobe PhotoShop.

Includes CD-ROM with Sample Programs

The companion CD-ROM includes samplers of:

- Toshiba's Photo/Graphic Viewer
- MicroTek's Photo Star graphic utility
- PCD photo examples used in the book
- Collection of popular shareware graphics utilities including:
  - JASC'S PaintShop Pro
  - Graphics WorkShop
- Several industry standard Phillips CD-I software drivers

Author: Heinz von Buelow and Dirk Paulissen
Order Item: #B293
ISBN: 1-55755-293-2

SRP: $34.95 US/$46.95 CAN includes CD-ROM

To order direct call Toll Free 1-800-451-4319

In US and Canada add $5.00 shipping and handling. Foreign orders add $13.00 per item. Michigan residents add 6% sales tax.

Productivity Series books are for users who want to become more productive with their PC.

Zipping for Beginners
"No Experience Required"

What is zipping?

Zipping is a way to "crunch" files. By zipping, you can save hard disk space, reduce on-line connect time and make it easier for you to pass files onto friends and business associates.

Zipping for Beginners is a no-nonsense introductory guide to using the two most popular zipping utilities – PKZip and WinZip. These step-by-step instructions will turn you into a zipping (and unzipping) expert in just a few short minutes.

Book highlights:
- What's a "zipped" file?
- Viewing a compressed file
- Zipping several files at once
- Zipping to multiple diskettes
- Creating a self-extracting zip file

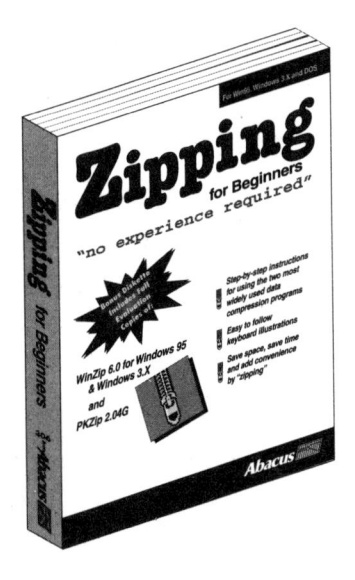

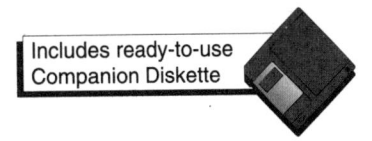

Includes a companion diskette with full evaluation copies of WinZip 6.0 for Windows 95 & Windows 3.X and PKZip 2.04G.

Author: Abacus Group
Order Item: #B306
ISBN: 1-55755-306-8
Suggested retail price: $14.95 US/ $19.95 CAN with companion diskette

To order direct call Toll Free 1-800-451-4319

In US and Canada add $5.00 shipping and handling. Foreign orders add $13.00 per item. Michigan residents add 6% sales tax.

Software

ZIP KIT

Learn to Use the World's Most Popular Data Compression Programs!

Start Using WinZip and nine other fully functional evaluation versions of the most popular data compression shareware in the universe today.

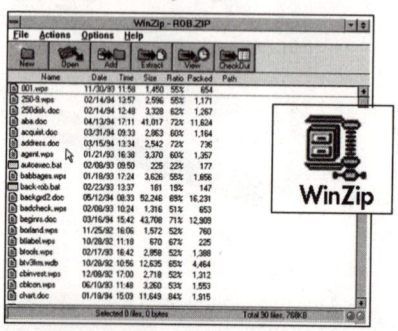

PKZip   ARJ   LH-ICE

PKLite   LHArc   LZH

This Windows-based utility makes unlocking the treasures of the information superhighway a breeze. Zip and unzip. Drag-and-drop. Virus scanning support.

Graphic & Video Utilities

Special graphic and video programs in the **ZIP KIT** will help you work with dozens of different formats.

Learn to convert and compress numerous graphic formats with unique image processing software: ART, BMP, DIB, GIF, IFF, ICO, LBM, MSP, PCX, RLE, TIF, WPG, CUT, EXE, HRZ, IMG, JPG, MAC, PIC, RAS, TGA, and TXT.

Discover the world of compressed video files: FLI, AVI, MPG, FLC, and MCI.

ZIP KIT
Item #S287
ISBN 1-55755-290-8
UPC 0 90869 55290 1

SRP: $34.95 US/ $46.95 CAN

To order direct call Toll Free 1-800-451-4319

In US and Canada add $5.00 shipping and handling. Foreign orders add $13.00 per item. Michigan residents add 6% sales tax.

Order Form 1996 Ancestry Catalog

Phone Orders 1(800)Ancestry *1(800)262-3787 including Canada)*
FAX Orders 1(801)531-1798

Ancestry's Research Club is a full service organization that offers genealogical products and services to family researchers at economical prices. You can save on every order from Ancestry.

Choose One: ☐ Ancestry's Guide to Research ☐ Writing the Family Narrative ☐ Killing Cousins
#904/905/906 $29.95/year

Total Membership Dues: $ _____

Books and Other Items

Item#	Qty.	Title or Description	Price Each	Total

Total Books and Other Items: $ _____

Shipping, Handling, and Insurance

Amount of Purchase	Via UPS	Via U.S. Post	Canada	2 Day Air
$0-10	5.00	3.00	4.00	7.00
10-25	6.00	4.00	5.50	8.50
25-50	7.00	5.50	7.50	10.00
@ add 25	2.00	2.50	2.50	3.00

Office Use Only

Note: No shipping charge on Genealogical Computing or Ancestry magazine in U.S.; Canada and Mexico $5.00, per year ordered; other foreign $10.00, per year ordered.

Phone Count _____ Phone Search Surname _____
Limiting Options: City/Cities _____ State(s) _____
Given Name _____
Report Form: Line Listings _____ Labels _____

Total S, H, & I: $ _____
Utah Residents 6.13% Sales Tax: $ _____
Total Amount Due: $ _____

Payment

☐ Check (U.S. Bank) or Money Order
☐ Invoice Institution (signature required)
☐ Credit Card (circle one)   VISA   MasterCard   Discover

Account Number _____ Exp. _____

Signature _____

Place label (from back of catalog) here, or fill in if label is missing. Please make any address corrections.

Your Name _____
Street _____
City, State, Zip _____
Telephone number during business hours (_____) _____

Please return this form to
ANCESTRY, INC., P.O. Box 476, Salt Lake City, UT 84110-0476

"Family Calendar for Windows"
Order Form

Command Line Software
3431 Florida Dr.
Loveland, CO 80538
970-667-4566
east@frii.com

$5.00 Discount

Name: _____

Address: _____

_____

City: _____

State/Prov _____ Zip/Postal Code _____

Country: _____

Email: _____

Order by Mail

Registered version of "Family Calendar"	$25.00
Book bundling discount	-5.00
Shipping & Handling ($6.00 intl)	3.00
Total	**$23.00**

Please make checks payable to: **Command Line Software**

Order On-line (http://www.frii.com/~east)

Pay with a credit card. Download immediately and save shipping charges.
You can order the Registered Version of "Family Calendar" directly from our Web Site and still receive your $5.00 discount/rebate using this form.

☐ I ordered on-line please mail my $5.00 discount/rebate to the address above.

Benefits to Registering "Family Calendar"

- Receive the latest version with the latest features including:
  - Importing of genealogy GEDCOM files.
  - Sizing of printed calendars.
  - More printed reports and other new features.
- Free updates via our Internet Web Site.
- Free support via email, Web Site and phone.
- Free laser printed, 12 month calendar using your calendar data.
- Removal of all Shareware screens and watermarks on printouts.

Discover your Family Roots!

Virginia
W. Virginia
N. Carolina
Georgia
& others

Iberian Publishing Company

_ To order by phone, call
1-800-394-8634
M-F, 8-6 EST
Saturday, 8-Noon, EST
Customer Service Questions, please call 1-706-546-6740
548 Cedar Creek Drive
Athens, GA 30605-3408

Family Tree For Windows V1.1

REGISTRATION FORM

Please print (this information will appear in your registration code):

Given-name (First): _____

Middle Initial: _____

Sur-name (Last): _____

Mailing address: _____

_____

_____

_____

_____

E-Mail (Optional): _____

FT4WIN Version: _____

Complete the above and send

  US $40 payable to:

      David Simmonds
      1725 - 147th Place S.E.
      Bellevue, Washington, 98007-6819
      USA

OR

      CAN $50 payable to:
      Gavin Jacobs
      12523 Lake Geneva Road S.E.
      Calgary, Alberta, T2J 2S4
      Canada

              *** OR ***

You can now register online with CompuServe by selecting GO SWREG. The registration ID is 3231.

Thankyou for registering FT4WIN!

ORDER FORM

First Name

Last Name

Company
Address

City _____ ST_____ ZIP_____
Country
Phone _____ FAX _____

Qty	Title	Price Each	Extended Price
		Total	

(Visa, MC, Check or Money Order only)

You may register NavRoad on-line with your credit cards (Visa, MasterCard, American Express, Novus brand cards), via REGNET by clicking on the following links:
Single User Licensing - http://www.xmission.com/~wintrnx/regnet/232p.htm
Site Licensing - http://www.xmission.com/~wintrnx/regnet/233p.htm
Royalty Free Licensing - http://www.xmission.com/~wintrnx/regnet/234p.htm
Please note there is an additional Service & Handling fee of US$5 if you register via REGNET.
REGNET can also be contacted by Phone 1 800 WWW2REG (1 800 999-2734) (Toll Free, U.S. & Canada) (805) 288-1827 (International) Fax (805) 288-1867
****To avoid any possible delays, please inform me by email once you have registered.
You may register via mail by Cheque (in US dollars), American Express Money Order (found at post offices or convenience stores) Cash (for safety reason please send me an email first)
Please make your cheque / money order payable to FAI GODFREY KO
Send to:

FAI GODFREY KO
PO BOX 710
MT GRAVATT 4122
QLD, AUSTRALIA

ORDER FORM

First Name: ☐☐☐☐☐☐☐☐☐☐☐☐☐☐☐

Last Name: ☐☐☐☐☐☐☐☐☐☐☐☐☐☐☐

Company
Address _____
_____
City _____ ST_____ ZIP_____
Country _____
Phone _____ FAX _____

Qty	Title	Price Each	Extended Price
		Total	

(Visa, MC, Check or Money Order only)

Orders:
Address: Pik A Program, Inc.
              13 Saint Marks Place
              New York, NY 10003
              USA
Toll-Free Phone: 1-800-867-3447
Phone: 212 598-4936
FAX: 212 228-5879
CompuServe: 74777,3233
Internet: 74777.3233@compuserve.com

Support:
Address: Cumberland Family Software
              385 Idaho Springs Road
              Clarksville, TN 37043
Phone: 615 647-4012
CompuServe: 70713,3476
Internet: 70713.3476@compuserve.com

ORDER FORM

First Name

Last Name

Company
Address

City   ST_____ ZIP_____
Country
Phone   FAX

Qty	Title	Price Each	Extended Price
		Total	

(Visa, MC, Check or Money Order only)

To Contact Progeny Software Inc.

Address: 5518 Prospect Road
New Minas, Nova Scotia
Canada   B4N 3K8

Telephone: 1-902-681-1131
Fax: 1-902-681-2042
E-Mail: support@progeny2.com
CompuServe: 71652,3205

Order Line: 1-800-565-0018
(call 001-902-681-1151 from overseas)

ORDER FORM

First Name

Last Name

Company Address

City
Country
Phone   ST_____ ZIP_____
                                  FAX

Qty	Title	Price Each	Extended Price
		Total	

I can now offer you two ways to pay the registration fee. If you are able to procure a money order or check drawn on a US bank for $20 US currency, then you may send it directly to me at:

**Eugene W. Stark
14 Landing Lane
Port Jefferson, NY 11777
USA**

You can also send me a US $20 bill, however you should wrap it in paper and be aware that there is some risk involved in sending cash through the postal service. My bank can also handle checks written in Canadian currency, for a fee of $2 US, so if you wish to pay that way you can do it, but please send an amount in $CDN that will cover the exchange and the fee.

ORDER FORM

First Name

Last Name

Company
Address

City   ST_____ ZIP_____
Country
Phone   FAX

Qty	Title	Price Each	Extended Price
		Total	

If you would like to address comments or questions about the CCFINDER II program, contact:

Ray Cox   Internet: 75503.1540@compuserve.com
17410 Huntersglen   Compuserve: 75503,1540
Humble, TX 77396   Voice: 713-454-6074

ORDER FORM

First Name

Last Name

Company Address

City
Country
Phone _____ ST_____ ZIP_____
                        FAX_____

Qty	Title	Price Each	Extended Price
		Total	

GENIUS Order Information

Requirements: Windows 3.1 in Enhanced mode or Windows 95.
386 or better computer with at least 4 Mbytes of RAM
Hard Disk with at least 1Mb of space

Registration: Australian $55 (includes shipping) to receive disk with
latest version and manual.

Author: Peter Resch, PO Box 720, Woodridge, Qld. 4114, Australia
Compuserve: 100245,1204
Internet: 100245.1204@Compuserve.com

Genealogy Book Catalogs Button

Contains many catalogs from the best genealogical book publishers, booksellers and other companies serving the family historian. This is quite possibly one of the largest collections of genealogy books and supplies you will find in one place (over 1300 pages). The companies who were so generous to contribute include:

- A J Morris
- Ancestry
- Ancestor Publishing
- Family Line
- Global Heritage
- Hearthstone Books
- Genealogical Publishing Company
- Heritage Books
- Hope Farm
- Iberian
- Parks Books
- TLCWillow Brook
- Yates Publishing
- Everton's

I highly recommend browsing these catalogs if you want to advance your family research.

Web Site Button

Contains various examples of world wide web pages created with several of the genealogy programs. It also contains several text files of resources. In writing this book I've compiled a comprehensive collection of Internet web sites that I have visited and researched that are of special interest to family history buffs. I have consolidated them into one bookmark file called FAMTREE.HTM different folders so that they will be easier for you to use.

Additional Demo's Button

This menu contains a wide variety of genealogy utilities and demonstrations of Family Calendar by Command Line Software, Inc., Graphic Work Shop by Alchemy Mindworks, GEDCOM to HTML by Gene Stark, GEDCOM to Tiny Tafel utility by Andrew Koppenhaver, Easy Photo Demo by Storm Technologies, Photo Works Demo by Seattle Film Works, Calendar Explorer by Albert Collver III, ThumbsPlus! Graphic and Photography programs by Cerious Software Inc. and more.

What's On the Companion CD-ROM

The CD-ROM included with this guide will be an indispensable source of reference material as well as a sampler of selected software. To run the CD-ROM in Windows 3.X, select "Run..." from the File pull-down menu located at the top left corner of your screen (this is the Windows' Program Manager screen). Type "D:\MENU.EXE" (where "D:" is the letter assigned to your CD-ROM drive) and click OK. Click OK again and the menu program will be loaded. To run the CD-ROM in Windows 95, click the "Start" button, select "Run...," type "D:\MENU.EXE" and click OK. This will load the CD's menu program. With a little exploration on your part, you'll discover some great tools and techniques to help you write your own family history.

Genealogy Program Demos

Contains evaluation and demonstration genealogy programs including Brother's Keeper Shareware by John Steed, Family Tree Maker Demo by Banner Blue Div., Broderbund Software, Family Origins Demo by Parsons Technology, Roots IV and V Slide Shows by CommSoft, Inc., Cumberland Family Tree Shareware by Cumberland Family Software, Family Tree for Windows Shareware by FT4W Software, Inc., PAF Mate Demo by Progeny Software, CCFind Shareware by Ray Cox, Genius Genealogy Shareware by Peter Resch and more.

See Chapter 7 for more information about the companion CD-ROM